Investing
in Zero Coupon
Bonds

PERSONAL COMPUTER SOFTWARE ORDER FORM

Mail to: LARRY ROSEN CO.
          7008 Springdale Road
          Louisville, Ky. 40222

Please send me the computer program indicated below. My check payable to Larry Rosen Co. is enclosed for
$_____ at $89.00 per disk. (Please indicate quantity in the boxes if more than one copy is desired. For orders
of three or more disks, deduct 15 percent.)

☐ **The Complete Bond Analyzer (CBA) Disk No. 1**

☐ **The Financial and Interest Calculator (FIC) Disk No. 2**

☐ **Investment Analysis (after tax) for Stocks, Bonds, and Real Estate (IASBR)** Disk No. 3

Name: _____

Street: _____

City: _____ State: _____ Zip: _____

Computer: _____ RAM: ____k Operating System: _____

Computer is compatible with (fill in if applicable): _____

Spreadsheet: _____ Spreadsheet Version: _____

Type of Disk Drive to be Used: ☐ 5 1/4 inch ☐ 3 1/2 inch

Telephone (office): (   ) ____-_____   (home): (   ) ____-_____

ADDITIONAL INFORMATION: **Full documentation** is on the disks explaining how to use the programs. All
programs may be used with various computers including the following and their **compatibles:**

Apple][	Apple][+	Apple //e and //c
Apple ///	MacIntosh	Lisa
IBM PC	IBM PC, Jr.	IBM XT
IBM AT		Commodore 64 & 128

Investment Analysis (after tax) for Stocks, Bonds, and Real Estate (Disk No. 3) is used with a spreadsheet.
Among the spreadsheet versions are: Appleworks, Lotus 1-2-3, VisiCalc, Symphony, SuperCalc, MagiCalc, Excel,
3 E-Z Pieces, Multiplan, Jazz, AceCalc, and FlashCalc. It is also available for the CP/M operating system with
Multiplan and SuperCalc. The minimum RAM (memory availability before booting the spreadsheet) is 64k. We
are continuously adding additional computers and spreadsheets, so if your configuration (spreadsheet and computer) is not listed, we encourage you to order anyway. If your order can not be promptly filled, your money will
be immediately refunded.

Investing in Zero Coupon Bonds

All about CATS™, STRIPS, TIGRs, LIONS, TRs, and TBRs

LAWRENCE R. ROSEN

JOHN WILEY & SONS
New York   Chichester   Brisbane   Toronto   Singapore

This publication is designed to provide accurate and
authoritative information in regard to the subject
matter covered. It is sold with the understanding that
the publisher is not engaged in rendering legal, accounting,
or other professional service. If legal advice or other
expert assistance is required, the services of a competent
professional person should be sought. *From a Declaration
of Principles jointly adopted by a Committee of the
American Bar Association and a Committee of Publishers.*

Library of Congress Cataloging in Publication Data:

Rosen, Lawrence R.
  Investing in zero coupon bonds.

  1. Zero coupon securities.   I. Title

HG4651.R77   1986   332.63′232   86-9262
ISBN 0-471-84707-0

Printed in the United States of America

10 9 8 7 6 5 4 3 2 1

Preface

Not since the go-go years of the late 1960s and the stir created by the tremendous growth of IOS has the investment world been mesmerized by any development as it has by zero coupon bonds. Since their introduction in 1982, some $200 billion in face value of Treasury zero coupon bonds has been originated and sold. Zeros have not only become the hottest new investment medium for tax-exempt investors, but have also created new markets for U.S. Treasury securities, which are the foundation and backing for most zero coupon bonds. And, municipal zeros offer unusual possibilities for taxable investors.

The advertisements for zeros present an enticing picture for investors:

"Quadruple your money in 11 years"
"Safety"
"Backed by U.S. Treasuries"
"Eliminate reinvestment risk"
"Security"

"Invest $33,000 now—start earning $10,000 a year tax
free in 11$^{1}/_{2}$ years"
"Tax free income"

Are zeros the answer to everyone's investment dilemma? Def-
initely not! To successfully invest in zeros, timing is crucial.

Surprisingly, some of the most enticing aspects of zero coupon
bonds are not advertised. Three noteworthy examples of such
features are:

The noncallable nature of most zero coupon bonds. This feature
alone can be worth its weight in gold to an investor who has
bought fortuitously in a period of near peak interest rates. Consider the value of being able to hold a bond yielding 15 percent
for 30 years rather than being forced to surrender it for redemption after five years, and being forced to reinvest at a then
current rate of 7 percent.

*The possible usage of zeros to increase a company's market
value and earnings per share by reducing pension plan costs
through "dedicating" zero coupon bonds to match certain specified
pension plan liabilities for benefits.*

The possible benefit from the Federal Reserve policy of allowing
up to 100 percent borrowing *against the full market value of
Treasury zeros—and the opportunity to make profits as high as
100 percent in a year, after taxes.*

This book provides you with the vital information you must
have if you own zero coupon bonds or if you are thinking of
investing in them. Among the subjects covered are:

How knowledge of volatility may make you rich! **Rich indeed.
The annual return was an astounding 184 percent for a
STRIP investment for the year ended March 1986, with-
out leverage.**

What the **risks and benefits** really are!

How **taxes** affect your investment decision.

How to buy and sell at a **fair market price** and not be gouged by brokers.

Whether **"locking in"** an interest reinvestment rate is advantageous.

How to compare zeros to alternative investment opportunities.

How to **get back your money** if you've been deceived by a broker and lost.

The fortunes made by some broker–dealers by charging huge mark-ups in retailing zero-coupon bonds to the public, and **how to protect yourself** from becoming a victim.

What price the **"callable tail"** of a zero coupon bond is worth.

When and why the U.S. Treasury decided to nurture the zero coupon market with its program called STRIPS.

The **magnitude** of zeros **price fluctuation** compared to conventional bonds.

The **hidden dangers** of municipal (tax-exempt) zeros.

When **tax-exempt** bonds produce **taxable** income.

The relationship of **prices at which zeros should sell** to the **"theoretical spot rate curve."**

How to construct a "theoretical spot rate curve."

When zeros should sell at **higher** yields than **comparable** maturities of Treasury bonds.

Why you **can't always believe** what you read **in the press,** including repeated financial blunders in some of our most respected publications, and proof that they are wrong.

Zero coupon bonds are an innovative addition to the investment scene. Yet, contrary to much of the publicity surrounding them, there are many complex issues with which investors owe it to themselves to be familiar. *The result of unfamiliarity with such issues can be financially devastating.* With the knowledge which you will gain from this book, your chances of reaping a fortune through zero coupon bonds, though far from guaranteed, will certainly be enhanced.

Good luck with your investing!

LAWRENCE R. ROSEN

Louisville, Kentucky
July 1986

Acknowledgments

A great many brokerage firms provided sales literature, for which I am grateful. For the most part, such literature extolled the virtues of zero coupon securities but generally failed to present a balanced picture. If such literature had been more objective, there would have been substantially less need for this book.

A noteworthy exception to the foregoing applies to Salomon Brothers' literature, which I have received in abundance for which thanks are due to Thomas E. Klaffky, Managing Director. The materials published by Salomon Brothers, which I have read with interest, are complete, objective, and informative.

Additional thanks are due to the Federal Reserve Bank of St. Louis and Megan Walsh of the research department for providing up-to-the-minute information about STRIPS; Larry Steinberg, Partner, Touche Ross & Co., was most helpful in providing company digests of the ever changing Internal Revenue Code; special thanks are due, also, to Missy Dorch of Hilliard-Lyons, who provided brokerage literature; and Ivan Diamond, partner of Greenebaum, Doll & McDonald, for reviewing Appendix B.

L.R.R.

Contents

Table of Charts

Table of Graphs

Table of Tables

Investing
in Zero Coupon
Bonds

1

Zero Coupon Bonds Take Investment World by Storm

The most popular new investment for IRA's, Keoghs, and company pensions is backed by full faith and credit obligations of the U.S. government. At current rates, it guarantees to double your money in six years, triple it in 10 or multiply it five times in only 14 years. The investment is the zero coupon Treasury. It is the simplest, safest and probably most sensible approach to investing retirement funds that exists today.

A zero coupon Treasury gives the owner the right to a single future interest or principal payment from a U.S. Treasury bond. Zero coupon Treasuries pay no interest. Instead, they are purchased at a discount and return one lump sum to the holder when they mature at face value. The discounted purchase price of a zero establishes the rate of return on the investment. In effect, both principal and interest compound automatically at this fixed and guaranteed rate until the bond comes due.

The power of this compounding is nowhere more evident than in the deeply discounted prices on intermediate and longer term zeroes. Those due in 10 years sell at 33 cents on the dollar; in 15 year maturities at 19 cents on the dollar; in 20 years, at less than 12 and in 25 years, the longest maturity, at less than 8 percent of face value. . . . They make it possible to plan for the future with 100 percent confidence and certainty.

Special Memorandum of Gabriele, Hueglin & Cashman, November 1, 1984.

Not since the creation of common stock has a new investment medium attracted brokers and investors as have zero coupon bonds. Investment brokers use different names to refer to these instruments. For example, they are called: CATs (certificates of accrual on treasury securities, a variety established by Salomon Brothers); TIGRs (Merrill Lynch), TRs (Treasury Bond Receipts, E.F. Hutton); and LIONS (Shearson Lehman/American Express).

Each different name is accompanied by appropriately descriptive brokerage company literature, for instance:

They're relatively new investments that offer exceptional growth and a high degree of safety for your money. . . . Zero coupon bonds offer a truly dramatic rate of growth. For example, an investment in a zero coupon bond yielding 11% would double in six years, triple in $9^{1}/_{2}$ years, and quadruple in 11 years. . . . Zero coupon bonds can play an important role in your total financial plan for very apparent reasons:

Security

High yields

Small initial investment

Ready liquidity

Flexible maturities

No reinvestment risk

U.S. Government-backed zeros are commonly known as CATS— Certificates of Accrual on Treasury Securities. CATS represent direct interests in U.S. Treasury notes or bonds and, as such, possess a very high degree of safety.

Zeros are liquid. You will find an active secondary market for all types of zeros. Compared to conventional bonds, zeros offer significantly greater trading leverage and more limited downside exposure when market interest rates adjust.

> From brochure issued by Prudential-Bache Securities, 1985.

Will your money work for you, year after year, toward a specific financial goal? Will you have a guarantee of your investment's performance? Even in an uncertain financial world, you can still answer yes to these questions—with the help of E.F. Hutton Zero Coupon Treasury Bond Receipts.

> From E.F. Hutton Treasury Bond Receipts—government-guaranteed returns
> for planning-oriented investors.

Zero Coupon Bonds offer capital gains that may equal as much as 25 times your original investment, depending on the length of maturity you choose. Furthermore, these gains are exempt from all federal taxes and, in many cases, state and local taxes, too. Zero Coupon Municipal Bonds can give you the comfort of knowing exactly how much money you will have at a time of need in the future. We know of no other investment that can make that promise. Of course, some investors may wish to sell their bonds before they mature. If unforeseen needs for capital arise, an active secondary market for Zero Coupon Municipal Bonds should enable you to liquidate at current market value at that time.

> From Zero-Coupon Municipal Bonds, E.F. Hutton.

Zero-Coupon bonds, like Big Macs, enjoy very wide appeal. Don't be embarrassed about liking them, even if you do understand what's inside.

> Personal Affairs, edited by William G. Flanagan, Forbes, May 1984

Stripped Treasuries, backed by the full faith and credit of the U.S. Government, are in great demand for IRAs, Keoghs and pension plans.

> Paine Webber Viewpoint, May 29, 1984

Do you have an investment that can

Double in 6 years

Triple in 9¹/₂ years

Quadruple in 11 years

Zero Coupon Bonds from Prudential-Bache Securities can.
A Prudential-Bache Securities Advertisement in The Wall Street Journal,
November 1, 1984.

If your portfolio has declined significantly and you feel exposed to further downside risk, we recommend that you replace the security, whether it be a common stock, preferred stock or a bond, with quality zero coupon bonds.
Shearson Lehman/American Express Weekly Newsletter, June 18, 1984

If everything were true that you have just read there would be no reason for this book. Alas, the need for this book is undeniable because investment in zero coupon bonds can:

Result in your losing 50 percent or more of your investment

Leave you vulnerable to disastrously high income taxation

Cost you more than it should due to the excessive markups some brokers charge (**surprisingly, the yield on zeros should sometimes be higher, even significantly higher, than the yield on conventional Treasury bonds of the same maturity**)

This book will give you an in-depth knowledge of zeros that will take you far beyond the sales pitch of Wall Street. You will be in a position to make intelligent decisions about investments in zero coupon instruments—with full knowledge of the important considerations that are a prerequisite to investment success.

2

Quick Zero Coupon Calculations

A short review of the principles of simple compound interest is a prerequisite to understanding the pros and cons of investing in zero coupon bonds.

SIMPLE ANNUAL INTEREST

The following discussions are taken from the *Dow Jones-Irwin Guide to Interest*. If you invest $1000 today at 4 percent simple annual interest, after one year the account is worth $1040; after two years, $1080, and so on. A $1000 investment maturing in 10 years would thus have a value of $1400 at maturity— $1000 + $40 (year 1) + $40 (year 2) + $40 (year 3) and so on until year 10. The formula for calculating simple interest is

$$I = P \times i \times T$$

where I = interest earned
        P = principal (e.g., $1000)
        i = rate of annual interest (e.g., 4 percent, or 0.04)
        T = time in years (e.g., 1 year).

Thus in the example given, after one year the interest earned (I) is $1000 × 0.04 × 1, or $40.

The value of the account (S) is the original principal ($1000) plus the interest earned ($40). Thus

$$S = P + I$$

and since

$$I = P \times i \times T$$

and

$$S = P + P \times i \times T \quad \text{or} \quad S = P(1 + iT)$$

After two years, the value of the account, with 4 percent simple annual interest, is

$$S = P(1 + iT)$$
$$= 1000(1 + 0.04 \times 2)$$
$$= 1000(1.08)$$
$$= 1080$$

However, this calculation fails to take into consideration the interest earned in the second year on the $40 interest from the first year. Interest paid only on the original principal is called "simple interest."[1]

COMPOUND INTEREST

Compound interest is calculated as shown in the following 10-year table:

Year	P Principal at Beginning	I Annual Interest Earned During Year at 4% ($P \times i \times T$)	S Value at End of Year ($P + I$)
1	1000.	40.	1040.
2	1040.	41.6000	1081.6000
3	1081.6000	43.2640	1124.8640
4	1124.8640	44.9946	1169.8586
5	1169.8586	46.7943	1216.6529

(continued)

[1]Lawrence R. Rosen, *Dow Jones-Irwin Guide to Interest,* Dow Jones-Irwin, Homewood, IL, 1981.

Year	P Principal at Beginning	I Annual Interest Earned During Year at 4% ($P \times i \times T$)	S Value at End of Year ($P + I$)
6	1216.6529	48.6661	1265.3190
7	1265.3190	50.6128	1315.9318
8	1315.9318	52.6373	1368.5691
9	1368.5691	54.7428	1423.3118
10	1423.3118	56.9326	**1480.2444**

The formula for determining S, the value of an account after a period of years n (e.g., 10), started with an original investment, P (e.g., 1000), at i annual compound interest (e.g., .04), is[2]

$$
\begin{aligned}
S &= P(1 + i)^n \\
&= 1000(1.04)^{10} \\
&= 1000(1.480244) \\
&= \$1480.244
\end{aligned}
$$

Thus the account earning compound interest is worth $80.24 more than the account earning simple interest ($1480.24 less $1400).

This identical compound interest formula is that which is used to calculate the purchase price, or total value, or compound rate of interest earned in a zero coupon bond investment. In the case of a zero coupon security, S is the value at maturity, i is the annual (or periodic) interest rate, n is the number of years or periods the investment is held, and P is the purchase price.

[2]Lawrence R. Rosen, *The Dow Jones-Irwin Guide to Calculating Yields,* Dow Jones-Irwin, Homewood, IL, 1985.

USING THE GRAPHS TO QUICKLY FIND SOLUTIONS TO COMPOUND INTEREST PROBLEMS: EXAMPLES

Example 1: Refer to Graph 2-1. After eight years, how much is $1000 worth if it earns 6 percent compound annual interest? The value would be $1593.85. The formula is

$$S = P(1 + i)^n$$
$$= 1000(1.06)^8$$
$$= 1000(1.59385)$$
$$= \underline{\$1593.85}$$

Example 2: Similarly, a $100 investment at 6 percent after eight years would be worth $159 and an original $10,000 investment about $15,939.

Example 3: Marshall McGrewder has $10,000 today and estimates that he can earn 5 percent per year compounded. How many years will it take for his investment to reach $30,000 if no withdrawals are made?

To find the solution in Graph 2-2, the problem may be restated as follows: At 10 percent compound interest, how long does it take an investment of $1000 ($10,000) to increase to $3000 ($30,000)?

As the dotted line shows, it would take about 11.5 years.

Example 4: How long would it take $4000 to increase to $40,000 at 10 percent compound interest? Rephrased, the question is: How long would it take $4000 to multiply itself 10 times? The solution to the problem is equivalent to the time required for $1000 to grow to $10,000. This would require 24.1 years.

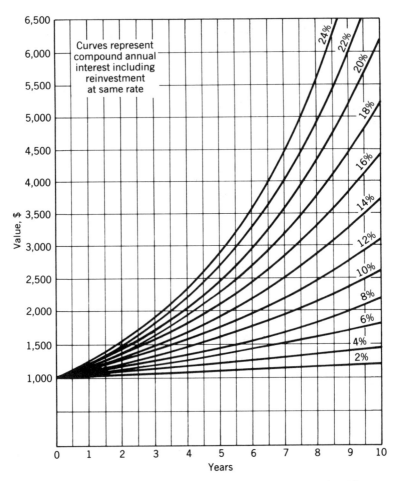

Graph 2-1. Zero Coupon Bonds, 1–10 Years to Maturity (*Source:*
Lawrence R. Rosen, *Dow Jones-Irwin Guide to Calculating Yields—Quick
Solutions for Investment Selection Using Computer Generated Internal Rate
of Return Analysis,* Dow Jones-Irwin, Homewood, IL, 1985).

Note: For tax brackets above 0 percent, before using the graph, multiply
the compound interest rate by [1 − tax bracket] and use the amount so determined as the curve in the graph.

Example: Tax bracket   50%   0.20 × (1 − 0.5) = 0.20 × 0.5

Compound interest   20%   = 10%

Use the 10% curve

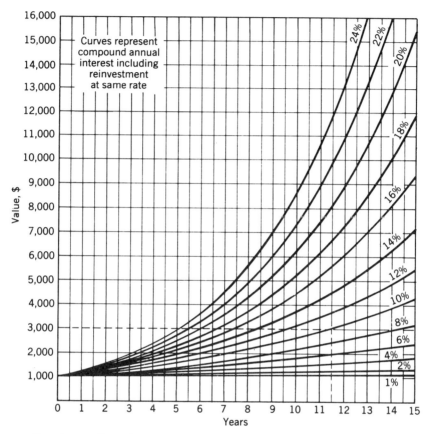

Graph 2-2. Zero Coupon Bonds, 1–15 Years to Maturity (*Source:*
Lawrence R. Rosen, *Dow Jones-Irwin Guide to Calculating Yields—Quick
Solutions for Investment Selection Using Computer Generated Internal Rate
of Return Analysis,* Dow Jones-Irwin, Homewood, IL, 1985).

Note: For tax brackets above 0 percent, before using the graph, multiply
the compound interest rate by [1 − tax bracket] and use the amount so determined as the curve in the graph.

Example: Tax bracket   30%
        Compound interest   10%
        $0.10 \times (1 - 0.3) = 0.10 \times 0.7$
                         $= 7\%$

        Use the 7% curve

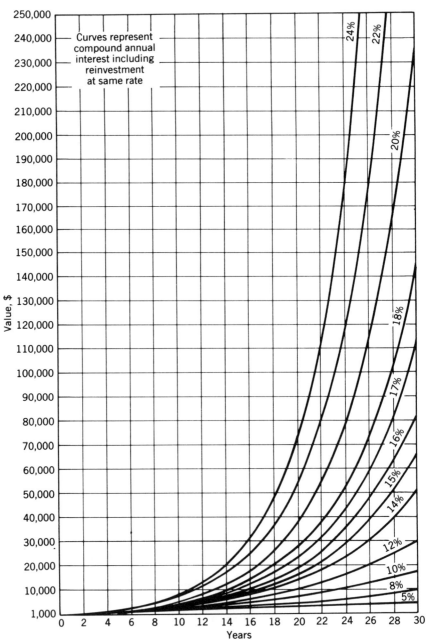

Graph 2-3. Zero Coupon Bonds, 1–30 Years to Maturity (*Source:*
Lawrence R. Rosen, *Dow Jones-Irwin Guide to Calculating Yields—Quick
Solutions for Investment Selection Using Computer Generated Internal Rate
of Return Analysis,* Dow Jones-Irwin, Homewood, IL, 1985).
(See Note on page 15)

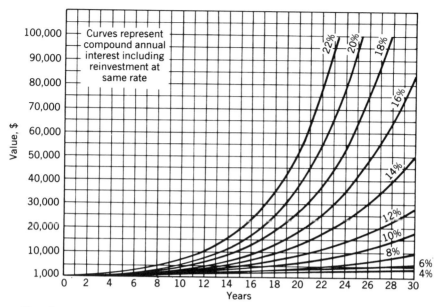

Graph 2-4. Zero Coupon Bonds, 1–30 Years to Maturity (expanded).

Refer to Graph 2-3. Your goal is to have $50,000 at the end of 19 years. Assuming money can earn 17 percent compounded, how much must be invested today? Start on the bottom axis of the graph at 19 years, proceed up to the 17 percent curve, then horizontally to the left axis. This shows that $1000 will grow to $20,000 after 19 years at the 17 percent rate.

The problem then is as follows. Where x is the sum that must

Note (for Graph 2–3): For tax brackets above 0 percent, before using the graph, multiply the compound interest rate by [1 − tax bracket] and use the amount so determined as the curve in the graph.

Example: Tax bracket   50%

Compound interest   20%

0.20 × (1 − 0.5)   = 0.20 × 0.5
                                = 10%

Use the 10% curve

be invested today to reach $50,000 after 19 years at 17 percent compounded:

$$\frac{\$1000}{\$20,000} = \frac{x}{\$50,000}$$
$$\$20,000x = \$50,000 \times \$1000$$
$$x = \underline{\$2500}$$

Hence, $2500 invested today will be worth $50,000 at 17 percent compounded after 19 years.[3]

See Graph 2-4 for a "blow-up" or expanded picture covering the $1,000 to $100,000 range of values.

INTERNAL RATE OF RETURN FOR SINGLE INVESTMENTS

A single investment of, say, $1000 paying 10 percent per year simple interest ($100) is equivalent to an internal rate of return (IRR) of 10 percent. Simple interest by definition means that interest is calculated on the original investment (principal) only (i.e., cash flows are not reinvested). If cash flows were reinvested, and if interest were calculated on the combined principal and previously reinvested interest, then the interest would be compound rather than simple. Thus the cash flows for a single investment at simple interest would be as follows:

Initial negative cash flow is the initial investment

Annual cash flows equal the initial investment times the interest rate

Cash flow in the final year is the annual interest plus the return of the original investment

The IRR is equal to the simple interest rate[4]

[3]*Ibid.*
[4]*Ibid.*

The IRR is the same as yield to maturity (YTM). The YTM or IRR may be defined as follows: the interest rate that equates the expected or scheduled cash inflows (e.g., interest receipts and proceeds of sale) from an investment to the initial (and subsequent, if any) cash outlays (cash investment). The process of "equating" the initial investment to the future cash flows requires discounting each future cash flow back to the present using the YTM as the discount factor for the relevant period of time. No reinvestment of cash flows is assumed in determining YTM or IRR. If reinvestment is taken into consideration (at whatever rate), the cash flows increase from those which were the case prior to such reinvestment, and the new higher return on investment is called "Revised IRR or Revised YTM." It is discussed in considerable detail in *The Dow Jones-Irwin Guide to Calculating Yields—Quick Solutions for Investment Selection Using Computer Generated Internal Rate of Return Analysis.*

Unless otherwise defined, the YTM or IRR is quoted before income and capital gains taxes. As a pre-tax measure, it is of value to tax-exempt entities (Keogh Plans, etc.), but taxpayers would be well advised to use after-tax IRRs or YTMs. After all, what matters from the standpoint of return on investment is not what you receive but what you are able to keep after the government takes its share.

In the case of zero coupon bonds, there is only one future cash flow, the maturity value (or sales proceeds if sold before maturity). As a result, the YTM or IRR for a zero coupon bond will always be equal to its "compound realized yield, realized compound yield or compound realized return (CRR)." The CRR was coined as a term in 1972 by Sidney Homer and Martin Leibowitz in *Inside the Yield Book* as "the total effective compound yield obtained from a bond purchased at a given price when the coupon income is reinvested and thus compounded at a specified reinvestment rate over the entire life of the bond." In other words, CRR is simply the compound rate of interest that equates the initial investment in a bond to its terminal value, where the terminal value is the value at maturity of all the cash flows from the bond including reinvested interest, if any. Since the CRR is sometimes referred to in literature, it is mentioned at this point. Often the CRR is erroneously confused with YTM and IRR. The CRR is normally not the same as IRR or YTM. The only case in which YTM or IRR equals the CRR is when the interest from a bond is reinvested at a percentage rate equal to the YTM at purchase. Since the imputed (theoretical annual accretion in value) cash flows from a zero are required to be reinvested, it holds true that for a zero YTM or IRR will always equal CRR.

An example of YTM, Revised YTM, and CRR is: a $1000 investment at 10 percent simple interest has cash flows of a negative $1000 at the beginning (the initial investment), $100 per year thereafter for five years, plus, in the fifth and final year, an additional $1000 return of principal. (Cash outflows such as the initial investment are treated as negative (minus) numbers and cash inflows (interest receipts, etc.) are treated as positive numbers.)

The IRR is 10 percent. The future cash flows discounted at 10 percent add up to the initial $1000 investment.

$$1000 = \frac{100}{1.1^1} + \frac{100}{1.1^2} + \frac{100}{1.1^3} + \frac{100}{1.1^4} + \frac{1100}{1.1^5}$$

$$1000 = 90.91 + 82.64 + 75.13 + 68.30 + 683.02$$

$$1000 = 1000$$

Continuing with the same example, the compound realized return is 8.45 percent. $1000 compounded at 8.45 percent for five years equals the $1500 terminal value ($1000 plus 5 times $100).

$$1000 \times 1.0845^5 = 1500$$

No reinvestment is required to achieve the IRR. At the lower compound realized return rate of 8.45 percent there are also no reinvestment earnings.[5] If the cash flows are reinvested at the 10 percent YTM, the terminal value at the end of five years increases to $1610.50 (from $1500), the Revised YTM is 11.95 percent, and the CRR is 10 percent.

SINGLE INVESTMENTS WITH COMPOUNDED INTEREST

Single Sum at Maturity as in Zero Coupon Bond Investment

With a zero coupon bond an investment is made today and no cash flow is received until maturity. There are no intervening cash flows. The only cash flows are the initial investment, which is negative, and the amount received at maturity, which is positive. For example, a $1000 initial investment that matures in 30 years and is compounded annually at 10 percent will be worth $17,449 at maturity. The cash flows are a negative $1000 at the beginning and a positive $17,449 at the end of 30 years. There is zero cash flow in the intervening years between the beginning and the end. The IRR is 10 percent. (See Graph 2-3.) (For a $1000 investment at 10 percent simple interest, the initial investment is $1000, and the sum received at maturity is $4000 (which is the $1000 maturity value plus $3000 in interest). In this case, the IRR is 4.73 percent.)

To achieve the same $17,449 result, one could buy a $1000 bond at par, paying $100 per year interest, and reinvest all the interest at a reinvestment rate of 10 percent, for a revised IRR

[5]*Ibid.*

of 19.13 percent. In this situation, the terminal value of $17,449 is comprised of:

Maturity value	$ 1,000
Interest on interest	$13,449
Regular interest	$ 3,000
Revised IRR	19.13%

A single investment (e.g., $1000) compounded to maturity (e.g., $17,449) at an interest rate of x percent (e.g., 10%) is the same as investing the amount of the single investment (e.g., $1000) in a conventional par bond, purchased at an IRR or yield to maturity of x percent (e.g., 10%), reinvesting all interest income at a rate of x percent (e.g., 10%), to obtain a resulting revised IRR of "greater than" x percent (e.g., 19.13%).[6]

Cash Flows Reinvested Periodically

The second possibility is when a single investment occurs, annual (periodic) distributions are received, and those distributions are reinvested at a reinvestment percentage rate. For example, $10,000 is invested for three years in Bond A, which returns 10 percent simple interest. In Bond B, interest is reinvested at a reinvestment rate of 10 percent. In Bond C, $10,000 is invested at the beginning, no intervening cash flows are received, and $13,310 is recouped at the end of three years.[7] The cash flows and IRRs are:[8]

---

[6]*Ibid.* See Chapter 9, What Zero Coupon "Yield" Really Means for a more detailed discussion of the foregoing.

[7]Bond A is a conventional bond, with no reinvestment; Bond B is a conventional bond with reinvestment at the same IRR (10 percent) as the IRR at purchase; Bond C is comparable to a zero coupon bond bought at a 10 percent IRR or YTM.

[8]*Ibid.* Lawrence R. Rosen, *The Dow Jones-Irwin Guide to Calculating Yields*, Dow Jones-Irwin, Homewood, IL, 1985.

	Bond A	Bond B	Bond C
Initial investment	$10,000	$10,000	$10,000
IRR	10%	10%	10%
Reinvestment rate	0%	10%	Compulsory 10%
Terminal value	$13,000	$13,310	$13,310

		Bond A				Bond B	
Year	Interest	Principal	Beginning Balance	Interest on Interest	Interest	Ending Balance	Cash Flow
0	0	− 10,000	0	0	0	0	− 10,000
1	1,000		0	0	1,000	1,000	1,000
2	1,000		1,000	100	1,000	2,100	1,100
3	1,000	+ 10,000	2,100	210	1,000	3,310	11,210

Cash Flows Summary and IRR

	Bond A		Bond B		Bond C
Year	10 Percent Simple	Cumulative	Cash Flows Reinvested at 10 Percent	Cumulative	Single Sum at Maturity
0	− 10,000		− 10,000		− 10,000
1	1,000	1,000	1,000	1,000	
2	1,000	2,000	1,100	2,100	
3	11,000	13,000	11,210	13,310	13,310
Revised IRR	10%[a]		10.96%[b]		10.96%[c]

[a]$11,000 \ (1.1)^{-3} + 1,000 \ (1.1)^{-2} + 1,000 \ (1.1)^{-1} = 10,000$
[b]$11,210 \ (1.1096)^{-3} + 1,100 \ (1.1096)^{-2} + 1,100 \ (1.1096)^{-1} = 10,000$
[c]$13,310 \ (1.1)^{-3} = 10,000$

Bond A's cash flow is not reinvested. If Bond A's cash flow were reinvested at a 10 percent rate, then Bond A would be transformed into Bond B. The terminal value of Bond B is equal to that of Bond C, $13,310. Bond A is inferior to Bond C at reinvestment rates below 10 percent and superior to Bond C at reinvestment rates greater than 10 percent. At a 10 percent reinvestment rate, Bond A and Bond C are equivalent with a revised IRR of 10.96 percent for both. Bond C's IRR (which is fully compounded) is 10 percent, and the progression of annual values is:

	Value	Change
Year 1 (beginning)	$10,000	
Year 1 (end)	11,000	+1,000
Year 2	12,100	+1,100
Year 3	13,310	+1,210

The revised IRR for Bond C is determinable by the imputed cash flows ($1000, $1100, and $11,210) that are automatically and irrevocably reinvested at the IRR rate of 10 percent. These imputed cash flows are identical to Bond B's, as is the revised IRR of Bond C, 10.96 percent.[9]

The zero coupon graphs earlier in this chapter allow the user to quickly determine the Yield to Maturity (YTM) or Internal Rate of Return (IRR) resulting from almost any zero coupon bond investment situation. The graphs (1) assume a zero tax bracket or tax-exempt investor and (2) do not take into effect possible call provisions that could cause the bond to be retired or redeemed prior to the stated maturity.

Example 1: Roger Shafer, a stock broker, calls a prospective investor, David Melin, an affluent elderly man, with the following proposition:

ROGER: "David, I've got a hot investment for you! It couldn't be safer (or my name isn't Shafer)—it's based on U.S. Treasury bonds. Now, what could be safer than the government?

---

[9]*Ibid.*

You simply invest $33,378 now and in 30 years you get back $1 million. That's almost 30 times or 3000 percent of your investment. The actual Treasury bonds are held by H & M Bank and Trust Co. as custodian and the bank issues to you a certificate of ownership. Shall I go ahead and buy it for you?"

DAVID: "Just a minute, please, Roger. I'd like to look at a book I just bought for a moment before I decide."

Melin turns to Graph 2-3. Let's see, he reasons, $1 million at maturity divided by the purchase price of $33,378 is 29.96. So the proposed investment would multiply by about 30 times in 30 years. That would produce the same return (IRR) as an increase from $1000 to $30,000 in 30 years. Melin draws a line horizontally across the graph starting from the $30,000 point on the left vertical axis. He then finds 30 years on the bottom axis and draws a vertical line up until the $30,000 line is reached. The curve that passes through (or closest to) this junction or point of intersection of the two lines indicates the IRR. In this case, the IRR is about 12 percent. So, Melin asks himself, why should I invest at a 12 percent YTM or IRR when much higher yields are currently available to me? "No thanks, not today," he says to Roger.

Example 2: John McClain reads an ad that says "Quadruple your investment in government bonds!" The small print says the investment is for 14.5 years and no earnings are paid until maturity. John wonders what the true YTM or IRR really is.

He turns to Graph 2-2. Quadrupling would be equivalent to $1000 growing to $4000. He enters the graph on the left vertical axis at $4000 and draws a horizontal line across the graph. Then he finds the 14.5-year mark on the bottom horizontal axis and draws a vertical line up the graph toward the top of the page. At the point it intersects the $4000 horizontal line, the nearest curve indicates the IRR or YTM, which in this case is about 10 percent.

Example 3: Emma Striver is 30 and she wants to retire at 60 with $500,000 cash. She now has $10,000. At what rate would her $10,000 have to grow to reach the desired sum?

It must increase by 50 times (500,000 divided by 10,000 is 50). Use Graph 2-4. Enter the graph on the left axis at $50,000 and draw a horizontal line across the graph. Then draw a vertical line up from the 30-year point on the horizontal bottom axis. The curve closest to the point where the two lines intersect indicates the compound growth rate required for money to increase by 50 times in 30 years. In this case, that is about 14 percent.

Thus if Emma buys a 30-year maturity zero coupon bond, yielding 14 percent, she should have a maturity value of about $500,000.

3

Beware of Zero Coupon Volatility

FACTORS AFFECTING VOLATILITY

The following is taken from *The Dow Jones-Irwin Guide to Calculating Yields*. The volatility, that is, the percentage price change of a bond is a function of three factors: maturity, coupon rate, and the starting level of yields. The longer the maturity, the lower the coupon rate, and the higher the initial yield to maturity, the greater is the price volatility. Conversely, the shorter the maturity, the higher the coupon rate, and the lower the initial yield to maturity, the lower is the price volatility.[1]

Beware of zero coupon price volatility. Some zero coupon bonds (those with longer time periods until maturity) are extremely volatile in price. That is, *small* changes in market interest rates cause much larger percentage changes in the market value of the zero coupon bond. For example, Sally Abelson buys zero coupon bonds for $3338 at 12 percent fully compounded (12 percent IRR with compulsory reinvestment at a 12 percent rate). But, if the market interest rate, 12 percent fully compounded, **increases by 25** percent (to 15 percent), then the market value of the bonds will **fall by 55 percent,** from $3338 to $1510. Compare the investment results between a conventional 30-year Treasury bond and a 30-year zero coupon bond between March 31, 1983 and March 31, 1984:[2]

Conventional 30-year Treasury bonds fell 3 percent.

The price of 30-year zeros fell 25 percent.

Thus, for a *given* increase in market interest rate levels during that one-year period of time, Treasury bonds dropped a mere 3 percent while zeros dropped 25 percent. Thus the tremendous volatility of zeros is evident. The price of the conventional Treasury bonds fell much more than 3 percent, but the negative

---

[1]Lawrence R. Rosen, *The Dow Jones-Irwin Guide to Calculating Yields,* Dow Jones-Irwin, Homewood, IL, 1985.
[2]Salomon Brothers' "CATS Market Update—March 1984," by Thomas E. Klaffky and Frances Sirianni; and Randall Smith, "Zero-Coupon Bonds' Price Swings Jolt Investors Looking for Security," *The Wall Street Journal,* June 1, 1984.

return was reduced to 3 percent by the positive benefit of one year's interest receipts. Had interest rates in general fallen the zeros would have outperformed the Treasury bonds, in price appreciation.

The magnitude of changes in bond price as the result of a change in interest rate levels is known as volatility.

It is well known that as economic conditions change, the yields to maturity and thus the prices of bonds fluctuate. If yields increase 5 percent and the value of your bond falls 50 percent, your bond is said to be more volatile than a bond which declines only 3 percent under the same conditions. Volatility measures the percentage price fluctuations of bonds, and relative volatility is a comparison of such fluctuations between different bonds. Volatility varies according to:

Coupon Rate. *Low* coupon issues are *more* volatile than those with high coupons.

Maturity. The *more distant* the maturity the higher the volatility.

Initial Yield to Maturity. Issues with *higher* yields to maturity at time of purchase are more volatile than issues with lower yields to maturity at time of purchase.[3]

Table 3-1 summarizes the factors that influence volatility.

Table 3-1. Price Volatility

Bond Feature	Characteristics of Low Volatility	Characteristics of High Volatility
Coupon rate	Higher coupons	Lower coupons
Maturity	Near or short	Distant
Initial yield to maturity	Lower	Higher

Source: Lawrence R. Rosen, *The Dow Jones-Irwin Guide to Calculating Yields,* Dow Jones-Irwin, Homewood, IL, 1985.

[3]Lawrence R. Rosen, *The Dow Jones-Irwin Guide to Calculating Yields,* Dow Jones-Irwin, Homewood, IL, 1985.

BOND PRICE VOLATILITY—SHORT VERSUS LONG MATURITIES[4]

A given change in bond yield to maturity has a progressively greater effect on the bond price as the time until maturity lengthens. Compare, for example, a 6 percent coupon, $1000 bond, bought at par to yield 6 percent until maturity with a zero coupon bond bought at a 6 percent yield. Table 3-2 shows for various maturities the change in bond price that results from an increase in yield to maturity from 6 percent at the time of purchase to 9 percent sometime thereafter.

While the price volatility generally increases with longer maturities, the incremental increases diminish as maturity lengthens. As shown in Table 3-2, for the 6 percent coupon bond, a 50 percent increase in yield to maturity results in an **11.7** percent **drop** in bond price for a **five**-year maturity versus a **30.8** percent **drop** for a **30-year** maturity. For a zero coupon bond, the price decreases after a 50 percent increase in yield range from 13 percent for a five-year bond to 56.7 percent for a 30-year maturity. Thus for a 30-year maturity the price decline of the zero coupon bond, 56.7 percent, is substantially more than the coupon bond's decline of 30.8 percent.

BOND PRICE VOLATILITY—HIGH VERSUS LOW COUPONS[5]

The lower the coupon rate of a bond, the greater is the change in the bond price that takes place from a given change in yield to maturity. For example, consider a 6 percent coupon, $1000 bond, bought at par to yield 6 percent until maturity. Table 3-3 shows the change in bond price that results from an increase in yield to maturity from 6 percent to 9 percent for a bond with a 20-year maturity for various coupon rates.

[4]*Ibid.*
[5]*Ibid.*

Table 3-2. Maturity Effect on Volatility

Years to Maturity	Yield to Maturity			6% Coupon Bond Price			Zero Coupon Bond Price		
	Original	Revised	Percent Change	Original	Revised[a]	Percent Change	Original	Revised[a]	Percent Change
5	6%	9%	50%	$1000	$883	−11.7%	$747	$650	−13.0%
10	6	9	50	1000	807	−19.3	558	422	−24.4
15	6	9	50	1000	758	−24.2	417	274	−34.2
20	6	9	50	1000	726	−27.4	312	178	−42.8
25	6	9	50	1000	705	−29.5	233	116	−50.2
30	6	9	50	1000	692	−30.8	174	75	−56.7

Source: Lawrence R. Rosen, *The Dow Jones-Irwin Guide to Calculating Yields*, Dow Jones-Irwin, Homewood, IL, 1985.

[a]Revised price after yield to maturity increases from 6 to 9 percent.

Table 3-3. Coupon Effect on Volatility

	Yield to Maturity			Bond Price		
Coupon	Original	Revised	Percent Change	Original	Revised[a]	Percent Change
12%	6%	9%	50%	$1688	$1274	−24.5%
10	6	9	50	1459	1091	−25.2
8	6	9	50	1229	909	−26.1
6	6	9	50	1000	726	−27.4
4	6	9	50	771	544	−29.5
2	6	9	50	541	361	−33.3
0	6	9	50	312	178	−42.8

Source: Lawrence R. Rosen, *The Dow Jones-Irwin Guide to Calculating Yields,* Dow Jones-Irwin, Homewood, IL, 1985.
[a]Revised, after yield increases from 6 to 9 percent.

Thus with a $120 coupon (12 percent), a 50 percent increase in yield to maturity results in a price drop of 24.5 percent, but with a $20 coupon (2 percent), the price decreases by 33.3 percent from the same yield change, and for a zero coupon bond the price decreases by 42.8 percent.

BOND PRICE VOLATILITY—MAGNITUDE OF YIELD TO MATURITY AT PURCHASE[6]

Is volatility greater if the yield to maturity at the time of purchase is *low* (for example, 2 percent) as compared to *high* (for example, 8 percent)? The answer is emphatically **no.** The *higher* the yield to maturity at time of purchase, the *greater* is the bond price volatility. This principle is evidenced by Table 3-4.

Table 3-4 shows that a 50 percent increase in yield to maturity results in only a 12.6 percent drop in bond price at a 2 percent

[6]*Ibid.*

Table 3-4. Volatility and Yield at Purchase

Yield to Maturity			Coupon Bond Price[a]			Zero Coupon Bond Price		
Initial	Revised	Percent Change	Initial	Revised[b]	Percent Change	Initial	Revised[b]	Percent Change
2%	3%	50%	$1,654	$1446	−12.6%	673	554	−17.7
4	6	50	1272	1000	−21.4	456	312	−31.7
6	9	50	1000	726	−27.4	312	178	−42.8
8	12	50	804	552	−31.3	215	104	−51.7

Source: Lawrence R. Rosen, *The Dow Jones-Irwin Guide to Calculating Yields*, Dow Jones-Irwin, Homewood, IL, 1985.
[a]Bond Price based on $60 coupon, 20 years to maturity with interest paid annually.
[b]Price for revised yield to maturity.

yield at purchase but results in a much larger, 31.3 percent, drop
at an 8 percent yield at purchase level. In other words, the *higher*
the yield to maturity at purchase, the *greater* is the volatility.
Zero coupon bonds exhibit even larger price declines for a given
increase in yields. As shown in Table 3-4, zero coupon bond price
declines range from 17.7 percent for a 2 percent yield to maturity
at purchase to 51.7 percent when the yield to maturity at purchase is 8 percent.

DURATION: A MEANS OF PREDICTING PRICE FLUCTUATION

The fluctuation of bond prices resulting from changes in yields
to maturity is known as *volatility*. A method of attempting to
measure such volatility is through a concept known as *duration,*
which was introduced by F.R. Macaulay (*Some Theoretical Problems Suggested by Movements on Interest Rates, Bond Yields,
and Stock Prices in the United States since 1856;* New York:
National Bureau of Economic Research, 1938).

Duration gives a useful but limited indication of the volatility
of a bond. It is essentially a time-weighted present value measure.

A view of how *duration* is regarded in the bond industry is
provided by Gabriele, Hueglin & Cashman, Inc. in their newsletter, "Special Memorandum," dated November 1, 1984:

> Crudely defined, duration is the average life of all the payment
> received from a bond investment. Because duration considers in-
> terest as well as principal, it is the more accurate measure (as
> compared to maturity alone) of the life of an investment and a
> much more useful gauge of interest rate risk and price volatility.

Calculating Duration

Duration is a measure of the average time that it takes to realize
the present value of the projected cash flows from an investment.

The formula for its calculation is

$$D = \frac{\left[\dfrac{c*1}{(1 + r)} + \dfrac{c*2}{(1 + r)^2} + \dfrac{c*3}{(1 + r)^3} \cdots \dfrac{c*n}{(1 + r)^n} + \dfrac{m*n}{(1 + r)^n}\right]}{P}$$

where D = duration (in years)
c = annual coupon payment (or semiannual)
n = number of annual time periods (or semiannual) at maturity
$*$ = symbol for multiplication or "times"
P = the price of the bond or its market value
r = IRR ($r/2$ if semiannual)
m = maturity value

Duration is calculated in Table 3-5 for a 10-year $1000 bond, with $60 coupon, selling at par for a yield to maturity or IRR of 6 percent. The formula values $c*1$, $c*2$, and so forth are shown in column c of Table 3-5. Column d is the present value of the amounts in column c discounting at the YTM rate. The duration in this case is 7.8.

For a zero coupon bond the duration is equal to the number of years to maturity. If the bond just described above had been a zero coupon issue, the duration would have been 10. The formula for duration for a zero coupon bond reduces to just the following:

$$\frac{n*m}{(1 + r)^n} \bigg/ \frac{m}{(1 + r)^n} = n$$

So the duration of a zero coupon bond is always equal to the number of years until its maturity. A coupon bond's duration will always be less than the number of years until its maturity. The duration is a measure of volatility and the higher the duration, the more volatile the price fluctuations of the bond.

Table 3-5. Calculation of Duration

	$1000	Purchase price
	$60	Coupon
	10	Years

(a)	(b)	(c)	(d)
			(years $\times$ CF)
		Years $\times$	
Cash Flows	Year	Cash Flow	$(1 + YTM)^n$
-1000	0	0	—
60	1	60	56.6
60	2	120	106.8
60	3	180	151.1
60	4	240	190.1
60	5	300	224.2
60	6	360	253.8
60	7	420	279.3
60	8	480	301.2
60	9	540	319.6
1060	10	10600	5919.0
Total			7802
Duration			7.8
$-$Duration $\times$ YTM change			-23.4
$\dfrac{-\text{Duration}}{(1 + \text{YTM})} \times$ YTM change			-23.2

Modified Duration Allows Price Fluctuation Estimation

A slight modification to the duration allows a rule-of-thumb estimation as to the specific bond price fluctuation that will occur. The modification to duration is simply to divide it by $(1 + r/2)$ where r is the yield to maturity.

For the bond in Table 3-5, the modified duration is

$$\frac{7.80}{(1 + .06/2)} = \frac{7.80}{1.03} = 7.57$$

To predict or estimate a price change in a bond, using the modified duration, the method is simply

price change = − modified duration
             × percentage change in yield to maturity

For example, if the yield to maturity increases from 6 to 9 percent, the percentage change in yield to maturity is 3. And the product of the negative modified duration (− 7.57) and the 3 percent change is − 22.7 percent. The actual price change would be − 19.3 percent. Thus the rule of thumb is not a very accurate estimator.

Table 3-6 shows the relationship for a change in yield of 3 percent (from a 6 percent yield to maturity to 9 percent) on price and compares such price changes to the "duration estimates."

Inspection of Table 3-6 shows the duration method to be a meager estimator of price changes for the conditions shown. And the greater the time period until maturity, the poorer the estimates become. If the YTM increases from 6 to 9 percent, for a 30-year maturity, for example, the price of the bond declines from $1000 to $692, a decline of 30.8 percent. But, the adjusted or modified duration is 14.17 which multiplied by the 3 percent change in yield estimates the price decline at 42.5 percent. And a decline of 42.5 percent is 138 percent greater than the actual decline.

The discrepancies decrease as the magnitude of the changes in yield decrease. The forecasting ability of modified duration improves accordingly.

Factors Affecting Duration

Duration is affected by the same three factors that affect volatility—high or low coupons, level of yield to maturity, and years until maturity. Short durations correspond to reduced volatility.

Table 3-6. Duration and Price Changes

	Purchase price of bond	$1000
	Coupon	$60
	Yield to maturity at purchase	6 percent

Maturity	Duration	Price at 9 Percent YTM	Actual Percent Change in Price	Modified Duration	Estimated Price Change by Duration Method	Relative Accuracy of Estimate
5	4.47	883	−11.7	4.34	−13.0	111%
10	7.80	807	−19.3	7.57	−22.7	118
15	10.29	758	−24.2	9.99	−30.0	124
20	12.16	726	−27.4	11.81	−35.4	129
25	13.55	705	−29.5	13.16	−39.5	134
30	14.59	692	−30.8	14.17	−42.5	138

Thus a higher bond coupon (as compared to an otherwise comparable bond with a lower coupon) means a shorter duration and less volatility. Other characteristics of lower volatility and shorter duration are lower levels of yield to maturity and shorter time periods until maturity.

IMMUNIZATION, DEDICATION, AND PENSION PLANS

Pension plans, life insurance annuity policies, and other insurers have the problem of having to pay a fixed, determinable, or estimable benefit in the future. In the case of a pension plan, it is the payment of monthly income for life or as provided in the pension plan. Managers of pension plans, insurance assets, and so forth, have the problem of meeting those future liabilities by investing their assets in a manner that will produce enough cash flow at as low a cost to the sponsor or corporation as possible while maintaining a sensible level of risk.

The cash flows of a bond investment portfolio consist of interest, redemptions of bonds at maturity, and the interest-on-interest earned from reinvestment. With normal coupon bond investments, the interest-on-interest proceeds in the future are unpredictable because the rate at which future reinvestment will occur is unknown. *Zero coupon bond investment provides a valuable tool for portfolio management in locking in a reinvestment rate and eliminating that unpredictable element in managing pension plan assets.*

Immunization Immunization is the term that applies to the attempt to insulate or immunize a bond portfolio from the risks of interest rate fluctuation. As just mentioned, the primary risk is that of the rate to be earned on reinvestment. Zero coupon bonds do a magnificent job of immunizing.

Another technique which preceded the availability of zero coupon bonds involves the concept of duration.

The three elements of total return from a bond, if one reinvests the income, are coupon interest, interest-on-interest from reinvesting, and maturity value. Let's say as a pension plan manager you plan to meet a $1 million liability in x years with $600,000 in bonds, with a coupon annually of $70,000 and interest-on-interest from reinvesting at a 9 percent rate. The first step is to match the average durations of both the assets and liabilities. If the bonds are selected so that the portfolio also has an average duration of x years, and the portfolio is continuously adjusted to maintain that duration, then it should be possible to wind up with the targeted $1 million no matter what happens to interest rates in the interim. If the durations are equal and interest rates decline, then capital gains from the bond portfolio will offset the reduced interest-on-interest from reinvesting. Should rates rise, then the capital losses from the bond portfolio will be offset by the higher rate earned on reinvestment.

The mathematics involved is such that it may be impossible to immunize a portfolio for as long a time period as desired. As noted earlier, the duration (except for zero coupon bonds) is shorter than the bond's term to maturity. *Zero coupon bonds offer a solution because their duration is equal to their maturity; hence a 30-year zero coupon bond has a duration of 30 as well.*

Dedication of Pension Assets   A variant of immunizing a portfolio is the concept of dedication. The objective of dedication is to raise the actuarial funding rate assumption used. A higher rate allows reduction or elimination of contributions to the plan by the plan sponsor. Alternatively, unfunded pension liabilities may be funded or benefit levels may be increased. To accomplish this objective, certain fund liabilities such as those of already retired persons are determined actuarially. Then an immunized bond portfolio is structured to provide the cash flows that will be needed to meet fully such future liabilities. As compared to the actuarial assumed rate (e.g., 7 percent) used for a certain pension plan, it may be that the yield is much higher (say, 13 percent) on this particular portfolio dedicated to meeting the specified liabilities. Discounting the future liabilities at 13 percent (with the actuary's consent) instead of 7 percent will produce a materially smaller present liability. In other words, certain of the pension plan's assets are "dedicated" to meeting a specified portion of the plan's liabilities.

Again, zero coupon bonds lend themselves beautifully to this concept because of the ability to lock in the rate at which reinvestment will occur. With any other bond, an actuary is not likely to agree to a reinvestment rate assumption of 13 or 14 percent. But if the high rate is locked in with a zero coupon bond, what choice does the actuary have? *The actuary's agreement to the high rate locked in by the zero means the pension plan needs less money and management can make a lower contribution while earning a higher income, higher earnings per share, and a higher market price.*

4

Beware of Taxation with Conventional Zeros

Brokerage firms extol the virtues of investing in zero coupon bonds. Their sales literature emphasizes the magical effects of compounding interest (always shown on a pre-tax basis) and the safety of a government-backed security. In some cases, zero coupon bonds are touted for pension, Keogh, IRA, and other tax-exempt investors.

Rarely does the literature dwell on the details of the taxability of such investments. But taxation must be dealt with, and failure to consider its effect may prove to be an expensive object lesson.

The annual taxable income is determined each year by multiplying the "accreted value" at the end of the previous year by the IRR. Note that the IRR method using semiannual compounding is applicable for bonds with original issue discount issued after July 1, 1982. For bonds issued July 1, 1982 or before, straight line amortization may be used. That accretion is then multiplied by the owner's percentage tax rate to determine the tax due and payable. Thus the cash flows each year are negative (due to the tax payable) until the year of maturity.

TAXABILITY OF NONMUNICIPAL ZEROS

The Internal Revenue Service (IRS) requires that the annual compound increase in value be treated as taxable interest, even though such interest is not payable until maturity. In other words, the purchaser of nonmunicipal zeros must pay tax each year on income which has *not* yet been received!

Table 4-1 shows the gory details for an investor who bought zero coupon bonds with an $8678 initial purchase. The bonds mature in 20 years for $100,000. The nontaxed yield to maturity (YTM) or internal rate of return (IRR) in this case is 13 percent. If taxed, however, the IRR plummets to a mere 6.5 percent.

The after-tax results are the same as if an $8678 bond was purchased at par (i.e., the purchase price and maturity value are identical). Such a par bond would annually earn $1128 (13

Table 4-1. Zero Coupon Bonds—After Tax

20	Number of years until maturity	
13.00%	Yield to maturity or IRR	
50.00%	Federal income tax bracket	
8,678.23	Purchase price of zero coupon Treasury bond	
100,000	Maturity value of bond	
11.5	Multiplier	

Year	Year-End Value	(Accretion) Pre-Tax Imputed Interest	Annual Tax	(Cash Flow) After Tax
0	8,678			−8,678
1	9,806	1,128	564	−564
2	11,081	1,275	637	−637
3	12,522	1,441	720	−720
4	14,150	1,628	814	−814
5	15,989	1,839	920	−920
6	18,068	2,079	1,039	−1,039
7	20,416	2,349	1,174	−1,174
8	23,071	2,654	1,327	−1,327
9	26,070	2,999	1,500	−1,500
10	29,459	3,389	1,695	−1,695
11	33,288	3,830	1,915	−1,915
12	37,616	4,328	2,164	−2,164
13	42,506	4,890	2,445	−2,445
14	48,032	5,526	2,763	−2,763
15	54,276	6,244	3,122	−3,122
16	61,332	7,056	3,528	−3,528
17	69,305	7,973	3,987	−3,987
18	78,315	9,010	4,505	−4,505
19	88,496	10,181	5,090	−5,090
20	100,000	11,504	5,752	94,248
Totals		91,322	45,661	45,661

Yield to Maturity or IRR
Pretax   13,000%
After Tax   6.500%

Table 4-2. Conventional Bonds, After Tax with Reinvestment

50%	Tax bracket of investor
20	Number of years until maturity
$8,678.23	Maturity Value: 60% of long-term gain untaxed
13%	Reinvestment rate earned before tax
$8,678.23	Purchase price of bond
$1,128.17	Coupon rate in dollars

			Interest Reinvestment			
Year	Cash Flows Each Year Before Reinvestment of Earnings	Balance Before Reinvestment	Original Balance	Annual Interest on Interest	Ending Balance with Reinvestment	Cash Flow per Year with Reinvestment
0	−8,678	0	0	0	0	−8,678
1	564	564	0	0.00	564	564
2	564	1,128	564	36.67	1,165	601
3	564	1,692	1,165	75.71	1,805	640
4	564	2,256	1,805	117.30	2,486	681

5	564	2,820	161.59	2,486	3,212	726
6	564	3,385	208.76	3,212	3,985	773
7	564	3,949	259.00	3,985	4,808	823
8	564	4,513	312.50	4,808	5,684	877
9	564	5,077	369.47	5,684	6,618	934
10	564	5,641	430.15	6,618	7,612	994
11	564	6,205	494.78	7,612	8,671	1,059
12	564	6,769	563.61	8,671	9,799	1,128
13	564	7,333	636.91	9,799	11,000	1,201
14	564	7,897	714.97	11,000	12,279	1,279
15	564	8,461	798.11	12,279	13,641	1,362
16	564	9,025	886.55	13,641	15,092	1,451
17	564	9,589	980.95	15,092	16,637	1,545
18	564	10,154	1081.38	16,637	18,282	1,645
19	564	10,718	1188.33	18,282	20,034	1,752
20	9,242	19,960	1302.24	20,034	30,579	10,545
	19,960		10,6̄9			30,579

Without reinvestment, the result is   Regular   IRR   6.50%

With reinvestment, the result is   Revised   IRR   10.33%

Source: Lawrence R. Rosen, "Investment Analysis—After Tax IRR for Stocks, Bonds and Real Estate," Copyright 1984 by L. R. Rosen, 7008 Springdale Road, Louisville, KY. Unauthorized reproduction is prohibited.

45

percent of the purchase price) in pre-tax interest and 6.5 percent per year after 50 percent tax, which translates to $564 per year. Note that in this case, none of the annual interest need be reinvested to achieve the IRR.

The year-by-year cash flows are shown in Table 4-2. The table also shows that if the after-tax income each year is reinvested to earn 13 percent before tax, the revised IRR (after reinvestment and tax) increases to 10.33 percent.

Technically, the applicable tax rules are those for bonds purchased with an *original issuance discount*. The interest included as taxable income each year is added to the cost basis of the bonds. Thus at sale either prior to or at maturity the capital gain or loss is based upon the difference between the sales price and the adjusted cost basis. For example, if the bond described in Table 4-1 is sold at the end of the tenth year for $34,459, a taxable capital gain of $5000 is realized. The gain is the sales price of $34,459 less the accreted value of $29,459 at the end of the tenth year.

GIFTS OF ZEROS TO MINOR CHILDREN

Zero coupon bonds are often recommended as an excellent means of building an education fund for minor children. The underlying theory is that since children are generally in a zero tax bracket, or a very low one, the resulting tax treatment will not be adverse. Let us test this theory. A grandfather gives his 10-year-old grandson $1000 to buy zero coupon bonds. The grandfather is registered as custodian. The bonds mature in 10 years. The grandson has no earnings from employment or from other investments. Tax rates remain unchanged during the period of the analysis. The analysis assumes the grandson's personal exemption is $1000. The bonds are purchased at a 13 percent pre-tax IRR. The IRR for the child after tax remains unchanged at 13 percent. Thus investing for the child would not have adverse tax

Table 4-3. Gift to Minors—After Tax

10	Number of years until maturity
13%	Yield to maturity or IRR
$1000	Purchase price of zero coupon Treasury bond
$3395	Maturity value of bond
3.4	Multiplier

Year	Year-End Value	(Accretion) Pre-Tax Imputed Interest	Income after $1000 Personal Exemption	Annual Tax	(Cash Flow) After Tax
0	1000				−1000
1	1130	130	0	0	0
2	1277	146	0	0	0
3	1443	166	0	0	0
4	1631	187	0	0	0
5	1842	212	0	0	0
6	2082	239	0	0	0
7	2353	270	0	0	0
8	2658	305	0	0	0
9	3004	345	0	0	0
10	3395	390	0	0	3395
Internal Rate of Return or Yield to Maturity (after tax)					13.0%

consequences in this instance. If $10,000 were invested for the same child, the tax difficulties would increase dramatically, however. The analysis is shown in Table 4-3.

ORIGINAL ISSUE DISCOUNT

Zero coupon bonds are taxed under the IRS's original issue discount rules. Original issue discount (OID) is the difference between the redemption price of a bond (say, $1000) and the issue price (say, $100 for a zero coupon bond). The OID in this case is

$900 (i.e., $1000 less $100). The OID rules discussed below do not apply to government securities which are payable without interest not more than one year from the date of issue (e.g., Treasury bills), tax-exempts, and U.S. savings bonds.

The OID may result in ordinary income (as in the case of an individual buying a CATS, TIGR, or STRIPS) or the OID may not be taxable as ordinary income (as in the case of a tax-exempt zero coupon bond). Tax-exempt municipal zero coupon issues are discussed in Chapter 6, Taxability of Municipal Zero Coupons.

An exception to the tax measures applying to OID may occur for certain "small" OIDs. In this case "small" means an OID at original issue not in excess of 1/4 of 1 percent (.0025) multiplied by the redemption price at maturity ($1000) multiplied by the number of complete years to maturity (e.g., 30). In this example, $75 is the limit. If the OID is $75 or more, then the entire amount is treated as OID. If the computation is less than $75, then OID may be totally disregarded. Since stripped coupons and bonds stripped of coupons were not originally issued at a discount, it is probable that the foregoing exception does not apply to them.

NUMEROUS TAX LAW CHANGES

There have been numerous tax law changes affecting the taxation of zero coupon bonds. Basically, the tax depends on when the bonds were issued and when they were acquired. Such governing dates include:

Pre-1955
Pre-May 28, 1969
July 1, 1982
July 18, 1984

Corporate Bonds Issued After 1954 and Before May 28, 1969
Government Bonds Issued After 1954 and Before July 2, 1982

No accrual of OID is required (i.e., a part of the OID does not have to be considered income each year).

Gain realized at sale or redemption is allocated, partly as ordinary income and partly as capital gain. If at the issuance of the bond there was no intention to call the bonds, then a gain is ordinary income to the extent of the OID attributable to the time the bonds were held. For example, Sam Shrewd buys a $1000 par bond at issue for $400, due in 15 years (180 months). If Sam sells the bond on the market five years later for $900, his long-term capital gain is $300. The OID is $600. The amount taxed as ordinary income is $200—the OID ($600) multiplied by the portion of the total life of the bonds that Sam owned the bonds (60 months divided by 180 months). In other words, the proceeds, $900, exceeded Sam's investment ($400) by $500, of which $200 is ordinary income and $300 is long-term capital gain.

Bond Issued Prior to 1955

These bonds are taxed as described in the preceding section (after 1954 and before May 28, 1969) except that for bonds issued with interest coupons or in registered form, at redemption capital gain or loss results.

Corporate Bonds Issued After May 27, 1969, and Before July 2, 1982

A ratable (straight-line method) portion of the OID must be included in income each year (even though such interest may not have been received in cash). The tax or adjusted basis is increased each year by the amount of OID included in income for that year. (If the bond is held to maturity, by such time the tax basis will equal the maturity value, thus eliminating any gain or loss at maturity.) For example, Gina Genius buys a 360-month bond for $640 at issuance. The OID is $360 (i.e., $1000 less $640). Straight-line amortization of the OID is $1 per month for the 360 months remaining until maturity. The annual ratable portion of the OID that is ordinary income is $12 per year. Thus the $360 OID is amortized by the straight-line method at the rate of $12 per year. During each full year of ownership Gina must report as ordinary interest income $12 per bond. And she increases the "tax adjusted basis" of the bond by the same $12. When the bond is sold or redeemed, the proceeds less "taxable basis" is taxable as follows: (1) if at issuance of the bonds there was no intention to call the bond, any gain or loss on disposition is a capital gain or loss; but (2) if there was (at issue) an intent to call, then any gain on disposition is ordinary to the extent of the unamortized OID.

The buyer, before July 2, 1982, of stripped coupons or a stripped bond reports interest income as the coupons mature. Resale of the coupons results in a capital gain or loss.

Subsequent Buyers (After Original Issuance)   A subsequent buyer of a bond issued with OID must continue to amortize the unamortized portion of the OID after deduction of amounts paid which are greater than the seller's adjusted taxable basis.

Freddie First buys a taxable bond at issue for $600, which matures at $1000. Freddie's OID is $400 ($1000 less $600). After a period of time he amortizes or accrues OID of $200, at which point his unamortized OID is $200 ($400 less $200) and his taxable adjusted basis is $800 (purchase price of $600 plus $200 accrued OID). Freddie now sells the bond at its market value to Paula Subsequent.

If Paula Subsequent pays $800 or less, then she must continue to amortize the OID at the same rate as did Freddie First prior to the sale—and Freddie First has a capital loss for the amount by which the sales proceeds are less than his $800 adjusted basis.

If Paula Subsequent pays $1000 or more, no further amortization of OID is required (and Freddie has a capital gain of $200 or more). If Paula Subsequent pays more than $800 but less than $1000, the remaining OID is reduced by the difference between Paula's cost and $800.

Bonds Issued After July 1, 1982

The OID must be amortized by the IRR method (i.e., compound semiannual amortization rather than straight line). This produces less taxable income than straight-line amortization in the early years and results in a lower taxable basis.

The buyer of stripped coupons or a stripped bond is subject to the OID rules.

Bonds Issued after July 18, 1984, and Market Discount

Historically, if one bought a taxable discount bond (bought for let's say, $700, originally issued at par of $1000) in the market (other than at the original issuance), the interest received during the year was taxable as ordinary income and a gain at redemption or earlier sale was a long- or short-term capital gain. After-tax yields were based on application of ordinary rates to the periodic interest. Long-term capital gain rates were generally applicable to the gain disposition. NO MORE! The Deficit Reduction Act of 1984 quietly changed the rules of the ball game, and amazingly few people seem to be aware of the changes. For bonds issued after July 18, 1984, on disposition of an obligation with an original maturity of over one year, taxpayers (except certain foreigners) are required to report as ordinary income any part of the gain, up to the amount of any market discount on the obligation that accrued while the taxpayer held the obligation.

The market discount rules do not apply to obligations maturing within a year, municipal bonds, installment sale obligations, and U.S. savings bonds. The market discount is considered to be zero and is disregarded if the market discount is less than 1/4 of 1 percent of the redemption price times the number of years to maturity.

Generally, the market discount (MD) (e.g., $200) is the excess of the sum of (1) the issue price (e.g., $1000) (IP) and (2) any accrued original issue discount (AOID) accrued to the date of purchase (e.g., $0 for most nonzero coupon bonds) OVER the taxpayer's purchase price (PP) (i.e., $800). Thus the determination of market discount is

$$MD = IP + AOID - PP$$

The accrued market discount (AMD) is generally determined by multiplying the market discount (MD) by a fraction the numerator of which is the number of days the taxpayer held the obligation (n) and the denominator of which is the number of days after the taxpayer acquired the obligation through the date of maturity (T). Thus the formula is

$$AMD = MD \times (n / T)$$

For example, Sally Ableson buys a taxable interest paying bond maturing in eight years from a broker for $800. Two years after the purchase, Sally sells the bond to Sam Subsequent for $835. What is Sally's tax situation with respect to the sale? The market discount (MD) at purchase is $200 (i.e., $1000 less $800). The accrued market discount (AMD) at sale is $50, determined as follows:

$$AMD = MD \times (n/T)$$
$$= 200 \times (2/8) = 50$$

The realized gain is \$35 (\$835 sales proceeds less \$800 cost). This gain is ordinary income to the extent of accrued market discount up to the date of disposition. Thus the entire gain is ordinary income. If the realized gain were greater than \$50 (the accrued market discount), then only \$50 of the gain would have been taxed as ordinary income and the excess of the gain over \$50 would have been long-term capital gain.

Sam Subsequent's tax situation is different. Sam's initial cost basis is \$835 and his market discount is \$165 (\$1000 less \$835).

Taxpayers are permitted to calculate the accrued market discount on a compound interest basis (i.e., YTM or IRR) instead of the straight-line method illustrated previously. Normally, the taxpayer will benefit by electing the compound interest method (YTM or IRR) because the calculated accrued market discount will be less than with straight line.

Severe limitations were placed by the 1984 Tax Reform Act on the deductibility of interest paid to purchase (after July 18, 1984) or carry market discount obligations. (An election, when possible, should be made to deduct the interest deferral amount.)

Buyers of discount bonds issued after July 18, 1984, may find that both OID and MD rules apply. For example, the issuance price after July 18, 1984, is \$900 for a \$1000 bond. The OID is \$100. At a time when the accrued OID is \$30, the original buyer sells it later for \$800 to Sam Subsequent. In Sam's hands, the bond has unamortized OID of \$70 (the original \$100 less \$30 accrued by the first owner) and market discount of \$130, determined as follows:

$$MD = IP + AOID - PP$$
$$= 900 + 30 - 800 = 130$$

Congress has seen fit to make the rules exceedingly complex. To determine the tax treatment of a bond a myriad of dates and rules must be considered.

Nevertheless, the moral of this chapter is simple: "What's good for the Keogh plan or pension plan is *not* good for its owner." Check out the tax consequences of proposed investments carefully before investing and consult your tax advisor. Remember, its the after-tax (not the pre-tax) IRR that matters!

Municipal Zero Coupons

Beware of Call and Redemption Dangers

For the individual investor who is a taxpayer, there is another "breed of CAT." This is the zero coupon municipal bond, which is frequently referred to as a tax-exempt. The principal characteristic of such bonds is that their owners normally do not pay taxes on interest but are still subject to capital gains taxation. Primarily, such bonds have been brought out by state housing development agencies.

MUNICIPALS AND CALL PROVISIONS

At the time of underwriting a municipal issue, call features or special redemption features are one of the items negotiated between the issuers and the underwriters. Naturally, the municipal issuer wants to have as short (i.e., sooner in time) a call provision as possible so that if rates fall, it can refund the higher-rate issue with the proceeds of a lower-rate borrowing. Conversely, the bond purchasers want to have call protection for as long as possible. (Treasury bonds are generally noncallable except for the last five years of the original issue, the "callable tail.") In recent issuances, buyers of ordinary municipals have been protected against calls for 10 years from the date of original issue.

Redemption Provisions

Before purchasing any such bonds, read the prospectus carefully. Concentrate on such topics as special redemption, optional redemption, and sinking fund redemption. For example, the prospectus for a $15 million issue for residential mortgage revenue bonds, series 1984 in the City of Louisville, contains the following:

> Redemption of Bonds. The bonds are subject to redemption at par prior to maturity at the times described herein, including special

mandatory redemption in whole or in part from prepayments on the mortgage loans, from undisbursed bond proceeds reserved for the purpose of purchasing mortgage loans and from moneys received from certain other sources. It is anticipated that a portion of the bonds may be redeemed at par prior to their scheduled maturity pursuant to the special mandatory redemption provisions provided by the indenture.

In other words, an investor who thinks he or she has purchased a 20-year bond may be unpleasantly surprised to have it redeemed at par in only a year or two.

Redemption at par in this case means at the accreted value—in other words, the original issuance price compounded at the initial yield (IRR) to the date of redemption. The effect of such redemption possibilities at the issuer's option is onerous to the investor: If interest rates decline dramatically, the price of a noncallable bond would soar! If the bonds are called at the accreted value, however, the investor is robbed of possibilities of appreciation. Worse yet, if one purchases a callable bond (or one subject to redemption prior to maturity) in the secondary market, at a price in excess of the accreted value, and if that bond is called or redeemed at par, (i.e., the formula accreted value), an unexpected capital loss may be realized.

Some bonds, particularly housing finance issues, contain extraordinary call provisions that allow the issuer to use unloaned funds to call bonds by random lot. In this context, unloaned funds are (1) the portion of the bond issue that the finance authority was unable to lend to home buyers to finance home purchases and (2) the proceeds of prepaid home mortgages.

Sinking Fund Calls

Many revenue bonds also have sinking funds that are, in effect, reserves set aside annually from which debt is retired by a sinking fund call, through random lot selection, at or near par or accreted value. These calls can and do occur prior to the first ordinary call provision date.

Stover Glass & Co., a municipal bond broker-dealer, points out in its newsletter: If you buy a new issue bond at par that is subject to a sinking fund call, it is somewhat like playing Russian roulette. If your bond is called when rates are low, you will be forced to reinvest at the low rates and if called when rates are high, you'll be able to cash your bond in early and get a higher yielding bond. The real risk here is that the bond you bought for $1000 may be trading at $1200 when you are forced to sell to the sinking fund at or near $1000. If you buy a secondary market bond that is subject to a sinking fund call and selling at a premium, be sure you know how active the sinking fund is, because if the bond is suddenly called, it could result in a loss. However, if you buy a bond at a price below the accreted value, you can only gain from a sinking fund call.

Investigate Investors ought to obtain full details of redemption and call provisions before investing. If your broker thinks a "call date" is when you are expecting the broker to next telephone you, or if the broker thinks a "sinking fund" is a mutual fund that is declining in price, then find yourself another broker.

FORMULA FOR YIELD TO CALL

The formula for any bond's yield to call is

$$A = R \left[\frac{1 - (1 + i)^{-n}}{i} \right] + S (1 + i)^{-n}$$

where A = purchase price
R = annual interest (zero for zero coupon bonds)
n = years to call
S = call price
i = yield to call

For zero coupon bonds, the formula simplifies to

$$A = S (1 + i)^{-n} \quad \text{or} \quad S = A (1 + i)^n$$

This equation may be solved by trial-and-error values for i.[1]

Suppose an investor, Sally Abelson, is considering buying a North Carolina Housing Finance Authority bond in the secondary market. The zero coupon municipal was issued a few years ago at a 13 percent IRR. But since the time of issuance, rates have declined to 10 percent for bonds with 15 years remaining to maturity. Thus the value of the bond has risen. The present accreted value of the bond, as measured from its original issuance, is $15,989 (its maturity value in 15 more years is $100,000). But the purchase price to yield 10 percent is $23,939.

BEWARE, SALLY! If any of the variety of redemption possibilities (sinking fund, special redemption, etc.) is exercised, Sally may be forced to sell the bonds that just cost her $23,939 for as little as the accreted value of $15,989! The accreted value in five more years will be $29,459. Suppose Sally buys the bond now and it is called five years hence at $29,459. The yield to call is

$$\$23,939 = \$29,459 (1 + i)^{-5}$$
$$0.8126 = (1 + i)^{-5}$$
$$0.8126^{-0.2} = (1 + i)$$
$$1.0424 = (1 + i)$$
$$i = .0424, \text{ or } 4.24 \text{ percent}$$

Thus with a call five years later, Sally realizes only 4.24 percent instead of the 10 percent she anticipated earning. The moral of the story is: remember to investigate call and redemption provisions carefully before investing.

---

[1]The equation may also be solved by computer programs included in software called "The Complete Bond Calculator," published by Larry Rosen Co., or by means of graphs in *The Dow Jones-Irwin Guide to Calculating Yields.*

6

Taxability of Municipal Zero Coupons

MUNIs ARE NOT COMPLETELY TAX-EXEMPT!

Contrary to conventional wisdom, tax-exempt municipals are not wholly tax-exempt. Such bonds are exempt from the federal income tax on interest—but they may still be subject to state tax on interest (from out-of-state issuers), and are subject to the federal capital gains tax, on sale, as well as gift and estate taxes, and, in addition, their ownership may trigger the taxability of otherwise untaxable Social Security benefits.

Municipal bond interest receipts are not taxed, nor is the accrual of interest (as in the case of a zero coupon municipal). The interest accrued by either straight-line or yield-to-maturity (YTM) method (depending on dates of issuance or acquisition involved) is added to the purchase price to obtain the tax adjusted basis of the bond. Thus the accrual reduces the taxable capital gain on sale or redemption by increasing the tax basis.

Carefully check the tax opinion in the prospectus as well as with your own tax advisor. One possible pitfall is that an issue which was tax-exempt at original issuance may become disqualified. However, such an eventuality is unlikely. The prospectus describes the itemized risks of disqualification for a particular issue.

The manner in which municipal zero coupon bonds are taxed depends on the date at which the bonds were issued. The differing tax treatment results from a series of periodic changes enacted by Congress to the Internal Revenue Code.

Issuance Prior to June 9, 1980

For zero coupon bonds issued prior to June 9, 1980, at redemption the entire (earned or unearned) original issuance discount (OID) is excluded from gross income or deducted from the gain to determine taxable gain. At sale (as opposed to redemption), the earned or accrued OID for the time period the bond was held is excluded from the capital gain from sale. For example, if the original issuance was at $100 and redemption is $1000, the OID was $900. The gain at redemption is $900 ($1000 less $100). The taxable gain is that $900 gain less OID of $900, that is, zero gain.

Or, if a 240-month bond was sold for $400 prior to redemption after being held for 24 months, and the OID was $800 (purchase price was $200 at issuance), the taxability of the sales proceeds is as follows: The accrued or earned OID is 24/240 times 800, that is, $80. The adjusted tax basis is the $200 purchase price plus the earned OID of $80, that is, $280. The $80 accrued original issuance discount (AOID) is tax-exempt. But $400 sales proceeds less the $280 adjusted basis is a long term capital gain of $120, which is taxable. Another way of looking at this is that the gain on disposition is taxable only to the extent that it exceeds the "earned or accrued" OID.

Issuances On or After June 9, 1980

For zero coupon bonds issued on or after June 9, 1980, at redemption or sale, only the earned OID is excluded from gross income or added to the taxable basis—that is, deducted from the gain. Determination of the earned OID and the resulting addition to taxable basis may be by either the straight-line method or YTM or IRR method, depending on the dates.

Straight-Line Method—Issuances Pre-July 1, 1982

For zero coupon municipal bonds issued before July 1, 1982, the total amount of interest payable at the maturity of each bond is apportioned by a straight-line method among the original and succeeding holders of the bond. Thus each holder is entitled to treat (for Federal income tax purposes) as tax-exempt interest that portion of the total interest which the number of days the bond is owned by such holder bears to the total number of days from the date of issuance to the stated date of maturity. (For the bond shown in Table 6-1, the annual interest allocable would be $4566—1/20(100,000 − 8678). The former method, described previously, allowed a larger sum to be treated as tax-free interest and added to the bond's purchase price to determine the tax basis. Artificial tax losses could be recognized by selling the bond at lower market prices.

If the amount realized from the sale or redemption of the bond is in excess of the holder's cost plus such holder's pro rata portion of the bond's total interest, then the holder will recognize taxable capital gain to the extent of such excess. Conversely, a capital loss may also be recognized.

Yield to Maturity or Internal Rate of Return Method— Post-September 3, 1982 Issuances

For zero coupon municipal bonds issued after September 3, 1982, and acquired after March 1, 1984, for purposes of determining capital gain or loss, each holder of the bond (i.e., original buyer and subsequent purchasers) would be entitled to treat as tax-exempt interest the accretion in value (for the precise time period involved) based on the YTM or IRR (compounded semiannually) at issuance and the original issuance price compounded over the life of the bond. (For the bond shown in Table 6-1, such annual interest increases each year, and starts at $1128 in the first year.) Such interest would add to the holder's original cost basis for determining gain or loss at sale or redemption. Nevertheless, for purposes of tax on interest, such accretion during the period held would be nontaxable. The application of this method of taxation to tax-exempts arose in the Deficit Reduction Act of 1984.

The result of having to use the YTM method (and not straight line) is that less income is "accreted" and thus the taxable basis is less, resulting in *more capital gain* that is subject to tax on disposition.

Table 6-1. Municipal Zero Coupon Bonds—After Tax

20	Number of years until maturity
13.00%	Yield to maturity or IRR
0%	Federal income tax bracket
8,678.23	Purchase price of zero coupon Treasury bond
100,000	Maturity value of bond
11.5	Multiplier

		(Accretion) Pre-Tax		(Cash Flow)	Yield to Maturity or IRR	
Year	Year-End Value	Imputed Interest	Annual Tax	After Tax	Pre-Tax	After Tax
0	8,678			−8,678		
1	9,806	1,128	0		13.000%	13.000%
2	11,081	1,275	0			
3	12,522	1,441	0			
4	14,150	1,628	0			
5	15,989	1,839	0			
6	18,068	2,079	0			
7	20,416	2,349	0			
8	23,071	2,654	0			
9	26,070	2,999	0			
10	29,459	3,389	0			
11	33,288	3,830	0			
12	37,616	4,328	0			
13	42,506	4,890	0			
14	48,032	5,526	0			
15	54,276	6,244	0			
16	61,332	7,056	0			
17	69,305	7,973	0			
18	78,315	9,010	0			
19	88,496	10,181	0			
20	100,000	11,504	0	100,000		
Totals		91,322	0	91,322		

Table 6-2. Conventional Municipal Bonds, After Tax, with Reinvestment

50%	Tax bracket of investor
20	Number of years until maturity
$8,678.23	Maturity value: 60% of long-term gain untaxed
50%	1 less tax bracket
26%	Reinvestment % rate earned before tax
$8,678.23	Purchase price of bond
$1,128.17	Coupon rate in dollars

Interest Reinvestment

Year	Cash Flows Each Year Before Reinvestment of Earnings	Balance Before Reinvestment	Original Balance	Annual Interest on Interest	Ending Balance with Reinvestment	Cash Flow per Year with Reinvestment
0	-8,678	0	0	0	0	-8,678
1	1,128	1,128	0	0.00	1,128	1,128
2	1,128	2,256	1,128	146.66	2,403	1,275
3	1,128	3,385	2,403	312.39	3,844	1,441
4	1,128	4,513	3,844	499.66	5,471	1,628

5	1,128	5,641	711.28	5,471	7,311	1,839
6	1,128	6,769	950.41	7,311	9,389	2,079
7	1,128	7,897	1,220.63	9,389	11,738	2,349
8	1,128	9,025	1,525.97	11,738	14,392	2,654
9	1,128	10,154	1,871.01	14,392	17,392	2,999
10	1,128	11,282	2,260.90	17,392	20,781	3,389
11	1,128	12,410	2,701.48	20,781	24,610	3,830
12	1,128	13,538	3,199.33	24,610	28,938	4,328
13	1,128	14,666	3,761.91	28,938	33,828	4,890
14	1,128	15,794	4,397.62	33,828	39,354	5,526
15	1,128	16,923	5,115.97	39,354	45,598	6,244
16	1,128	18,051	5,927.71	45,598	52,654	7,056
17	1,128	19,179	6,844.97	52,654	60,627	7,973
18	1,128	20,307	7,881.48	60,627	69,636	9,010
19	1,128	21,435	9,052.74	69,636	79,817	10,181
20	9,806	31,242	10,376.26	79,817	100,000	20,183
	31,242		68,758.00		100,000	100,000

Without reinvestment, the result is   Regular   IRR   13.00%

With reinvestment, the result is   Revised   IRR   24.18%

67

In other words, a particular tax-exempt zero coupon bond generates $x of tax-exempt interest, and $x is apportioned (based on the time period the bond is held) among the original and subsequent holders (who increase their tax basis by such apportionment for determining taxable gain or loss at sale or redemption).

A gain attributable to *market discount* (MD) is includible in gross income without diminution. Such gain is treated as short- or long-term capital gain since tax-exempts are excluded from the market discount rules (discussed in Chapter 4, Beware of Taxation with Conventional Zeros). For example, Judy Blank buys a municipal for $400 that was originally issued for $1000 and which matures at $1000. The market discount is $600 and her taxable basis is $400. If market discount rules apply, when the bond is redeemed or matures at $1000, the $600 would be ordinary income. But such rules do not apply and Sally's capital gain or loss is the difference between her taxable basis of $400 and the redemption or sale price.

There are certain exceptions to the nontaxability of interest. For example, if funds were borrowed in order to buy or carry the municipals, the interest could be taxable.

Sally Abelson buys a municipal zero coupon bond for $8678.23 which matures 20 years later at $100,000—a 1150 percent increase. The yield to maturity or IRR (after tax, since there is no tax on the interest) is 13 percent, as shown in Table 6-1.

Sally could achieve the same results by buying a 13 percent coupon municipal at par of $8678 and holding it until maturity (of $8678). Provided that annual interest is reinvested to earn 13 percent after tax (26 percent pre-tax in a 50 percent tax bracket), the terminal or ending value is the same as for the zero coupon bond bought for $8678 and held until its $100,000 maturity. Table 6-2 shows the cash flows for the entire time period. Note that the end result in the column entitled Ending Balance with Reinvestment is $100,000.

The breakdown of the $100,000 end result is

Maturity value	$8,678
Interest, normal	22,564
Interest-on-interest	68,758
Total	$100,000

For both the zero coupon bond and the conventional bond, the results of reinvesting at 13 percent after tax produce a revised IRR (with reinvestment) of 24.18 percent.

7

Wall Street in Wonderland

Once upon a time, Sidney Sharp, an enterprising Wall Street executive, was inspired by an idea. It was a rather simple idea, as many brilliant ideas are. This little idea, though, stood to earn Sidney a quick $28 million profit for a very short-term investment. Not bad.

MAKE THE PARTS WORTH MORE THAN THE WHOLE

This was Sidney's idea: Buy $100 million of Treasury bonds, maturing in, let's say, 30 years and yielding the current market at purchase of 13 percent. Thus, Sidney would buy 100,000 bonds at par. He then planned to divide the bonds into two segments: (1) the coupons (paying $13 million per year in interest for each of the next 30 years); and (2) the sum of $100 million payable at maturity. Finally, Sidney's stroke of genius: Sell the right to the annual income from each individual coupon and the maturity value separately to different investors. So the investors who buy the coupon due in five years will receive $13 million in five years—but no income until then. And the investors who buy the maturity value of the bond—$100 million in 30 years—will receive just that with nothing during the intervening period.

Resell at Lower Yields

The next step is to sell the new package to investors at a lower yield (i.e., higher price) than the 13 percent yield at which the bonds were purchased. And, Sidney reasoned, using a lot of sales pizazz would make the offering appealing. Advertising slogans such as "Become a Millionaire for Only $57,309" or "Get 17 Times Your Money Back by Investing in U.S. Government Bonds!" can certainly attract customers.

The ads are, of course, basically correct: Because $57,309 is the present value of $1 million due in 30 years discounted to the present at 10 percent per year. Conversely, $57,309 will grow to $1 million in 30 years at 10 percent compound interest. And $1 million is 17 times the cost of buying the bonds today. Having devised this scheme, Sidney wanted to be sure that no one would come along to steal it. So he planned ahead. Once the bonds are sold to the public, they will be relatively inactive, because the investors who buy will be seeking to meet long-term objectives with the projected long-term gains. E.F. Hutton so stated such long-term objectives in its sales brochure:

> Why should I invest in a bond that pays no income? Because you have goals—a comfortable retirement, education for your children, a second home, a yacht, a trip around the world. Zero-coupon Municipal Bonds may offer goal-oriented investors a better way to reach their objectives than traditional tax-free, fixed income investments.

And, Sidney reasoned, since there won't be much trading in the bonds, it won't take much of a capital commitment to make a market in the bonds and make certain that in the after-market the yield to maturity (sold to the public at 10 percent) stays low, and the price of the component parts (128 million in the aggregate) stays high. In this way, more and more of such transformations can take place, and the brokers can justify their pricing policies by saying that the yields are "in line with market prices." Sidney felt that other firms would be quick to follow this path to easy riches. Sidney's firm would not be alone in the market for long.

Lack of Attention to Rates

But, you may be thinking, people are not stupid enough to buy bonds at a 10 percent yield when they could be getting 13 percent. Where is the Securities and Exchange Commission? This is where a bit of sleight of hand comes into play. And this is Sidney's masterpiece. The packaging was done so creatively that, for the most part, neither the unsuspecting public nor their trusted brokers and advisors knew what was happening. How could this be?

First, the public is not terribly discriminating when it comes to small differentials between interest rates. (How else did banks manage for decades to hang on to billions of no-interest deposits?) One or 1 1/2 percentage points just don't deter many investors from buying or not buying—especially when one of Sidney's persuasive account executives is doing the selling. Such a difference in rates should make a difference, even if it is only 1/10 of 1 percent. More about that later.

Stepladder Setting of Yields

Second, the broker–underwriter practice has been to price the long-term zero coupon issues, say the 30-year maturities, near but below the prevailing Treasury bond long-term trading rate. Thus a 30-year zero bond might be sold to yield 13 percent at a time when 30-year treasuries are selling at 13.5 or 13.75 percent yields to maturity. But here's the catch: Each preceding year's zero coupon bond (e.g., 29, 28, 27 . . . etc.) may be priced at successively lower yields to maturity (12.9 percent, 12.8 percent, 12.6 percent, etc.). And this produces the great profitability to the underwriter because he bought the Treasuries at the 30-year, 13.5 or 13.75 percent yield to maturity rate, and is marking them up by marking their yields down to that commensurate with short-term maturities. Yields on short-term maturities (say two years or so) are usually, but not always, substantially less than yields on longer-term issues.

The result: The purchaser is happily looking forward to the day that her $57,000 investment in U.S. debt makes her a millionaire; the sales force is doubly happy, because they have a happy customer and because of all those sales commissions from the sale of the investment; and Sidney is ecstatic because he's retired to Switzerland with his cut from all those underwriting profits. So what is the problem? All concerned parties are content with the outcome. The problem is the potential for financial loss to the consumer.

A Little Interest Makes a Big Difference

For example, Ingrid Investor buys $57,309 of zero coupon bonds through her broker at the market rate of 10 percent fully compounded yield to maturity. At the end of the 30-year period, the zero matures for $1 million. If Ingrid chooses to purchase the same amount of conventional Treasury bonds at a 13 percent yield to maturity, and reinvests the income at 13 percent, her bonds at maturity, including the proceeds of the reinvestment, would be worth $2,241,693. Thus if Ingrid overpaid for her bonds by buying at a 10 percent yield rather than 13 percent, 30 years later she will be poorer to the extent of $1,241,693.

8

Wonderland Is Not Wonderful

(If You're a Customer)

REGULATORS INVESTIGATE EXCESSIVE BROKER MARKUPS

In Chapter 7, Wall Street in Wonderland, hypothetical broker Sidney Sharp bought Treasury instruments at factory prices and marked them up to an stratospherically high retail price for sale to his customers in the form of zero coupon issues. (In dealing with bonds, the lower the yield the higher the price; and vice versa, the higher the yield the lower the price.)

In the "Personal Finance" column of the *The New York Times*, January 27, 1985, Deborah Rankin reported the following:

Some dealers who sell to the public may be adding an excessive markup above the bonds' wholesale cost. Both the Securities and Exchange Commission and the National Association of Securities Dealers are looking into the brokerage industry's pricing practices on zero-coupon bonds, and the issue has sparked at least one lawsuit. . . . The problem is that some dealers are apparently employing the same markup procedures when pricing zeros that they use in pricing ordinary bonds—that is, figuring the markup on the face value of the bond rather than its purchase price. The difference is small if you buy a regular bond for close to its face value, but the markup may be very steep; when expressed as a percentage of a deeply discounted zero-coupon bond. . . . But some observers maintain that individuals who buy zeros are routinely being charged mark ups of 15 percent or more. . . . Although the Securities dealers association began its investigation of pricing practices last July (1984), it is vague about when the study, which was to have been concluded by September (1984), will be finished. . . . In the meantime, the rule of the marketplace is caveat emptor. "There's not a fixed formula for determining markups," said one marketing executive with a large brokerage firm. "It depends upon the maturity, the client and the situation of the bond market. We go at it from the point of what yield is the client going to walk out with and is it competitive? There's no way the customer is going to know what the markup is, other than the yield." For example, a recent spot check found a spread of 0.30 to 0.35 of a point on the yield of several identical long-term treasury zeros offered by several large brokerage firms.

In a syndicated column appearing in the February 14, 1985, Louisville *Courier-Journal* Jane Bryant Quinn stated:

An even greater risk—which is just now coming to light—is that all brokers may not be figuring the yield in a straightforward or uniform way.

Take the class-action lawsuit recently brought by a group of Michigan investors against the brokerage firm Merrill Lynch.

The investors' lawyer, Nelson Chase of West Bloomfield, MI, says that when his clients bought the bonds in 1983, they were priced at seven cents on the dollar. Just two weeks later, their value had unaccountably fallen to 5.4 cents on the dollar, a 22 percent loss. Nelson charges that the drop was due in good part to a large and undisclosed markup on the bonds that profited the securities firm.

MARKUPS

The question of markups, and the reasonableness thereof, depends on whether the broker is acting as a principal (dealer) or simply as an agent and charging a commission. Since commissions would be openly disclosed, it is probable that the abuses occur in the broker's activity as a dealer, where the broker is acting as a principal. In that case, it is not reasonable to compare the price at which a broker sells to its customer to the cost price when the broker brought the zero coupon bond, unless the purchase and sale occurred virtually simultaneously in a riskless transaction. Rather, when the broker is selling bonds from its inventory, what is relevant in determining the reasonableness of its pricing policies is the yield to the customer compared to the spot price and Treasury bond yield curves. This subject is discussed in detail in Chapter 10, Pricing Surprises.

COMPARING ZERO YIELDS TO CONVENTIONAL BOND YIELDS

To compare the yield to maturity (YTM) or Internal Rate of
Return (IRR) on a zero coupon issue, one must compare it to the
YTM or IRR from a normal or conventional bond. But the zero
requires reinvestment at the original YTM. The rate to be earned
on reinvesting income from a conventional bond is subjective
and will change. Alternatively, the revised IRR or revised YTM
of a conventional bond, after reinvesting all income at an assumed rate, produces a revised YTM that is directly comparable
to the revised YTM for a zero coupon bond.

A Little Change in Interest Makes a Big Difference

It is worthy of noting that *each percentage point* of the increased
IRR results in over $300,000 at maturity. Thus, $50,000 invested
at 10 percent compound interest for 30 years will be worth $872,470
(see Table 8-1); but at 13 percent it grows instead to $1,955,795,
a difference of $1,083,325 (see Table 8-2).

A 30-year zero coupon bond purchased at a 10 percent IRR or
YTM *is the equivalent of a conventional par bond purchased at
a 10 percent YTM or IRR, and reinvesting its $100 per year
interest income at a rate of 10 percent until maturity.* The revised
IRR for the 10 percent IRR zero coupon bond (after reinvestment)
works out to be 19.1 percent (see Table 8-3). However, for a 30-
year conventional Treasury bond purchased at a 13 percent IRR
and with the cash flow reinvested at 13 percent, the revised IRR
would be 25.45 percent (see Table 8-4).

To repeat, a zero coupon bought at 10 percent IRR is equivalent to buying a conventional bond at $1000, reinvesting the
$100 per year income at a reinvestment rate of 10 percent. How-
ever, with the zero coupon, one is locked in to the 10 percent
reinvestment rate. The buyer is stuck with it or benefits by it,
according to one's perspective, for the duration of the holding.
With the conventional bond, on the other hand, the reinvestment

Table 8-1. Nontaxable Zero Coupon Bonds—10 Percent YTM

30	Number of years until maturity
10.00%	Yield to maturity or IRR
0.00%	Federal income tax bracket
$50,000	Purchase price of zero coupon Treasury bond
$872,470	Maturity value of bond
17.4	Multiplier

Year	Year-End Value	(Accretion) Pre-Tax Imputed Interest	Annual Tax	(Cash Flow) After Tax	Yield to Maturity or IRR Pre-Tax	After Tax
0				50,000		
1	55,000	5,000	0	0	10.000%	10.000%
2	60,500	5,500	0	0		
3	66,550	6,050	0	0		
4	73,205	6,655	0	0		
5	80,526	7,321	0	0		
6	88,578	8,053	0	0		
7	97,436	8,858	0	0		
8	107,179	9,744	0	0		
9	117,897	10,718	0	0		
10	129,687	11,790	0	0		
11	142,656	12,969	0	0		
12	156,921	14,266	0	0		
13	172,614	15,692	0	0		
14	189,875	17,261	0	0		
15	208,862	18,987	0	0		
16	229,749	20,886	0	0		
17	252,724	22,975	0	0		
18	277,996	25,272	0	0		
19	305,795	27,800	0	0		
20	336,375	30,580	0	0		
21	370,012	33,637	0	0		
22	407,014	37,001	0	0		
23	447,715	40,701	0	0		
24	492,487	44,772	0	0		
25	541,735	49,249	0	0		
26	595,909	54,174	0	0		
27	655,500	59,591	0	0		
28	721,050	65,550	0	0		
29	793,155	72,105	0	0		
30	872,470	79,315	0	872,470		
Totals		822,470	0			

Table 8-2. Nontaxable Zero Coupon Bonds—13 Percent YTM

30	Number of years until maturity	
13.00%	Yield to maturity or IRR	
0.00%	Federal income tax bracket	
$50,000	Purchase price of zero coupon Treasury bond	
$1,955,795	Maturity value of bond	
39.1	Multiplier	

Year	Year-End Value	(Accretion) Pre-Tax Imputed Interest	Annual Tax	(Cash Flow) After Tax	Yield to Maturity or IRR Pre-Tax	After Tax
0				−50,000		
1	56,500	6,500	0	0	13.000%	13.000%
2	63,845	7,345	0	0		
3	72,145	8,300	0	0		
4	81,524	9,379	0	0		
5	92,122	10,598	0	0		
6	104,098	11,976	0	0		
7	117,630	13,533	0	0		
8	132,922	15,292	0	0		
9	150,202	17,280	0	0		
10	169,728	19,526	0	0		
11	191,793	22,065	0	0		
12	216,726	24,933	0	0		
13	244,901	28,174	0	0		
14	276,738	31,837	0	0		
15	312,714	35,976	0	0		
16	353,366	40,653	0	0		
17	399,304	45,938	0	0		
18	451,213	51,910	0	0		
19	509,871	58,658	0	0		
20	576,154	66,283	0	0		
21	651,054	74,900	0	0		
22	735,692	84,637	0	0		
23	831,331	95,640	0	0		
24	939,405	108,073	0	0		
25	1,061,527	122,123	0	0		
26	1,199,526	137,999	0	0		
27	1,355,464	155,938	0	0		
28	1,531,674	176,210	0	0		
29	1,730,792	199,118	0	0		
30	1,955,795	225,003	0	1,955,795		
Totals		1,905,795	0			

rate will be dependent upon rates at the time of each reinvestment and may average more or less than the original IRR or YTM.

As Chart 8-1 shows, the trend of interest rates since 1950 has generally been upward. If history repeats itself, locking oneself into reinvestment at today's rates could be a risky and costly endeavor.

ZEROS COMPARED TO CONVENTIONAL BONDS

Several other factors, besides the reinvestment rate, could upset this seeming equality between the zero and the conventional bond:

Income Taxes. For individual investors or other tax-paying entities, the zero coupon bond may become exceedingly unattractive because taxes are payable each year on the "presumed or imputed" interest earned by zeros. See Chapter 4, Beware of Taxation with Conventional Zeros.

Volatility Risk. On a day-to-day basis, zeros normally fluctuate much more in value than do conventional bonds. See Chapter 3, Beware of Zero Coupon Volatility.

Credit. Should the bond issuer go bankrupt, default, or become insolvent at some point, the conventional bond holder has at least received interest in cash up until that time, whereas the zero bond holder receives nothing until maturity. And all the incremental increase in value of the zero coupon bond, year by year, would be wiped out by the insolvency.

EVALUATING AN OFFERING OF ZEROS

At this point, we will analyze a current offering for a $395,687,500 issue of zero coupon bonds (called Treasury Receipts (TR) by

Table 8-3. Bonds, After Tax with Reinvestment—10 Percent Reinvestment Rate

0%	Tax bracket of investor
30	Number of years until maturity of bond
$1,000	Maturity value
10%	Reinvestment rate earned before tax
$1,000	Purchase price of bond
$100	Coupon rate in dollars

Year	Cash Flows Each Year Before Reinvestment of Earnings	Balance Before Reinvestment	Interest Reinvestment Original Balance	Annual Interest on Interest	Ending Balance with Reinvestment	Cash Flow per Year with Reinvestment
0	-1,000	0	0	0	0	-1,000
1	100	100	0	0.00	100	100
2	100	200	100	10.00	210	110
3	100	300	210	21.00	331	121
4	100	400	331	33.10	464	133
5	100	500	464	46.41	611	146
6	100	600	611	61.05	772	161
7	100	700	772	77.16	949	177
8	100	800	949	94.87	1,144	195
9	100	900	1,144	114.36	1,358	214
10	100	1,000	1,358	135.79	1,594	236

11	100	1,100	1,594	159.37	1,853	259
12	100	1,200	1,853	185.31	2,138	285
13	100	1,300	2,138	213.84	2,452	314
14	100	1,400	2,452	245.23	2,797	345
15	100	1,500	2,797	279.75	3,177	380
16	100	1,600	3,177	317.72	3,595	418
17	100	1,700	3,595	359.50	4,054	459
18	100	1,800	4,054	405.45	4,560	505
19	100	1,900	4,560	455.39	5,116	556
20	100	2,000	5,116	511.59	5,727	612
21	100	2,100	5,727	572.75	6,400	673
22	100	2,200	6,400	640.02	7,140	740
23	100	2,300	7,140	714.03	7,954	814
24	100	2,400	7,954	795.43	8,850	895
25	100	2,500	8,850	884.97	9,835	985
26	100	2,600	9,835	983.47	10,918	1,083
27	100	2,700	10,918	1,091.82	12,110	1,192
28	100	2,800	12,110	1,211.00	13,421	1,311
29	100	2,900	13,421	1,342.10	14,863	1,442
30	1,100	4,000	14,863	1,486.31	17,449	2,586
	4,000			13,449.70		17,449

Without reinvestment, the result is   Regular IRR   10.00%
With reinvestment, the result is   Revised IRR   19.13%

Source: Lawrence R. Rosen, "Investment Analysis—After Tax IRR for Stocks, Fonds and Real Estate," Copyright 1984 by L. R. Rosen, 7008 Springdale Road, Louisville, KY. Unauthorized reproduction is prohibited.

85

Table 8-4. Bonds, After Tax with Reinvestment—13 Percent Reinvestment Rate

0%	Tax bracket of investor
30	Number of years until maturity of bond
$1,000	Maturity value
13%	Reinvestment rate earned before tax
$1,000	Purchase price of bond
$130	Coupon rate in dollars

Year	Cash Flows Each Year Before Reinvestment of Earnings	Balance Before Reinvestment	Interest Reinvestment			Cash Flow per Year with Reinvestment
			Original Balance	Annual Interest on Interest	Ending Balance with Reinvestment	
0	−1,000	0	0	0	0	−1,000
1	130	130	0	0.00	130	130
2	130	260	130	16.90	277	147
3	130	390	277	36.00	433	166
4	130	520	443	57.58	630	188
5	130	650	630	81.96	842	212
6	130	780	842	109.52	1,082	240
7	130	910	1,082	140.65	1,353	271
8	130	1,040	1,353	175.84	1,658	306
9	130	1,170	1,658	215.60	2,004	346
10	130	1,300	2,004	260.53	2,395	391

11	130	1,430	2,395	311.29	2,836	441
12	130	1,560	2,836	368.66	3,335	499
13	130	1,690	3,335	433.49	3,898	563
14	130	1,820	3,898	506.74	4,535	637
15	130	1,950	4,535	589.52	5,254	720
16	130	2,080	5,254	683.06	6,067	813
17	130	2,210	6,067	788.75	6,986	919
18	130	2,340	6,986	908.19	8,024	1,038
19	130	2,470	8,024	1,043.15	9,197	1,173
20	130	2,600	9,197	1,195.66	10,523	1,326
21	130	2,730	10,523	1,368.00	12,021	1,498
22	130	2,860	12,021	1,562.74	13,714	1,693
23	130	2,990	13,714	1,782.80	15,627	1,913
24	130	3,120	15,627	2,031.46	17,788	2,161
25	130	3,250	17,788	2,312.45	20,231	2,442
26	130	3,380	20,231	2,629.97	22,991	2,760
27	130	3,510	22,991	2,988.77	26,109	3,119
28	130	3,640	26,109	3,394.21	29,633	3,524
29	130	3,770	29,633	3,852.35	33,616	3,982
30	1,130	4,900	33,616	4,370.00	39,116	5,500
	4,900			34,216.00		39,116

Without reinvestment, the result is   Regular   IRR   13.00%

With reinvestment, the result is   Revised   IRR   25.45%

Source: Lawrence R. Rosen, "Investment Analysis—After Tax IRR for Stocks, Bonds and Real Estate," Copyright 1984 by L. R. Rosen, 7008 Springdale Road, Louisville, KY. Unauthorized reproduction is prohibited.

LONG- AND SHORT-TERM INTEREST RATES

ANNUALLY

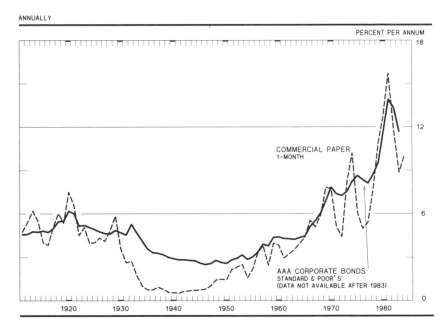

Chart 8-1. Long- and Short-Term Interest Rates (*Source:* Historical
Chart Book: Board of Governors of Federal Reserve System, 1985).

the sponsoring underwriters) being underwritten by Mosely,
Hallgarten, Estabrook & Weeden Inc.) in order to evaluate
the relationship between the price at which the zero coupons are
being offered to the public and the alternative investments
available in conventional bonds. We will also look at the prices
at which zero coupons are trading on the New York Exchange
Bond Market.

The following direct quotations are taken from the six-page
prospectus reproduced in Appendix A, Treasury Receipts Prospectus. Page numbers refer to prospectus page numbers.

TRs are being offered to the public by Mosely, Hallgarten, Estabrook & Weeden Inc. in negotiated transactions at varying prices

which will be determined at the time of sale and will be based upon market conditions at such time. [Page 1].

No payments will be made on TRs prior to the maturity of the corresponding interest or principal payments on the underlying Treasury Securities. In addition, in the event Treasury Securities underlying any Callable TRs are redeemed, no payments will be made on such Callable TRs with respect to interest payments due after such redemption. The face amount of each TR will be equal to the payment or payments to be received thereon, except that the face amount of Callable TRs will include interest payments on the underlying Treasury Securities which may not be made if such Treasury Securities are redeemed prior to maturity. . . . [Page 1.]

Any depositor of Treasury Securities who is acceptable to the Custodian ("Depositor") may offer the related TRs from time to time. Depositors intend to make a market in all TRs irrespective of which Depositor initially offered such TRs, but are not obliged to do so. . . . [Page 1.]

The offering is for 100,000 Treasury bonds with maturity November 15, 2012. The Treasury may call the bonds on or after November 15, 2007. The interest rate is 10.375 percent, which is $103.75 per bond, per year, payable semiannually in the amount of $51.875 per bond.

PROSPECTUS—A MONUMENT IN NONDISCLOSURE

The prospectus or "descriptive memorandum" is a monument in nondisclosure! The following questions cannot be answered even after reading the entire document:

Who is selling the Treasuries that are being marked up and sold to the public?

What was the cost to the sellers of the bonds being sold?

How much profit are the sellers making?

How is the price determined at which the TRs are being sold? What relationship does the yield to the buyer from the TRs bear to the yield that the buyer could obtain by buying conventional Treasury bonds?

The answers to these questions are vital to an informed investor. One of the brokers selling the issue provided the following pricing information:

July 3, 1984

Year of Maturity of TR	Yield to Buyer of TR
11/84	11.50 %
5/85	12.30
11/85	13.00
5/86	13.33
11/86	13.43
5/87	13.58
11/87	—
5/88	13.74
11/88	13.74
5/89	13.82
11/89	13.82
5/90	13.88
11/90	13.88
5/91 to 11/97	13.91
5/98 to 11/99	13.81
5/00 to 11/00	13.74
5/01 to 11/01	13.69
5/02 to 11/02	—
5/03 to 11/03	13.56
5/04 to 11/04	13.51
5/05 to 11/05	13.41
5/06 to 11/06	13.36
5/07 to 11/07	13.31
11/15/2012	13.26

The prospectus mentioned a vague pricing method. The quotes above are the actual prices at which the underwriters (or selling group members) were prepared to sell the TRs on the date indicated.

Remember that the yields shown to the buyer are with no income to the buyer until the maturity date, which makes the purchase equivalent to buying a normal Treasury bond of the same maturity, and reinvesting all the income at the purchase yield rate until such maturity.

Table 8-5 shows the pricing of Treasury issues on the same date, July 3. Note the price quotation for the identical Treasury issue that underlies the TRs: 10-3/8, 2007–12 Nov. The bid price was 76-18/32 and the asked price 76-26/32 at a yield of 13.61 percent. This compares to the yield offered by the broker for November 15, 2012, maturity of only 13.26 percent.

Table 8-5. Treasury Issues/ Bonds, Notes, and Bills.

Treasury Issues/ *Bonds, Notes & Bills*

Tuesday, July 3, 1984

Representative mid-afternoon Over-the-Counter quotations supplied by the Federal Reserve Bank of New York City, based on transactions of $1 million or more.

Decimals in bid-and-asked and bid changes represent 32nds; 101.1 means 101 1/32. a-Plus 1/64. b-Yield to call date. d-Minus 1/64. n-Treasury notes.

Treasury Bonds and Notes

Rate	Mat. Date	Bid	Asked	Chg.	Yld.
13⅛s,	1984 Jul n	100.6	100.10		8.09
6⅜s,	1984 Aug	99.17	100.1	+ .1	5.94
7¼s,	1984 Aug n	99.20	99.24	+ .1	9.29
11⅝s,	1984 Aug n	100.5	100.9	+ .1	9.37
13¼s,	1984 Aug n	100.10	100.14		8.78
12⅛s,	1984 Sep n	100.9	100.13	+ .1	10.03
9¾s,	1984 Oct n	99.19	99.23	+ .2	10.48
9⅞s,	1984 Nov n	99.15	99.19	+ .2	10.83
14⅝s,	1984 Nov n	101.3	101.7	+ .1	10.63
16s,	1984 Nov n	101.21	101.25		10.61
9⅝s,	1984 Dec n	99.3	99.7	+ .3	11.06
14s,	1984 Dec n	101.7	101.11	+ .1	11.05
9¼s,	1985 Jan n	98.24	98.28	+ .3	11.34
8s,	1985 Feb n	98.2	98.6	+ .4	11.14
9⅝s,	1985 Feb n	98.23	98.27	+ .4	11.51
14⅝s,	1985 Feb n	101.19	101.23	+ .2	11.64
9⅝s,	1985 Mar	98.12	98.16	+ .2	11.81
13⅜s,	1985 Mar n	101	101.4	+ .2	11.74
9½s,	1985 Apr n	98.3	98.7	+ .3	11.84
3¼s,	1985 May	94.8	95.8		9.11

Rate	Mat. Date	Bid	Asked	Bid Chg.	Yld.
4¼s,	1975-85 May	95	96	- .1	9.15
9⅞s,	1985 May n	98.1	98.5	+ .2	12.09
10⅜s,	1985 May n	98.26	98.30	+ .2	11.71
*4⅛s,	1985 May n	101.15	101.19	+ .1	12.12
14⅛s,	1985 May n	101.21	101.25	+ .1	12.14
14s,	1985 Jun n	101.20	101.24		12.06
10s,	1985 Jun n	97.30	98.2	+ .2	12.15
10⅜s,	1985 Jul n	98.7	98.11	+ .2	12.32
8¼s,	1985 Aug n	96.9	96.13	+ .3	11.79
9⅝s,	1985 Aug n	97.4	97.8	+ .2	12.35
10⅜s,	1985 Aug n	98	98.4	+ .3	12.42
13½s,	1985 Aug n	100.19	100.23	+ .2	12.41
10⅞s,	1985 Sep n	98.2	98.6	+ .3	12.50
15⅞s,	1985 Sep n	103.22	103.26	+ .3	12.46
10½s,	1985 Oct n	97.17	97.21	+ .3	12.48
9¾s,	1985 Nov n	96.12	96.16	+ .2	12.63
10½s,	1985 Nov n	97.7	97.11	+ .2	12.62
11¾s,	1985 Nov n	99.2	99.6	+ .2	12.42
10⅞s,	1985 Dec n	97.15	97.19	- .4	12.70
14⅛s,	1985 Dec n	101.22	101.26		12.75
10⅜s,	1986 Jan n	97	97.4	+ .3	12.70
10⅞s,	1986 Feb n	97.3	97.7	+ .3	12.79
13½s,	1986 Feb n	100.24	100.28	+ .2	12.88
9⅞s,	1986 Feb n	95.20	95.24	+ .3	12.88
14s,	1986 Mar n	101.16	101.20	+ .2	12.93
11½s,	1986 Mar n	97.22	97.26	+ .4	12.95
11¾s,	1986 Apr n	97.27	97.29	+ .3	13.08
7⅞s,	1986 May n	91.29	92.5	+ .3	12.74
9¾s,	1986 May n	94.2	94.6	+ .2	12.99
12⅝s,	1986 May n	99.4	99.6	+ .3	13.12

(*Continued*)

Table 8-5. Treasury Issues/ Bonds, Notes, and Bills.

(Continued)

Rate	Mat.	Date	Bid	Asked	Bid Chg.	Yld.
13¾s,	1986	May n	101.1	101.5	.....	13.03
13s,	1986	Jun n	99.26	99.28	+ .3	13.07
14⅞s,	1986	Jun n	103	103.8	+ .4	12.97
8s,	1986	Aug n	91.4	91.8	+ .7	12.86
11⅜s,	1986	Aug n	96.31	97.3	+ .5	12.99
12¼s,	1986	Sep n	98.13	98.17	+ .4	13.03
6⅛s,	1986	Nov	89.12	90.12	+ .6	10.85
11s,	1986	Nov n	95.27	95.31	+ .4	13.04
13⅞s,	1986	Nov n	101.12	101.20	+ .4	13.05
16⅛s,	1986	Nov n	105.27	106.3	+ .5	13.04
10s,	1986	Dec n	93.14	93.18	+ .5	13.12
ss,	1987	Feb n	90.31	91.3	+ .6	13.14
10⅞s,	1987	Feb n	94.30	95.2	+ .5	13.17
12¾s,	1987	Feb n	98.31	99.3	+ .5	13.17
10¼s,	1987	Mar n	93.4	93.8	+ .6	13.27
12s,	1987	May n	97.6	97.10	+ .5	13.16
12½s,	1987	May n	98.3	98.5	+ .5	13.30
14s,	1987	May n	101.18	101.22	+ .6	13.27
10½s,	1987	Jun n	93.5	93.9	+ .7	13.30
13¾s,	1987	Aug n	100.31	101.3	+ .7	13.31
11⅛s,	1987	Sep n	94.7	94.11	+ .6	13.33
7⅝s,	1987	Nov n	85.13	85.29	+ .8	12.93
12⅝s,	1987	Nov n	97.31	98.3	+ .6	13.35
11¼s,	1987	Dec n	94.4	94.8	+ .6	13.37
12⅜s,	1988	Jan n	97	97.8	+ .5	13.38
10⅛s,	1988	Feb n	90.19	90.27	+ .5	13.40
12s,	1988	Mar n	95.20	95.22	+ .5	13.51
13¼s,	1988	Apr n	99.15	99.23	+ .7	13.35
8¼s,	1988	May n	84.28	85.4	+ .7	13.30
9⅞s,	1988	May n	89.4	89.12	+ .6	13.49
13⅝s,	1988	Jun n	100.4	100.6	+ .5	13.56
14s,	1988	Jul n	101.12	101.20	+ .7	13.46
10½s,	1988	Aug n	90.14	90.22	+ .7	13.53
15⅜s,	1988	Oct n	105.23	105.31	+ .2	13.49
8¾s,	1988	Nov n	84.26	85.2	+ .5	13.38
11¾s,	1988	Nov n	94.1	94.9	+ .7	13.53
14⅝s,	1989	Jan n	103.10	103.18	+ .7	13.55
11⅜s,	1989	Feb n	92.13	92.21	+ .8	13.57
7½s,	1988-93	Aug	68.11	68.27	+ .7	13.56
8⅝s,	1993	Aug	73.19	73.27	+ .8	13.74
11⅞s,	1993	Aug n	89.31	90.7	+ 12	13.79
8⅝s,	1993	Nov	73.14	73.22	+ 11	13.70
11¾s,	1993	Nov	89.8	89.12	+ .13	13.81
9s,	1994	Feb	74.29	75.5	+ .11	13.73
4⅛s,	1989-94	May	89.25	90.25	+ .3	5.34
13⅛s,	1994	May	96.14	96.18	+ .12	13.77
8¾s,	1994	Aug	73	73.8	+ .11	13.72
10⅛s,	1994	Nov	80	80.8	+ .12	13.76
3s,	1995	Feb	90	91	+ .7	4.05
10½s,	1995	Feb	81.21	81.29	+ .12	13.80
10⅜s,	1995	May	80.28	81.4	+ .14	13.77
12⅝s,	1995	May	93.20	93.28	+ .14	13.73
11½s,	1995	Nov	86.30	87.6	+ .5	13.76
7s,	1993-98	May	60.24	61.8	+ .11	13.15
3½s,	1998	Nov	90.8	91.8	+ .6	4.32
8½s,	1994-99	May	67.16	68	+ .12	13.56
7⅞s,	1995-00	Feb	62.20	62.28	+ .14	13.70
8⅜s,	1995-00	Aug	65.16	65.24	+ .14	13.69
11¾s,	2001	Feb	86.26	87.2	+ .14	13.75
13⅛s,	2001	May	96.22	96.30	+ .15	13.59
8s,	1996-01	Aug	63.7	63.23	+ .18	13.48
13⅜s,	2001	Aug	98.1	98.9	+ .13	13.64
15¾s,	2001	Nov	115.10	115.18	+ .17	13.42
14¼s,	2002	Feb	103.8	103.16	+ .13	13.72
11⅝s,	2002	Nov	85.20	85.28	+ 15	13.75
10¾s,	2003	Feb	79.23	79.31	+ 15	13.76
10¾s,	2003	May	79.23	79.31	+ .15	13.75
11⅛s,	2003	Aug	82.6	82.14	+ .19	13.75
14⅜s,	1989	Apr n	102.16	102.24	+ .7	13.57
9¼s,	1989	May n	85.8	85.16	+ .7	13.40
11¾s,	1989	May n	93.11	93.15	+ .7	13.63
14½s,	1989	Jul n	102.27	103.3	+ .5	13.63
13⅞s,	1989	Aug n	100.21	100.23	+ .8	13.65
11⅞s,	1989	Oct n	93.12	93.20	+ .8	13.61
10¾s,	1989	Nov n	89.4	89.12	+ .7	13.61
10½s,	1990	Jan n	87.22	87.30	+ .7	13.68
3½s,	1990	Feb	89.12	90.12	− .9	5.52
10½s,	1990	Apr n	87.10	87.18	+ .7	13.68
8¼s,	1990	May	79.15	79.31	+ .15	13.27
10¾s,	1990	Jul n	87.25	88.1	+ .7	13.73
10¾s,	1990	Aug n	87.24	88	+ .4	13.71
11½s,	1990	Oct n	90.18	90.26	+ .6	13.73
13s,	1990	Nov n	97	97.8	+ .7	13.66
11¾s,	1991	Jan n	91.12	91.16	+ .6	13.77
12⅜s,	1991	Apr	93.31	94.3	+ .7	13.74
14½s,	1991	May n	102.30	103.6	+ .4	13.77
14⅞s,	1991	Aug n	104.23	104.31	+ .6	13.76
14¼s,	1991	Nov n	101.30	102.6	+ .5	13.77
14⅝s,	1992	Feb n	103.17	103.25	+ .2	13.81
13¾s,	1992	May n	99.17	99.25	+ .5	13.80
4¼s,	1987-92	Aug	89.13	90.13	+ .2	5.75
7¼s,	1992	Aug	69.21	70.5	+ .4	13.39
10½s,	1992	Nov n	83.28	84.4	+ .10	13.75
4s,	1988-93	Feb	89.24	90.24	+ .4	5.35
6¾s,	1993	Feb	66.16	67	+ .9	13.30
7⅞s,	1993	Feb	70.29	71.13	+ .10	13.61
10⅞s,	1993	Feb n	85.10	85.14	+ .6	13.82
10⅛s,	1993	May n	81.12	81.16	+ .8	13.81
11⅞s,	2003	Nov	87.20	87.28	+ .19	13.67
12⅜s,	2004	May	91	91.8	+ .20	13.66
8¼s,	2000-05	May	63.8	63.24	+ .18	13.48
7⅝s,	2002-07	Feb	58.24	59	+ .18	13.44
7⅞s,	2002-07	Nov	60.4	60.12	+ .17	13.48
8⅜s,	2003-08	Aug	63.11	63.19	+ .21	13.51
8¾s,	2003-08	Nov	65.14	65.22	+ .20	13.62
9⅛s,	2004-09	May	67.31	68.7	+ .23	13.63
10⅜s,	2004-09	Nov	76.28	77.4	+ .23	13.60
11¾s,	2005-10	Feb	86.8	86.16	+ .20	13.66
10s,	2005-10	May	74.7	74.15	+ .23	13.59
12¾s,	2005-10	Nov	93.14	93.22	+ .26	13.64
13⅞s,	2006-11	May	101.22	101.30	+ .13	13.60
14s,	2006-11	Nov	102.13	102.21	+ .17	13.62
10⅜s,	2007-12	Nov	76.18	76.26	+ .24	13.61
12s,	2008-13	Aug	88.2	88.6	+ .22	13.65
13¼s,	2014	May	98	98.4	+ .26	13.51

U.S. Treas. Bills

Mat. date	Bid Discount	Asked Discount	Yield	Mat. date	Bid Discount	Asked Discount	Yield
-1984-				10-25	10.03	9.95	10.41
7- 5	9.49	8.27	8.39	11- 1	10.13	10.07	10.56
7-12	9.70	9.60	9.75	11- 8	10.14	10.06	10.57
7-19	9.58	9.48	9.64	11-15	10.15	10.09	10.62
7-26	8.62	8.52	8.68	11-24	10.24	10.18	10.75
8- 2	9.05	8.99	9.18	11-29	10.29	10.23	10.82
8- 9	9.35	9.29	9.50	12- 6	10.33	10.27	10.89
8-16	9.37	9.31	9.54	12-13	10.38	10.32	10.97
8-23	9.36	9.30	9.55	12-20	10.41	10.33	11.00
8-30	9.35	9.27	9.53	12-27	10.39	10.33	11.02
9- 6	9.66	9.62	9.92	-1985-			
9-13	9.68	9.62	9.94	1-24	10.57	10.51	11.26
9-20	9.70	9.64	9.98	2-21	10.69	10.61	11.41
9-27	9.73	9.67	10.03	3-21	10.79	10.75	11.61
10- 4	9.98	9.94	10.33	4-18	10.89	10.81	11.74
10-11	10.00	9.94	10.36	5-16	11.00	10.94	11.96
10-18	9.95	9.89	10.32	6-13	11.02	10.98	12.09

Source: Wall Street Journal (Tuesday, July 3, 1984.)

It is immediately apparent that this "real world" case is analogous (but to a lesser extent) to the hypothetical example previously cited when Sidney Sharp sold zero coupons to investors at a 10 percent yield at a time when the market for conventional Treasuries was a 13 percent yield to maturity.

As the previous information shows, the underwriter (or selling group member) has marked up the price and written down the 13.6 percent Treasury yield to only 12.3 percent for the May 1985 offering to investors, to 13.0 percent for the November 1985 offering, and for the $100 million maturity value, in 2012, reduced the yield to 13.26 percent.

You will discover in Chapter 10, Pricing Surprises, that the spot rate, not the Treasury bond rate, is the appropriate standard of yield comparison. Nevertheless, it is evident that one needs to carefully investigate fair market prices for zeros among several sources before deciding where to buy or sell.

9

What Zero Coupon "Yield" Really Means

FORMULA FOR ZERO YIELD CALCULATION

The formula is established that equates the purchase price of a zero coupon bond to the sum received at maturity. It is the staid equation for compound interest, as follows:

$$S = P (1 + i)^n$$

where S = maturity value
P = purchase price
i = annual interest rate (IRR or YTM)
n = number of years until maturity

Consider the following example:

Purchase price $1000
Maturity value $17,449.40
Number of years   30

Find the Internal Rate of Return (IRR), or Yield to Maturity (YTM).

$$S = P (1 + i)^n$$
$$17,499.40 = 1000 (1 + i)^{30}$$
$$17.449 = (1 + i)^{30}$$
$$(17.499)^{1/30} = (1 + i)$$
$$1.1 = (1 + i)$$
$$i = .1 \quad \text{or} \quad 10\%$$

This means that $1000 will grow into $17,449.40 in 30 years at a compound interest rate of 10 percent. A compound interest rate requires that all earnings be reinvested. In the absence of reinvestment of earnings, there is nothing to compound. During the 30 years while the investment augments from $1000 to $17,449, the value of the investment is continually increasing.

The value at the end of the first year is 10 percent more than at the beginning; the value at the end of the second year is 10 percent more than at the end of the first year; and so forth.

Although there is no cash flow to the investor from a zero coupon bond, the nature of compounding is such that there is an *imputed cash flow* which is reinvested each year. The imputed cash flow is the value increase each year. Thus the first year it is $100, the second year $110, the third year $121, and so on.

The correct way to judge the return from such an investment is to consider (1) the initial investment to be the first (negative) cash flow and (2) the imputed cash flow each year is the cash flow, which is reinvested at a rate equal to the IRR (10 percent). In other words, this is the same as buying a bond for $1000 that pays $100 per year interest, which is reinvested at a reinvestment rate of 10 percent. Such a conventional bond will grow into $17,449 after 30 years. Thus the 10 percent compound realized yield is the same as investing at a 10 percent IRR and reinvesting the cash flows at a 10 percent reinvestment rate.

What, then, is the revised IRR, that is, the IRR after giving effect to the reinvestment of cash flows? It is 19.1 percent, determined by showing the progression in year-end values of the zero bond and the related imputed annual cash flow, as shown in Table 9-1. The zero bond is comparable to a conventional bond, purchased at par with a 10 percent IRR, and with all cash flow reinvested to earn 10 percent. As the column entitled "Cash Flow for the Year" shows, the cash flow from the conventional bond is the same as from the imputed cash flow of the zero.

FORMULA FOR TERMINAL VALUE CALCULATION

The formula for determining the future value (or terminal value) of a conventional bond (purchased at par) with interest reinvested at the rate of IRR is

Table 9-1. Zero Coupon Compared to Conventional Coupon Bond

		Zero Coupon Bond				Coupon Bond			
	Year	Year End Value of Bond	Imputed Annual Cash Flow	Maturity Value	Old Balance	Interest on Old Balance	Coupon for the Year	Cash Flow for the Year	New Balance
Maturity Value	0	1,000.00	-1,000.00		$0.00	$0.00	$0.00	$0.00	$0.00
$17,449.40	1	1,100.00	100.00	$1,000	0.00	0.00	100.00	100.00	100.00
Purchase	2	1,210.00	110.00	Purchase	100.00	10.00	100.00	110.00	210.00
Price	3	1,331.00	121.00	Price	210.00	21.00	100.00	121.00	331.00
$1,000	4	1,464.10	133.10	$1,000	331.00	33.10	100.00	133.10	464.10
Coupon	5	1,610.51	146.41	Coupon	464.10	46.41	100.00	146.41	610.51
$0	6	1,771.56	161.05	$100	610.51	61.05	100.00	161.05	771.56
Years until	7	1,948.72	177.16	Years til	771.56	77.16	100.00	177.16	948.72
Maturity	8	2,143.59	194.87	Maturity	948.72	94.87	100.00	194.87	1,143.59
30	9	2,357.95	214.36	30	1,143.59	114.36	100.00	214.36	1,357.95
Yield to	10	2,593.74	235.79	Yield to	1,357.95	135.79	100.00	235.79	1,593.74
Maturity	11	2,853.12	259.37	Maturity at	1,593.74	159.37	100.00	259.37	1,853.12
10%	12	3,138.43	285.31	at Purchase	1,853.12	185.31	100.00	285.31	2,138.43

13	3,452.27	313.84	10%	2,138.43	213.84	100.00	313.84	2,452.27
14	3,797.50	345.23	Rate earned	2,452.27	245.23	100.00	345.23	2,797.50
15	4,177.25	379.75	on interest	2,797.50	279.75	100.00	379.75	3,177.25
16	4,594.97	417.72	reinvestment	3,177.25	317.72	100.00	417.72	3,594.97
17	5,054.47	459.50	10%	3,594.97	359.50	100.00	459.50	4,054.47
18	5,559.92	505.45	Revised	4,054.47	405.45	100.00	505.45	4,559.92
19	6,115.91	555.99	Yield to	4,559.92	455.99	100.00	555.99	5,115.91
20	6,727.50	611.59	Maturity	5,115.91	511.59	100.00	611.59	5,727.50
21	7,400.25	672.75	19.13%	5,727.50	572.75	100.00	672.75	6,400.25
22	8,140.27	740.02		6,400.25	640.02	100.00	740.02	7,140.27
23	8,954.30	814.03		7,140.27	714.03	100.00	814.03	7,954.30
24	9,849.73	895.43		7,954.30	795.43	100.00	895.43	8,849.73
25	10,834.71	984.97		8,849.73	884.97	100.00	984.97	9,834.71
26	11,918.18	1,083.47		9,834.71	983.47	100.00	1,083.47	10,918.18
27	13,109.99	1,191.82		10,918.18	1,091.82	100.00	1,191.82	12,109.99
18	14,420.99	1,311.00		12,109.99	1,211.00	100.00	1,311.00	13,420.99
29	15,863.09	1,442.10		13,420.99	1,342.10	100.00	1,442.10	14,863.09
30	17,449.40	2,586.31[b]		14,863.09	1,486.31	1,100.00[a]	2,586.31[a]	17,449.40[b]
					$13,449.00	$4,000.00	$17,449.00	

Revised Internal Rate of Return.... 19.13%

[a]Includes $1,000 Maturity Value.
[b]Includes $1,000 purchase price.

$$S = \frac{R\,[(1 + i)^n - 1]}{i} + P$$

where S = value of the investment at maturity
R = annual interest payment
i = IRR before reinvestment at a rate on reinvestment of i
n = number of years until maturity
P = purchase price (maturity value for a par bond)

This formula can be manipulated as follows:

$$R = P \times i$$

Here the annual interest is the purchase price ($1000 times the IRR of 10 percent; that is, $100 per year. Substitute $P \times i$ in the formula for R:

$$S = (P \times i)\frac{[(1 + i)^n - 1]}{i} + P$$

Multiply the numerator and denominator of P by i

$$S = (P \times i)\frac{[(1 + i)^n - 1] + (P \times i)}{i}$$

$$S = (P \times i)\frac{[(1 + i)^n - 1 + 1]}{i}$$

$$S = P\,(1 + i)^n$$

Thus we have arrived back at the compound interest formula, which has been derived from the formula for interest reinvestment from a conventional bond. It is thus apparent that the return from a zero bond (purchased at a compounded yield of "x percent") is identical to that from a conventional bond (purchased at an IRR or YTM of "x percent") where all cash flows are reinvested at the rate of the initial IRR. The amount invested in the zero coupon bond, in this case, is used to purchase the same dollar amount of the conventional bond at par.

IRR AT PURCHASE AND EQUIVALENT REVISED IRR

Every zero coupon bond purchase irrevocably requires reinvestment at the percentage rate of the IRR at purchase. Thus for every IRR at purchase, there is a corresponding **revised IRR** which gives effect to reinvestment at the original IRR percentage rate. How does such revised IRR (after reinvestment) compare to the original IRR? As the maturity of a zero coupon bond lengthens, the revised IRR increases. The higher the level of the original IRR, the greater the magnitude of such increase. These relationships are illustrated in Table 9-2.

Table 9-2. Relationship of IRR to Revised IRR for Zero Coupon Bonds

Internal Rate of Return	Revised IRR after Reinvestment at Original IRR (%)					
	5 Years	10 Years	15 Years	20 Years	25 Years	30 Years
3.00%	3.18	3.41	3.65	3.90	4.10	4.30
4.00	4.32	4.73	5.15	5.55	5.93	6.28
6.00	6.71	7.63	8.53	9.32	9.98	10.50
8.00	9.26	10.86	12.30	13.45	14.27	14.84
10.00	11.95	14.36	16.34	17.72	18.60	19.13
12.00	15.00	18.30	20.30	22.00	23.00	23.20
14.00	17.74	21.97	24.78	26.32	27.11	27.52

The incremental changes in revised IRR do not follow a simple pattern of change as the maturity of the bond increases. Observe the 10 percent row in Table 9-2. For each five-year increase in years to maturity of a zero coupon bond purchased at an IRR or YTM of 10 percent, the absolute increase in revised IRR is:

Years	Absolute Change in Revised IRR (%)
0	—
5	—
10	2.41
15	1.98
20	1.38
25	0.88
30	0.53

For example, the revised IRR of a bond with a five-year maturity is 11.95 percent, and increases to 14.36 percent at a 10-year maturity, an increase of 2.41 percent.

There is no discernible pattern. Viewing the same data from the viewpoint of relative or percentage change from one revised IRR to the next provides:

Years	Percent Increase in Maturity	Percent Increase in Revised IRR
5	—	—
10	100	20
15	50	14
20	33	8
25	25	5
30	20	3

Again, no discernible pattern exists in comparing the change in revised IRR.

As the rates of original IRR or YTM at purchase increase, the revised IRRs increase too. However, the pattern of the rate of change of such increase is unclear. Consider a 20-year bond. As the initial IRR increases, observe the absolute change in revised IRR:

IRR at Purchase (%)	Revised IRR (%)	Change (%)
3	3.90	—
4	5.55	1.65
6	9.32	3.77
8	13.45	4.13
10	17.72	4.27
12	22.00	4.28
14	26.32	4.32

The relative change from one IRR to the next provides an equally unrevealing pattern of change:

IRR at Purchase (%)	Change in IRR at Purchase (%)	Change in Revised IRR (%)
3	—	—
4	33	42
6	50	68
8	33	44
10	25	32
12	20	24
14	17	20

Nevertheless, it is possible with the aid of graphs to quickly find a revised IRR, given the years until maturity and initial IRR at purchase.

QUICK SOLUTIONS TO FINDING REVISED IRR

If the YTM or IRR at purchase of a zero coupon bond is known, the revised IRR (after reinvestment) can be determined in seconds from either Graph 9-1 (Note: For a bond with 20 years until maturity, if purchased at an 8 percent IRR, the revised yield to maturity is 13.45 percent, an increase of 5.45 percent. But if purchased at a 12 percent IRR, the revised IRR is 22 percent, an increase of 10 percent as compared to the original IRR, as shown by the dashed lines.) or Graph 9-2 (Note: A zero coupon bond purchased at a 12 percent YTM or IRR is equivalent to earning with reinvestment for a five-year time period, 15 percent

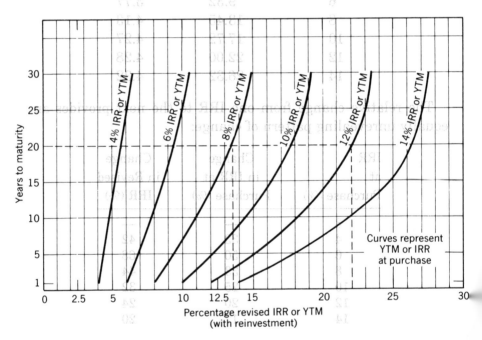

Graph 9-1. Finding Revised IRR, Given the IRR Relative to Maturity.

Note: For a bond with 20 years until maturity, if purchased at an 8 percent IRR, The Revised IRR is 13.45 percent, an increase of 5.45 percent. But, if purchased at a 12 percent IRR, The Revised IRR is 22 percent, an increase of 10 percent.

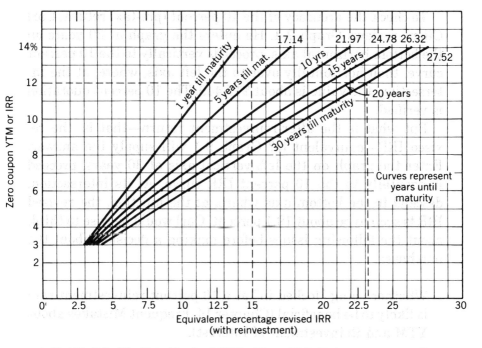

Graph 9-2. Finding Revised IRR, Given IRR Relative to IRR.

Note: A zero coupon bond purchased at a 12 percent IRR is equivalent to earning with reinvestment, for a 5 year maturity, 15 percent revised IRR; and for a 30 percent maturity, 23.2 percent revised IRR—as shown by the dashed lines.

revised IRR and for 30 years, 23.2 percent revised IRR, as shown by the dashed lines.) For example, consider the following offer from broker Sharpy McClintock to Carl Client to buy a 30-year zero coupon bond.

SHARPY McCLINTOCK: "I've got a terrific investment for your IRA (individual retirement account), Carl. Invest $1000 in a government-guaranteed bond and you'll get back $17,449 in 30 years."

CARL CLIENT: "What's the return on investment, Sharpy?"

SHARPY: "Ten percent yield."

To check the accuracy of the 10 percent (pre-tax) return, Carl Client reviews Graph 2-4. He enters the graph at 30 years on the bottom horizontal axis, proceeds vertically to the 10 percent curve, then horizontally over to the left axis, where, at the intersection, the value is about $17,449. The 10 percent quotation is verified.

But what is the after-reinvestment return—that is, the revised IRR—equivalent to? Graph 9-1 will supply the answer: Enter the graph on the left vertical axis at 30 years, proceed horizontally to the 10 percent IRR curve. At its intersection, descend to the bottom axis where, at the junction, the revised IRR is seen to be about 19.1 percent. Carl would be wise to think about the following issues before making a decision about the purchase:

Whether being "locked in" at a 10 percent reinvestment rate is likely to be beneficial (Chapter 14, Frequent Mistakes about YTM and Reinvestment of Interest).

The prognosis for interest rate changes that would affect the volatility of the proposed investment (Chapter 3, Beware of Zero Coupon Volatility).

The yield on 30-year conventional Treasury bonds.

The shape of the Treasury bond yield curve, to determine the reasonableness of the 10 percent yield offered (Chapter 10, Pricing Surprises).

Offerings of other brokers and banks for zero coupon bonds.

The tax consequences of the proposed investment (Chapters 4, Beware of Taxation with Conventional Zeros, and 6, Taxability of Municipal Zero Coupons).

Zeros versus Conventional Treasury Bonds

What is the practical significance of all this? Although "Invest $57,000 and receive $1 million in U.S. backed Treasuries" sounds exciting, consider what it means: The investment does not receive any cash flow for 30 years. You are obtaining a conventional 10 percent IRR or YTM and are reinvesting compulsorily all imputed cash flows at a reinvestment rate of 10 percent. This may be well and good—or it may not. The success depends on market conditions. In summary, if you had a choice between the purchase of a 30-year Treasury at a 12 percent IRR or a zero coupon bond at 10 percent, you would have to decide whether it would be wise to buy the Treasury and take your chances on whether the cash flow could be reinvested at rates averaging 10 percent.

10

Pricing Surprises

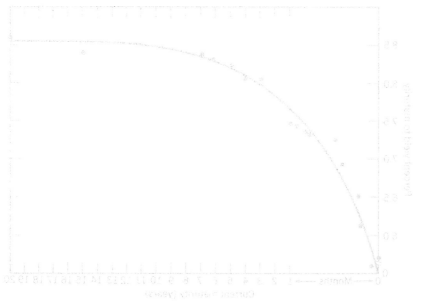

Yields to maturity, at purchase, of a zero coupon bond in some instances should be **higher** than the yield to maturity of a conventional Treasury bond. For example, if a 20-year Treasury bond is selling at par to yield 12 percent to maturity (i.e., 12 percent internal rate of return (IRR)), it is possible that a 20-year zero coupon bond should sell at a price to yield 13 percent or 14 percent to maturity. Conversely, it is also possible that zero coupon yields ought to be less than yields for comparable maturities of Treasury bonds.

Confused? There is a relationship between the yield level at which zero coupon bonds ought to sell and the yield for comparable maturities of conventional bonds. The relationship, which depends principally on the shape of the conventional Treasury

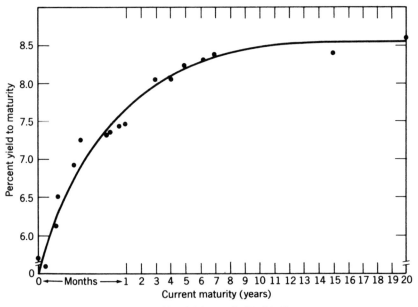

Dots represent observed yields; yield curve is fitted to them.

Chart 10-1. Yield Curve for U.S. Treasury Securities—Bills, Notes, and Bonds (August 19, 1975) (*Source:* Marcia Stigum, *The Money Market: Myth, Reality, and Practice,* Dow Jones-Irwin, Homewood, IL, 1978).

bond yield curve, can be determined mathematically. Secondarily the relationship depends on the level—for example, high versus low—of yields.

CONVENTIONAL YIELD CURVE

The conventional Treasury bond yield curve is a graphic display showing the relationship between yield to maturity and the maturity of the bond. Chart 10-1 shows a *yield curve*. Note that for 10-year bonds the yield to maturity is about 8.5 percent, and for three-year bonds the yield to maturity is about 8 percent. Chart 10-2 shows an *upward-sloping* yield curve. As the length of the bond (i.e., the number of years until the bond matures) increases, the IRR or percentage yield to maturity (YTM) increases. Chart 10-3 shows an *inverted* yield curve. For maturities of 1 to 11 years, the IRR or yield to maturity decreases with the passage

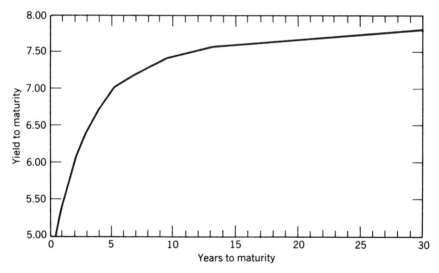

Chart 10-2. Upward-sloping U.S. Treasury Yield Curve (*Source: The Handbook of Fixed Income Securities,* Frank Fabozzi and Irving M. Pollack, eds., p. 753, Dow Jones-Irwin, Homewood, IL, 1983.

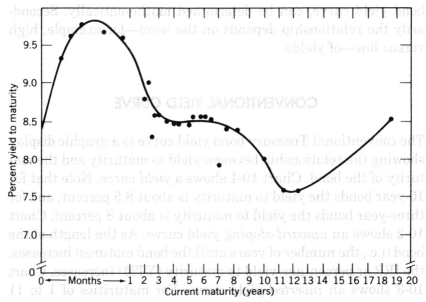

Chart 10-3. Inverted Yield Curve for U.S. Treasury Securities—Bills, Notes, and Bonds (August 30, 1974) (*Source:* Marcia Stigum, *The Money Market: Myth, Reality, and Practice,* Dow Jones-Irwin, Homewood, IL, 1978).

of time, but then the reverse occurs and yields to maturity increase for years 11 to 20.

WHAT IRR OR YTM REALLY MEANS

The YTM or IRR is that percentage rate which equates or makes equal the purchase price of the bond and all the future cash flows. By definition then, it is a single uniform (discount) rate which is applied to the future cash flows to obtain the bond purchase price. In a sense the IRR may be regarded as an "average compound rate." It may either be specified as a before-tax percentage or after taxes for a stated tax bracket.

It may be simpler to view the IRR or yield to maturity within the framework of a normal banking deposit relationship. If, for example, you deposit the amount of the purchase price of the bond into your bank account, and if the bank pays you an interest rate equal to the IRR or YTM, just enough interest (cash flow) will be earned to pay the periodic (semiannual) interest requirements and provide you with the maturity value at the end of the bond's life.[1]

Consider this example: The IRR or YTM is 10 percent for a three-year bond paying 10 percent per annum which is purchased at par of $1000. The discounted present value of each cash flow is determined by dividing each such cash flow by $(1 + i)^n$, where i is the periodic interest rate (e.g., 10 percent or 0.10 per year) and n is the time period in years (or the number of periodic intervals). Table 10-1 illustrates cash flows of this bond and their discounted present value at a 10 percent IRR or yield to maturity. Thus $1000 is the present value of the $1300 in future cash flows expected from ownership of this bond.

For periods of compounding other than annually, i is the *periodic* rate, for example, 5 percent semiannually, and n is the

---

[1]IRR is technically the rate earned on the adjusted investment balance (referred to misleadingly as "unrecovered investment"). In like manner, a bank interest rate is the rate earned on the bank balance. In any event you only earn at IRR or a bank rate on the balance in the account; and you don't earn on what you have withdrawn or recovered. The beginning adjusted balance is the initial investment (the purchase price of a bond). The ending adjusted balance is the disposition proceeds (the bond's maturity value or other sales proceeds). For a bond bought at par, the beginning and ending adjusted balances are the same, $1000. But, for premium, discount, and zero coupon bonds (which are just an extreme form of discount bonds), the beginning and ending adjusted balances are different. An annual modification (or amortization) of the adjusted balance gradually changes it, such that over the life of the holding, the initial difference between the beginning and ending balances is fully eliminated. The annual modification is determined as follows: [IRR times prior years adjusted balance] less cash flow distribution for the year. For a $30 coupon bond bought for $800 at an IRR of 8 percent, the first annual modification would be: [0.08 × 800] − 30; that is, 34. Thus the adjusted balance for the next year becomes $800 plus 34, that is, $834. So, the use of IRR allows an investor to earn at the IRR rate on the adjusted balance of an investment and it at the same time amortizes the difference, if any, between the initial beginning balance and the ultimate sales or disposition proceeds. The IRR is the magic number that makes the projected results happen; no more, no less. For further study, see *The Dow Jones-Irwin Guide to Calculating Yields*.

Table 10-1. Detail of IRR or YTM Calculation—Annual Interest

Time	Cash Flow	Discount Factor	Value of Discount Factor	Present Value (of Cash Flow)
0	—			
1	$ 100	$(1.1)^1$	1.1	$ 90.91
2	100	$(1.1)^2$	1.21	82.64
3	100	$(1.1)^3$	1.331	75.13
3	1000	$(1.1)^3$	1.331	751.32
Total	$1300			$1000.00

number of *periodic time intervals* (e.g., six semiannually), which is the same as the number of years (e.g., three) times the number of times interest is compounded (e.g., two) per year.

Provided the bond just discussed was purchased for $1000 with $50 interest coupons paid semiannually, the IRR or yield to maturity remains 10 percent (5 percent semiannually). The present value at that IRR of the cash flows is shown in Table 10-2.

Table 10-2. Detail of IRR or YTM Calculation—Semiannual Interest

Time	Cash Flow	Discount Factor	Value of Discount Factor	Present Value
0				
1	$ 50	$(1.05)^1$	1.05	$ 47.62
2	50	$(1.05)^2$	1.1025	45.35
3	50	$(1.05)^3$	1.157625	43.19
4	50	$(1.05)^4$	1.21551	41.13
5	50	$(1.05)^5$	1.27628	39.18
6	50	$(1.05)^6$	1.3401	37.31
6	1000	$(1.05)^6$	1.3401	746.22
Total	$1300			$1000.00

The foregoing examples show that the IRR or yield to maturity is the discount rate which equates all future cash flows from the bond investment to the initial investment. (Note that in practice some adjustment is required to account for payment of accrued interest on purchase and the nonuniform time period until the first coupon after purchase is payable; but such adjustment is not meaningful in most instances.)

IRR OR YTM IS AN AVERAGE RATE

The IRR or YTM is an **average rate** in the sense that the **same rate of IRR is applied to all cash flows** from a particular bond, **whether the first** such cash flow due in six months or less **or the last cash flow** which may be the maturity value 30 years hence.

Because the IRR or yield to maturity applies the same discount rate to all future cash flows, it is inappropriate to use the IRR or YTM of a conventional bond of "x" years maturity, and suggest or imply the same rate as a measure of yields for a zero coupon bond, where a single, unique duration is involved. Just because the IRR or YTM of a three-year conventional Treasury issue is 10 percent is no reason that a three-year zero coupon bond should be sold to yield 10 percent as well.

For the conventional bond, 10 percent may represent an average or compilation of an 8 percent yield for the first coupon payment, 9 percent for the second coupon, and 11 percent for the third, or an almost infinite variety of other combinations.

The relevant rate for a three-year zero coupon issue would be the 11 percent applicable to three-year maturities (and not the 10 percent average yield to maturity or IRR at which three-year bonds are selling). *Thus a completely different yield curve (as compared to the traditional Treasury bond yield curve) is required for zero coupon issues.* It exists and is appropriately identified as the *spot rate curve.*

THEORETICAL SPOT RATE CURVE

The "theoretical spot rate curve" depicts the yields that should be effective for varying maturities of zero coupon issues. To construct the theoretical spot curve, one needs both the Treasury bond yield curve and information about short-term rates. *The theoretical curve is based on the premise that the value of a bond should be the same irrespective of whether one owns it in the conventional manner (i.e., with all interest coupons attached) or whether one owns all the parts of a stripped bond.* The premise is that the whole (conventional bond) is worth no more and no less than the sum of its parts (after conversion to a series of zero coupon issues).

To determine the theoretical spot rate curve, each cash flow is discounted at the rate applicable to the pertinent period of time. Table 10-3 shows a two-year Treasury bond paying 10 percent annual interest (for simplicity). If one-year Treasury bills are selling at 6 percent yield to maturity or IRR, and two-year conventional bonds yield 10 percent, the calculation would be as shown in Table 10-3. The value of the zero coupon parts must equal the value of the whole conventional bond, $1000. For the zero bond, then, the present value of the second-year cash flows of the $100 coupon and the $1000 maturity must be equal to the $1000 value of the conventional bond less the $94.34 present value of the first-year coupon of the zero bond ($94.34 is the present value of $100 at a 6 percent discount factor and 6 percent is the rate at which one-year Treasury bills are selling). Thus the present value of the $1100 in the second-year cash flows is $905.66, which is $1000 less $94.34. So, where i is the second-year theoretical spot rate, i is now determinable by the customary present value compound interest formula, as follows:

$$\frac{\$100}{(1 + i)^2} + \frac{1000}{(1 + i)^2} = \$905.66$$

Table 10-3. Spot Rate Derivation—Two Years Until Maturity; 10 Percent Par Bond
Purchased to Yield 10 Percent

Time	Cash Flow	Discount Factor @10% YTM	Present Value at 10% YTM	Spot Discount Rate	Present Value at Spot Rate
0					
1	$ 100	1.1	$ 90.91		
2	100	1.21	82.64		
2	1000	1.21	826.45	1.06	$94.34
Total			$1000.00		

117

$$\frac{1100}{(1 + i)^2} = \$905.66$$

$$(1 + i)^2 = 1.2145838$$

$$(1 + i) = 1.1020815$$

$$i = 0.1020815 \quad \text{or} \quad 10.21\%$$

Now that the two-year theoretical spot rate has been determined, the present value of the conventional bond may be determined by discounting all cash flows at the applicable spot rates, as seen in Table 10-4.

THE WHOLE EQUALS THE SUM OF ITS PARTS

It is evident that the present value of the two-year conventional bond at the IRR of 10 percent is $1000—which is identical to the present value of a series of zero coupon bonds, priced to yield the spot rate of 6 percent for one year and the just-calculated 10.208 percent for two years.

Hence the value of the bond is unchanged, whether it remains as a conventional bond or is stripped of its coupons to become a series of zero coupon bonds. The spot rate for two years that causes the foregoing to occur is 10.208 percent versus the 10 percent yield to maturity for a two-year Treasury bond. If the two-year coupon of $100 or maturity value of $1000 is sold as a zero coupon security at the theoretical spot rate, it would be priced to yield 10.208 percent to the purchaser. *Note that this exceeds the 10 percent yield on two-year Treasury bonds.* In practice, the actual yield to the purchaser would be reduced from the theoretical spot rate by the broker-dealer's markup or profit. Chart 10-4 compares the Treasury bond yield curve and the spot rate yield curve, as described above. Note that the Treasury bond

Table 10-4. Spot Rates Applied to Conventional Bonds

Time	Cash Flow	Discount Factor—@ 10% (Divisor)	Present Value @ 10%	Spot Rate	Discount Factor-Spot (Divisor)	Present Value—@ Spot
0						
1	$ 100	1.1	$ 90.91	6%	1.06	$ 94.34
2	100	1.21	82.64	10.208	1.21458	82.33
2	1000	1.21	826.45	10.208	1.21458	823.33
Total			$1000.00			$1000.00

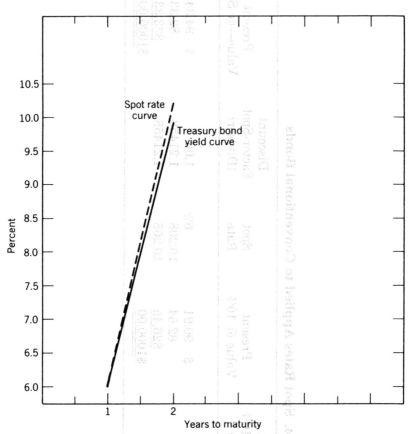

Chart 10-4. Two-Year Bond, Spot Rate Curves vs. Treasury Bond Curve

yield curve is upward-sloping, and the spot rates exceed the Treasury bonds' yields to maturity.

SUMMARY

In this chapter we have seen that in some instances zero coupon bonds should be priced at a higher YTM than Treasury bonds of the same maturity. We have determined that the YTM of a conventional bond is an average rate for its entire term, and that such an average rate is inappropriate for pricing a specific maturity of a zero coupon bond. For zeros the appropriate YTM is the spot rate, and the spot rate for a zero can be determined theoretically from the yields of Treasury bonds of various maturities. Although we have used a two-year bond as an example, the principles involved apply to any maturity and can be used to determine the expected YTM for any zero coupon bond as we shall see in Chapter 11, Construction of the Theoretical Spot Rate Curve.

11

Construction of the Theoretical Spot Rate Curve

YIELD CURVES

As discussed in Chapter 10, Pricing Surprises, the yield at which zero coupon bonds should sell is based on the spot rate yield curve. It is possible to construct an entire spot rate yield curve using the same principles as were outlined in the discussion of two-year bonds in Chapter 10.

The Treasury bond price/yield quotations at a random date are shown in Table 11-1. These yields have been plotted and the curve thus formed makes up the Treasury bond yield curve, as shown in Chart 11-1. Such a yield curve has historically been the benchmark of value against which all other yields in the fixed-income markets are measured and compared. Prior to 1985, the only way to judge the reasonableness of price for zero coupon bonds was to create a **spot rate yield curve** derived from the Treasury bond yield curve, and, in particular, the yields for individual, conventional coupon-paying Treasury bonds. The broad, liquid, and well-understood conventional Treasury bond market, in effect, served as the basis for the determination of appropriate yields for zero coupon instruments. The introduction of STRIPS (Separate Trading of Registered Interest and Principal of Securities) in 1985 is likely to change the benchmark from the Treasury bond yield curve (conventional coupon paying issues) to a "STRIPS yield curve." (STRIPS are discussed in Chapter 13, STRIPS.) If and when the STRIPS curve becomes the primary benchmark, the value of a coupon-paying Treasury can be calculated by the method described in Chapter 10, Pricing Surprises. The result of such calculation is referred to as a "synthetic par Treasury bond."

"Even those with no interest in zero-coupon bonds should understand STRIPS thoroughly because. . . . STRIPS may become the driving force behind the evaluation of the entire fixed-income market."[1]

---

[1]"STRIPS: The New Treasury Zeros," Thomas E. Klaffky and John D. Plum, Salomon Brothers, Inc. March 1985.

Table 11-1. Treasury Issues/Bonds, Notes, and Bills

Treasury Issues/*Bonds, Notes & Bills*

Wednesday, July 18, 1984

Mid-afternoon Over-the-Counter quotations; sources on request.

Decimals in bid-and-asked and bid changes represent 32nds; 101.1 means 101 1/32. a-Plus 1/64. b-Yield to call date. d-Minus 1/64. n-Treasury notes.

Treasury Bonds and Notes

Rate	Mat. Date		Bid	Asked	Bid Chg.	Yld.
13⅛s,	1984	Jul n.	100.1	100.5	.....	7.48
6⅜s,	1984	Aug.	99.20	100.4	.....	4.50
7¼s,	1984	Aug n.	99.22	99.26	.....	9.59
11⅝s,	1984	Aug n.	100.2	100.6	.....	9.54
13¼s,	1984	Aug n.	100.5	100.9	.....	8.79
12⅛s,	1984	Sep n.	100.4	100.8	.....	10.44
9¾s,	1984	Oct n.	99.19	99.23	.....	10.56
9⅞s,	1984	Nov n.	99.15	99.19	.....	10.89
14⅜s,	1984	Nov n.	100.29	101.1	.....	10.77
16s,	1984	Nov n.	101.13	101.17	.....	10.75
9⅜s,	1984	Dec n.	99.5	99.9	+ .1	11.01
14s,	1984	Dec n.	101.3	101.7	− .1	11.05
9¼s,	1985	Jan n.	98.27	98.31	+ .1	11.31
8s,	1985	Feb n.	98.5	98.9	.....	11.18
9⅝s,	1985	Feb n.	98.25	98.29	.....	11.51
14⅝s,	1985	Feb n.	101.16	101.20	.....	11.61
9⅝s,	1985	Mar.	98.18	98.22	+ .1	11.63
13⅜s,	1985	Mar n.	100.29	101.1	− .1	11.80
9½s,	1985	Apr n.	98.9	98.13	+ .1	11.69
3¼s,	1985	May.	95.3	96.3	.....	8.26
4¼s,	1975-85	May.	95.5	96.5	− .1	9.20
9⅞s,	1985	May n.	98.8	98.12	.....	11.90
10⅜s,	1985	May n.	98.30	99.2	+ .1	11.60
14⅛s,	1985	May n.	101.16	101.20	− .1	12.00
14⅜s,	1985	May n.	101.22	101.26	− .1	12.00
14s,	1985	Jun n.	101.21	101.25	+ .1	11.96
10s,	1985	Jun n.	98.5	98.9	+ .1	11.97
10⅝s,	1985	Jul n.	98.15	98.19	.....	12.12
8¼s,	1985	Aug n.	96.15	96.19	+ .1	11.72
9⅝s,	1985	Aug n.	97.14	97.18	.....	12.11
10⅝s,	1985	Aug n.	98.7	98.11	− .1	12.26
13⅛s,	1985	Aug n.	100.25	100.29	.....	12.20
10⅞s,	1985	Sep n.	98.13	98.17	+ .1	12.23
15⅞s,	1985	Sep n.	103.24	103.28	.....	12.30
10½s,	1985	Oct n.	97.25	97.29	.....	12.31
9¾s,	1985	Nov n.	96.22	96.26	− .1	12.43
10½s,	1985	Nov n.	97.17	97.21	.....	12.42
11¾s,	1985	Nov n.	99.6	99.10	.....	12.33
10⅞s,	1985	Dec n.	97.25	97.29	− .1	12.50
14⅛s,	1985	Dec n.	102	102.4	.....	12.47
10⅝s,	1986	Jan n.	97.12	97.16	.....	12.47
10⅞s,	1986	Feb n.	97.16	97.20	+ .2	12.54
13½s,	1986	Feb n.	'101.2	101.6	.....	12.64
9⅞s,	1986	Feb n.	96.1	96.5	+ .1	12.65
14s,	1986	Mar n.	101.25	101.29	.....	12.72
11½s,	1986	Mar n.	98.4	98.8	+ .2	12.68
11¾s,	1986	Apr n.	98.9	98.11	+ .1	12.82
7⅞s,	1986	May n.	92.10	92.18	+ .1	12.56
9⅜s,	1986	May n.	94.14	94.18	.....	12.81
12⅝s,	1986	May n.	99.16	99.18	+ .1	12.90
13¾s,	1986	May n.	101.12	101.16	+ .1	12.80
13s,	1986	Jun n.	100.7	100.9	+ .2	12.83
14⅞s,	1986	Jun n.	103.11	103.19	+ .3	12.83
8s,	1986	Aug n.	91.18	91.22	+ .2	12.68
11⅜s,	1986	Aug n.	97.12	97.16	+ .2	12.79
12¼s,	1986	Sep n.	98.29	99.1	+ .1	12.77
6⅛s,	1986	Nov.	89.18	90.18	+ .2	10.83
11s,	1986	Nov n.	96.11	96.15	+ .1	12.80
13⅞s,	1986	Nov n.	101.22	102.3	− .2	12.81

Rate	Mat. Date		Bid	Asked	Bid Chg.	Yld.
9⅞s,	1988	May n.	90.13	90.21	+ .4	13.06
13⅝s,	1988	Jun n.	101.15	101.17	+ .6	13.12
14s,	1988	Jul n.	102.24	103	+ .7	13.01
10½s,	1988	Aug n.	91.27	92.3	+ .6	13.06
15⅜s,	1988	Oct n.	106.29	107.5	+ .9	13.12
8¾s,	1988	Nov n.	86.4	86.12	+ .9	12.96
11¾s,	1988	Nov n.	95.17	95.25	+ .7	13.06
14⅝s,	1989	Jan n.	104.24	105	+ .7	13.12
11⅜s,	1989	Feb n.	94.2	94.10	+ .7	13.07
14⅜s,	1989	Apr n.	104.2	104.10	+ .8	13.12
9¼s,	1989	May n.	86.26	87.2	+ .11	12.94
11¾s,	1989	May n.	95	95.4	+ .8	13.15
14½s,	1989	Jul n.	104.19	104.27	+ .7	13.15
13⅞s,	1989	Aug n.	102.10	102.12	+ .8	13.20
11⅞s,	1989	Oct n.	95.1	95.9	+ .7	13.15
10¾s,	1989	Nov n.	90.24	91	+ .8	13.15
10½s,	1990	Jan n.	89.10	89.18	+ .8	13.24
3½s,	1990	Feb.	90	91	+ .6	5.39
10½s,	1990	Apr n.	88.31	89.7	+ .8	13.24
8¼s,	1990	May.	80.30	81.14	+ .7	12.88
10¾s,	1990	Jul n.	89.22	89.30	+ .11	13.24
10¾s,	1990	Aug n.	89.16	89.24	+ .12	13.26
11½s,	1990	Oct n.	92.17	92.25	+ .9	13.24
13s,	1990	Nov n.	98.29	99.5	+ .9	13.20
11¾s,	1991	Jan n.	93.12	93.16	+ .9	13.28
12⅜s,	1991	Apr.	96	96.4	+ .10	13.26
14½s,	1991	May n.	105.4	105.12	+ .8	13.28
13¾s,	1991	Jul n.	101.31	102.1	+ .9	13.29
14⅞s,	1991	Aug n.	106.28	107.4	+ .10	13.29
14¼s,	1991	Nov n.	103.30	104.6	+ .8	13.34
14⅝s,	1992	Feb n.	105.25	106.1	+ .10	13.34
13¾s,	1992	May n.	101.26	102.2	+ .8	13.32
4¼s,	1987-92	Aug.	89.28	90.28	+ .4	5.67
7¼s,	1992	Aug.	71.31	72.15	+ .6	12.82
10½s,	1992	Nov n.	85.28	86.4	+ .13	13.31
4s,	1988-93	Feb.	89.31	90.31	+ .3	5.33
6¾s,	1993	Feb.	68.14	68.30	+ .8	12.83
7⅞s,	1993	Feb.	73.1	73.17	+ .7	13.11
10⅞s,	1993	Feb n.	87.17	87.21	+ .13	13.33
10⅛s,	1993	May n.	83.20	83.24	+ .16	13.31
7½s,	1988-93	Aug.	70.18	71.2	+ .12	13.03
8⅝s,	1993	Aug.	75.24	76	+ .11	13.25
11⅞s,	1993	Aug n.	92.10	92.18	+ .13	13.31
8⅝s,	1993	Nov.	75.18	75.26	+ .10	13.21
11¾s,	1993	Nov.	91.18	91.22	+ .9	13.33
9s,	1994	Feb.	76.29	77.5	+ .8	13.29
4⅛s,	1989-94	May.	89.31	90.31	+ .3	5.32
13⅛s,	1994	May.	98.30	99.2	+ .9	13.30
8¾s,	1994	Aug.	75.4	75.12	+ .8	13.25
10⅛s,	1994	Nov.	82.13	82.21	+ .9	13.26
3s,	1995	Feb.	89.27	90.27	+ .3	4.07
10½s,	1995	Feb.	84.2	84.10	+ .8	13.31
10⅜s,	1995	May.	83.9	83.17	+ .8	13.29
12⅝s,	1995	May.	96.1	96.9	+ .10	13.28
11½s,	1995	Nov.	89.15	89.23	+ .8	13.28
7s,	1993-98	May.	62.6	62.22	+ .10	12.83
3½s,	1998	Nov.	89.27	90.27	+ .3	4.37
8½s,	1994-99	May.	69.8	69.24	+ .12	13.20
7⅞s,	1995-00	Feb.	65.1	65.9	+ .11	13.18
8⅜s,	1995-00	Aug.	67.29	68.5	+ .13	13.19
11¾s,	2001	Feb.	89.15	89.23	+ .10	13.30
13⅛s,	2001	May.	99.4	99.12	+ .12	13.22
8s,	1996-01	Aug.	64.30	65.14	+ .14	13.12
13⅜s,	2001	Aug.	100.12	100.20	+ .13	13.28
15¾s,	2001	Nov.	116.30	117.6	+ .11	13.20
14¼s,	2002	Feb.	106.5	106.13	+ .10	13.30
11⅝s,	2002	Nov.	88.7	88.15	+ .8	13.32
10¾s,	2003	Feb.	82.8	82.16	+ .12	13.31
10¾s,	2003	May.	82.7	82.15	+ .12	13.31

(Continued)

Table 11-1. Treasury Issues/Bonds, Notes, and Bills
(Continued)

Rate	Mat.	Date	Bid	Asked	Bid Chg.	Yld.	Rate	Mat.	Date	Bid	Asked	Bid Chg.	Yld.
16⅛s,	1986	Nov n...........	106.5	106.13+	.1	12.85	11⅛s,	2003	Aug............	84.24	85 +	.14	13.31
10s,	1986	Dec n............	94.3	94.7 +	.1	12.83	11⅞s,	2003	Nov............	90.6	90.14+	.13	13.26
9s,	1987	Feb n...........	91.24	91.28+	.4	12.81	12⅜s,	2004	May............	93.27	94.3 +	.10	13.22
10⅞s,	1987	Feb n............	95.17	95.21+	.2	12.91	13¾s,	2004	Aug............	103.5	103.7 +	.15	13.28
12¾s,	1987	Feb n...........	99.21	99.25+	.3	12.85	8¼s,	2000-05	May............	65.20	66.4 +	.15	13.00
10¼s,	1987	Mar n...........	93.29	94.1 +	.2	12.94	7⅞s,	2002-07	Feb............	61.2	61.10+	.16	12.95
12s,	1987	May n...........	97.30	98.2 +	.2	12.84	7⅞s,	2002-07	Nov............	62.16	62.24+	.16	12.98
12½s,	1987	May n...........	98.26	98.28+	.5	12.99	8⅜s,	2003-08	Aug............	65.22	65.30+	.17	13.04
14s,	1987	May n...........	102.9	102.13+	.3	12.96	8¾s,	2003-08	Nov............	67.26	68.2 +	.12	13.15
10½s,	1987	Jun n...........	93.29	94.1 +	.3	13.00	9⅛s,	2004-09	May............	70.15	70.23+	.15	13.14
13¾s,	1987	Aug n...........	101.24	101.28+	.4	12.99	10⅛s,	2004-09	Nov............	79.14	79.22+	.16	13.16
11⅛s,	1987	Sep n...........	95.4	95.8 +	.3	12.99	11¾s,	2005-10	Feb............	89.10	89.18+	.13	13.18
7⅞s,	1987	Nov n...........	86.8	86.24+	.3	12.63	10s,	2005-10	May............	76.18	76.26+	.12	13.17
12⅝s,	1987	Nov n...........	98.27	98.31+	.3	13.02	12¾s,	2005-10	Nov............	96.16	96.24+	.13	13.17
11¼s,	1987	Dec n...........	95.6	95.10+	.3	12.98	13⅞s,	2006-11	May............	104.26	105.2 +	.15	13.16
12⅜s,	1988	Jan n...........	98.6	98.14+	.4	12.95	14s,	2006-11	Nov............	105.28	106.4 +	.14	13.15
10⅛s,	1988	Feb n...........	91.27	92.3 +	.2	12.96	10⅜s,	2007-12	Nov............	79.4	79.12+	.13	13.17
12s,	1988	Mar n...........	96.28	96.30+	.2	13.07	12s,	2008-13	Aug............	91.2	91.6 +	.13	13.19
13¼s,	1988	Apr n...........	100.19	100.27+	.3	12.96	13¼s,	2014	May............	101	101.4 +	.15	13.10
8¼s,	1988	May n...........	85.31	86.7 +	.6	12.93							

Source: The Wall Street Journal, Thursday, July 19, 1984.

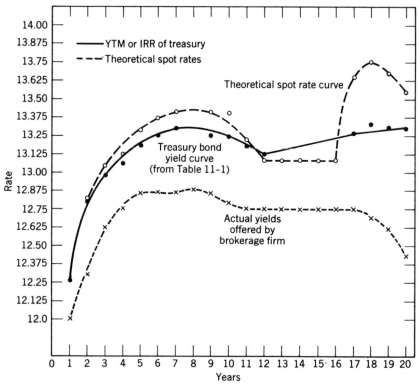

Chart 11-1. Theoretical Spot Rate Curve vs. Actual Broker Quotes.

Tables 11-2 through 11-16 contain the detailed calculations of the **theoretical spot rate**—which would indicate appropriate zero or strip yields—for years 1–20. For example, refer to Table 11-2. The theoretical, or calculated, spot rate for two years as shown in the table is 12.824 percent.

Note that with respect to Table 11-2, the horizontal rows are labeled from 1 to 48 and the vertical columns are designated from B to O. Each number in the table can be identified by its row and column designation. Such locations are often referred to as "cells." For example, the value at C 48 is $1127.90 (on the bottom line under the designation "Bond Cash Flow"). The value in cell C 47, $127.90, is found by "B12*B13"; that is, multiplying the value in cell B12 ($1000) by the value in B13 (0.1279). The theoretical spot rates thus calculated are then plotted on Chart 11-1 and a curve is fitted to such points to form the theoretical spot rate curve.

But how does the theoretical spot rate compare to the actual values at which zero coupon bonds traded on the same date? The yields being offered by an active (randomly selected) broker are shown in Table 11-17. For example, zero coupon bonds maturing approximately two years hence were quoted to yield 12.3 percent, at an August 15, 1986 maturity. And bonds maturing 20 years hence were quoted at a 12.45 percent yield. Those offered rates are plotted as "x's" on Chart 11-1.

Because the broker's yields for a given maturity are less than the spot rate, it is evident that the yields offered by the broker were too low and the bonds were overpriced. Table 11-18 presents a comparison of the same data. The yields offered by the broker are as much as 8 percent (relatively) less than the theoretical spot rate.

Only an informed public and more active surveillance on the part of the regulatory authorities will prevent this type of price-gouging from taking place.

A comparison of spot rates to the Treasury bond yield curve is shown in Table 11-19.

Table 11-2. Theoretical Spot Rate Calculation: 2 years

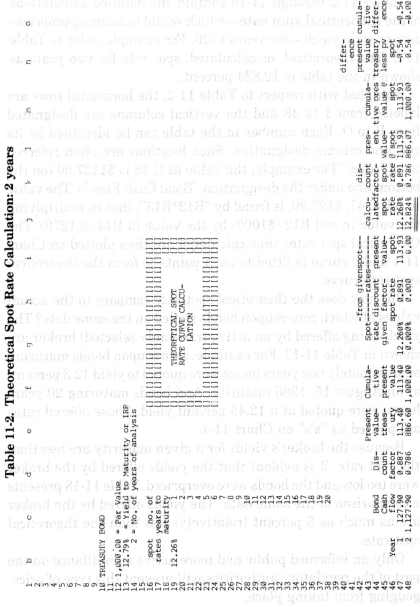

```
        b    c    d    e    f    g    h    i    j    k    l

 1  TREASURY BOND
 2
 3
 4
 5
 6
 7
 8
 9
10  TREASURY BOND
11  1,000.00  = Par Value
12  12.79%    = Yield to Maturity or IRR
13  2         = No. of years of analysis
14
15
16  spot      no. of
17  rates     years to
18  12.26%    maturity
19
20
```

THEORETICAL SPOT RATE CALCULATION

		Present value treasury	Discount factor	Cumulative present value	Spot rate given	rate discount factor given	present value @ spot	discount factor spot rate	calculated spot rate	cumulative pres value spot	treasury pv less spot pv difference	present value cumulative difference
Year	Bond Cash flow											
1	127.90	113.40	0.887	113.40	12.260%	0.0003%	113.93	0.891	12.260%	113.93	-0.54	-0.54
2	1,127.90	886.60	0.786	1,000.00	0.000%	0.000%	886.07	0.786	12.824%	1,000.00	-0.00	-0.00

Table 11-3. Theoretical Spot Rate Calculation: 3 years

	b	c	d	e	f	g	h	i	j	k	l	m	n	o

```
10  TREASURY BOND
11
12  1,000.00 = Par Value
13  12.99% = Yield to Maturity or IRR
14  3 = No. of years of analysis
15
16       spot   no. of
17      rates  years to
18             maturity
19  12.26%  1
20  12.82%  2
```

```
┌────────────────────────────────┐
│      THEORETICAL SPOT           │
│      RATE CURVE CALCU-          │
│      LATION                     │
│                                 │
└────────────────────────────────┘
```

Year	Bond Cash flow	Dis-count factor	Present value-treas-ury	Cumula-tive present value	Spot—from given spot—rates spot rate given	discount factor	present value spot rate	calcu-lated spot rate	dis-count latedfactor-spot rate	pres-ent value @spot rate	cumula-tive pres value @ spot	present value @ spot less pv spot	differ-ence present value treasury less pv	cumula-tive differ-ence
1	129.90	0.885	114.97	114.97	12.260%	0.891	115.71	12.26%	0.891	115.71	115.71	115.71	-0.75	-0.75
2	129.90	0.783	101.75	216.71	12.824%	0.786	102.05	12.824%	0.786	102.05	217.76	217.76	-0.30	-1.05
3	1,129.90	0.693	783.29	1,000.00	0.000%	0.000	0.000	13.043%	0.692	782.24	1,000.00	1,000.00	1.05	0.00

Table 11-4. Theoretical Spot Rate Calculation: 4 years

	b	c	d	e	f	g	h	i	j	k	l	m	n	o

TREASURY BOND

1,000.00 = Par Value
13.06% = Yield to Maturity or IRR
4 = No. of years of analysis

spot rates	no. of years to maturity
12.26%	1
12.82%	2
13.04%	3
	4

```
[][][][][][][][][][][][][][][][][][]
[]                                []
[]      THEORETICAL SPOT           []
[]   RATE CURVE CALCU-             []
[]        LATION                   []
[]                                []
[][][][][][][][][][][][][][][][][][]
```

Year	Bond Cash flow	Discount factor	Present value treasury	Cumulative present value	Spot rate given spot rate	from given spot rates — discount factor given	present value spot	calculated spot rate	discount factor spot rate	present value spot	cumulative pres value @ spot	cumulative present value treasury less pv @ spot	difference cumulative present value treasury difference spot
1	130.60	0.884	115.51	115.51	12.260%	0.891	116.34	12.260%	0.891	116.34	116.34	-0.82	-0.82
2	130.60	0.782	102.17	217.68	12.824%	0.786	102.60	12.824%	0.786	102.60	218.94	-0.43	-1.25
3	130.60	0.692	90.37	308.05	13.040%	0.692	90.42	13.040%	0.692	92.42	309.35	-0.05	-1.30
4	1,130.60	0.612	691.95	1,000.00	0.000%	0.000	0.00	13.113%	0.611	690.65	1,000.00	1.30	0.00

130

Table 11-5. Theoretical Spot Rate Calculation: 5 years

	b	c	d	e	f	g	h	i	j	k	l	m	n	o

```
TREASURY BOND

1,000.00 = Par Value
13.20% = Yield to Maturity or IRR
    5 = No. of years of analysis

 spot     no. of
rates    years to
         maturity
12.26%      1
12.82%      2
13.04%      3
13.11%      4
            5
            6
            7
            8
            9
           10
           11
           12
           13
           14
           15
           16
           17
           18
           19
           20
```

THEORETICAL SPOT RATE CURVE CALCULATION

Year	Bond Cash flow	Discount factor	Present value-treasury	Cumulative present value	Spot—from given spot rates given spot rate	discount factor	present value-spot	calculated spot rate	discount latedfactor-spot rate	pres-ent value @ spot	cumulative present value @ spot	difference present value treasury less pv spot spot	cumulative difference spot
1	132.00	0.883	116.61	116.61	12.26%	0.891	117.58	12.26%	0.891	117.58	117.58	-0.98	-0.98
2	132.00	0.780	103.01	219.62	12.82%	0.786	103.70	12.82%	0.786	103.70	221.28	-0.69	-1.66
3	132.00	0.689	91.00	310.62	13.04%	0.692	91.39	13.040%	0.692	91.39	312.67	-0.39	-2.05
4	132.00	0.609	80.39	391.00	13.11%	0.611	80.64	13.113%	0.611	80.64	393.30	-0.25	-2.30
5	1,132.00	0.538	609.00	1,000.00	0.000%	0.000	0.00	13.286%	0.536	636.70	1,000.00	2.30	0.00

131

Table 11-6. Theoretical Spot Rate Calculation: 6 years

	a	b	c	d	e	f	g	h	i	j	k	l	m	n	o

TREASURY BOND

1,000.00 = Par Value
13.26% = Yield to Maturity or IRR
6 = No. of years of analysis

spot no. of
rates years to
maturity

THEORETICAL SPOT
RATE CURVE CALCU-
LATION

	1	12.26%
	2	12.82%
	3	13.04%
	4	13.11%
	5	13.29%

Year	Bond Cash flow	Discount factor	Present value treasury	Cumulative present value
1	132.60	0.883	117.08	117.08
2	132.60	0.780	103.37	220.44
3	132.60	0.686	91.27	311.71
4	132.60	0.606	80.58	392.29
5	132.60	0.537	71.15	463.44
6	1,132.60	0.474	536.56	1,000.00

	—from given spot—rates—								differ-ence present value less pv	cumula-tive differ-ence
	Spot rate given	discount factor given	present value	spot rate	calcu-lated spot rate	dis-count factor spot	pres-ent value @ spot	cumula-tive pres value @ spot		spot
	12.260%	0.891	118.12	118.12	12.260%	0.891	118.12	118.12	-1.04	-1.04
	12.824%	0.786	104.17	164.17	12.824%	0.786	104.17	222.29	-0.80	-1.84
	13.040%	0.692	91.80	91.80	13.040%	0.692	91.80	314.09	-0.53	-2.38
	13.113%	0.611	81.00	81.00	13.113%	0.611	81.00	395.09	-0.42	-2.80
	13.286%	0.536	71.07	71.07	13.286%	0.536	71.07	466.16	0.08	-2.72
	0.000%	2.000	0.00	0.00	13.356%	0.471	533.84	1,000.00	2.72	0.00

Table 11-7. Theoretical Spot Rate Calculation: 7 years

TREASURY BOND

1,000.00 = Par Value
13.29% = Yield to Maturity or IRR
7 = No. of years of analysis

spot rates / no. of years to maturity	spot rate
1	12.26%
2	12.62%
3	13.04%
4	13.11%
5	13.29%
6	13.36%

THEORETICAL SPOT RATE CURVE CALCULATION

Year	Bond Cash flow	Dis-count factor	Present value-treasury	Cumula-tive present value	—from given spot rates— spot rate	given discount factor	present value spot	Spot—rates— calcu-lated spot rte	dis-count factor spot rate	pres-ent value @ spot	cumula-tive present value @ spot	differ-ence present value treasury less pv spot	cumula-tive differ-ence
1	132.90	0.883	117.31	117.31	12.26%	0.891	118.39	12.26%	0.891	118.39	118.39	-1.08	-1.08
2	132.90	0.779	103.55	220.86	12.82%	0.786	104.41	12.82%	0.786	104.41	222.79	-0.86	-1.93
3	132.90	0.688	91.40	312.26	13.04%	0.692	92.01	13.04%	0.692	92.01	314.80	-0.61	-2.54
4	132.90	0.607	80.68	392.94	13.11%	0.611	81.18	13.11%	0.611	81.18	395.98	-0.51	-3.05
5	132.90	0.536	71.21	464.15	13.28%	0.536	71.23	13.28%	0.536	71.23	467.21	-0.01	-3.06
6	132.90	0.473	62.86	527.01	13.36%	0.471	62.64	13.36%	0.471	62.64	529.85	0.22	-2.84
7	1,132.90	0.418	472.99	1,000.00	0.00%	0.000	0.000	13.38%	0.415	470.15	1,000.00	2.84	0.00

Table 11-8. Theoretical Spot Rate Calculation: 8 years

TREASURY BOND

1,000.00 = Par Value
12.82% = Yield to Maturity or IRR
8 = No. of years of analysis

spot rates	no. of years to maturity
12.26%	1
12.82%	2
13.04%	3
13.11%	4
13.29%	5
13.36%	6
13.39%	7

THEORETICAL SPOT
RATE CURVE CALCU-
LATION

Year	Bond Cash flow	Dis-count factor	Present value-treasury	Cumula-tive present value	Srot rate given	discount factor	present value	spot rate	calcu-latedfactor-spot rate	dis-count factor-spot rate	pres-ent spot value-@ spot	cumula-tive pres value @ spot	treasury less pv spot	present value treasury differ-ence spot
1	128.20	0.886	113.63	113.63	12.26%	0.891		114.20	12.26%	0.891	114.20	114.20	-0.57	-0.57
2	128.20	0.786	100.72	214.35	12.824%	0.786		100.71	12.824%	0.786	100.71	214.91	0.01	-0.56
3	128.20	0.696	89.27	303.63	13.040%	0.692		88.75	13.040%	0.692	88.75	303.67	0.52	-0.04
4	128.20	0.617	79.13	382.76	13.113%	0.611		78.31	13.113%	0.611	78.31	381.98	0.82	0.78
5	128.20	0.547	70.14	452.90	13.286%	0.536		68.71	13.286%	0.536	68.71	450.69	1.43	2.21
6	128.20	0.485	62.17	515.07	13.356%	0.471		60.43	13.356%	0.471	60.43	511.11	1.74	3.95
7	128.20	0.430	55.10	570.17	13.388%	0.415		53.20	13.388%	0.415	53.20	564.31	1.90	5.85
8	1,128.20	0.381	429.83	1,000.00	0.000%	0.000		0.00	12.62%	0.386	435.69	1,000.00	-5.85	0.00

134

	b	c	d	e	f	g	h	i	j	k	l	m	n	o

TREASURY BOND

1,000.00 = Par Value
13.25% = Yield to Maturity or IRR
9 = No. of years of analysis

spot no. of rates	years to maturity
1	12.26%
2	12.82%
3	13.04%
4	13.11%
5	13.29%
6	13.36%
7	13.39%
8	12.63%

THEORETICAL SPOT RATE CALCULATION

Year	Bond Cash flow	Dis-count factor	Present value-treasury	Cumula-tive present value	Spot from given spot rates — given spot rate	rate discount factor	present value spot	calcu-lated spot rate	dis-count factor @ spot rate	pres-ent value @ spot	cumula-tive pres value @ spot	difference present value treasury less pv spot	cumula-tive difference spot
1	132.50	0.883	117.00	117.00	12.260%	0.891	118.03	12.260%	0.891	118.03	118.03	-1.03	-1.03
2	132.50	0.780	103.31	220.31	12.824%	0.786	104.09	12.824%	0.786	104.09	222.12	-0.78	-1.81
3	132.50	0.688	91.22	311.53	13.040%	0.692	91.73	13.043%	0.692	91.73	313.85	-0.51	-2.32
4	132.50	0.608	80.55	392.08	13.113%	0.611	80.94	13.113%	0.611	80.94	394.79	-0.39	-2.71
5	132.50	0.537	71.13	463.20	13.286%	0.536	71.01	13.285%	0.536	71.01	465.81	0.11	-2.60
6	132.50	0.474	62.80	526.01	13.356%	0.471	62.45	13.356%	0.471	62.45	528.26	0.35	-2.25
7	132.50	0.419	55.46	581.46	13.388%	0.415	54.99	13.388%	0.415	54.99	583.24	0.47	-1.78
8	132.50	0.370	48.97	630.43	12.629%	0.386	51.17	12.629%	0.386	51.17	634.41	-2.20	-3.98
9	1,132.50	0.326	369.57	1,000.00	0.000%	0.000	0.00	13.305%	0.323	365.59	1,000.00	3.98	0.00

135

Table 11-10. Theoretical Spot Rate Calculation: 10 years

TREASURY BOND

1,000.00 = Par Value
13.25% = Yield to Maturity or IRR
10 = No. of years of analysis

spot no. of rates years to maturity	
1	12.26%
2	12.82%
3	13.04%
4	13.11%
5	13.29%
6	13.36%
7	13.39%
8	12.63%
9	13.39%
10	
11	
12	
13	
14	
15	
16	
17	
18	
19	
20	

```
□□□□□□□□□□□□□□□□□□□□
□□□□□□□□□□□□□□□□□□□□
□□□            □□□
□□□  THEORETICAL SPOT  □□□
□□□  RATE CURVE CALCU-  □□□
□□□     LATION     □□□
□□□            □□□
□□□□□□□□□□□□□□□□□□□□
□□□□□□□□□□□□□□□□□□□□
```

Year	Bond Cash flow	Dis-count factor	Present value-treasury	Cumula-tive present value	Spot-rate spot rate	rate discount given factor	present value spot	calcu-lated spot rate	dis-count spot rate	pres-ent value @ spot	cumula-tive pres value @ spot	differ-ence present value treasury less pv spot	cumula-tive differ-ence spot
					—from given spot rates—								
1	132.50	0.883	117.00	117.00	12.260%	0.891	118.03	12.260%	0.891	118.03	118.03	-1.03	-1.03
2	132.50	0.780	103.31	220.31	12.824%	0.786	104.09	12.824%	0.786	104.09	222.12	-0.78	-1.81
3	132.50	0.688	91.22	311.53	13.040%	0.692	91.73	13.040%	0.692	91.73	313.85	-0.51	-2.32
4	132.50	0.608	80.55	392.08	13.113%	0.611	80.94	13.113%	0.611	80.94	394.79	-0.39	-2.71
5	132.50	0.537	71.13	463.20	13.286%	0.536	71.01	13.286%	0.536	71.01	465.81	0.11	-2.60
6	132.50	0.474	62.80	526.01	13.356%	0.471	62.45	13.356%	0.471	62.45	528.26	0.35	-2.25
7	132.50	0.419	55.46	581.46	13.388%	0.415	54.99	13.388%	0.415	54.99	583.24	0.47	-1.78
8	132.50	0.370	48.97	630.43	12.629%	0.386	51.17	12.629%	0.386	51.17	634.41	-2.20	-3.98
9	132.50	0.326	43.24	673.67	13.386%	0.323	42.77	13.386%	0.323	42.77	677.19	1.46	-3.52
10	1,132.50	0.288	326.33	1,060.00	0.000%	0.000	0.000	13.373%	0.285	322.81	1,060.00	3.52	-0.00

Table 11-11. Theoretical Spot Rate Calculation: 11 years

```
9
10 TREASURY BOND
11
12 1,000.00 = Par Value
13 13.19% = Yield to Maturity or IRR
14    11  = No. of years of analysis
15
16       spot  no. of
17 rates years to
18       maturity
19 12.26%  1
20 12.82%  2
21 13.04%  3
22 13.11%  4
23 13.29%  5
24 13.36%  6
25 13.39%  7
26 12.63%  8
27 13.39%  9
28 13.37% 10
```

THEORETICAL SPOT RATE CURVE CALCULATION:

| | | | | | -from given spot-rates- | | | calcu- lated spot rate | dis- count factor @ spot | pres- ent value @ spot | cumula- tive pres value @ spot | differ- ence present value treasury less pv spot | cumula- tive differ- ence spot |
Year	Bond Cash flow	Dis- count factor	Present value- treas- ury	Cumula- tive present value	Spot rate given	discount factor	present value spot						
1	131.90	0.883	116.53	116.53	12.26%	0.891	117.50	12.26%	0.891	117.50	117.50	-0.97	-0.97
2	131.90	0.781	102.95	219.48	12.82%	0.786	103.62	12.82%	0.786	103.62	221.11	-0.67	-1.63
3	131.90	0.690	90.95	310.43	13.04%	0.692	91.32	13.04%	0.692	91.32	312.43	-0.36	-2.00
4	131.90	0.609	80.35	390.79	13.11%	0.611	80.57	13.11%	0.611	80.57	393.00	-0.22	-2.22
5	131.90	0.538	70.90	461.78	13.29%	0.536	70.69	13.28%	0.536	70.69	463.70	0.30	-1.92
6	131.90	0.476	62.72	524.50	13.36%	0.471	62.17	13.35%	0.471	62.17	525.87	0.55	-1.37
7	131.90	0.420	55.41	579.91	13.38%	0.415	54.74	13.38%	0.415	54.74	580.60	0.67	-0.69
8	131.90	0.371	48.95	628.86	12.63%	0.386	50.94	12.62%	0.386	50.94	631.54	-1.99	-2.68
9	131.90	0.328	43.25	672.11	13.39%	0.323	42.58	13.38%	0.323	42.58	674.12	0.67	-2.01
10	131.90	0.290	38.21	716.32	13.37%	0.285	37.60	13.37%	0.285	37.60	711.72	0.61	-1.40
11	1,131.90	0.256	289.68	1,000.00	0.00%	0.000	0.00	13.24%	0.255	288.28	1,000.00	1.40	-0.00

Table 11-12. Theoretical Spot Rate Calculation: 12 years

Row		
9	TREASURY BOND	
11		
12	1,000.00	= Par Value
13	13.12%	= Yield to Maturity or IRR
14	12	= No. of years of analysis

spot rates	no. of years to maturity
12.26%	1
12.82%	2
13.04%	3
13.11%	4
13.29%	5
13.36%	6
13.39%	7
12.63%	8
13.39%	9
13.37%	10
13.24%	11

THEORETICAL SPOT RATE CURVE CALCULATION

Year	Bond Cash flow	Dis-count factor	Present value-treas-ury	Cumula-tive present value	Spot rate given spot rate	rate discount factor given	present value spot rate	calcu-lated factor spot rate	dis-count factor spot rate	pres-ent value @ spot	cumula-tive pres value @ spot	differ-ence present value treasury less pv spot	cumula-tive differ-ence spot
1	131.20	0.884	115.98	115.98	12.260%	0.891	116.87	12.260%	0.891	116.87	116.87	-0.89	-0.89
2	131.20	0.781	102.53	218.51	12.824%	0.786	103.07	12.824%	0.786	103.07	219.94	-0.54	-1.43
3	131.20	0.691	90.64	309.15	13.040%	0.692	90.83	13.040%	0.692	90.83	310.77	-0.19	-1.62
4	131.20	0.611	80.13	389.28	13.113%	0.611	80.15	13.113%	0.611	86.15	390.92	-0.02	-1.64
5	131.20	0.540	70.83	460.11	13.286%	0.536	70.32	13.286%	0.536	70.32	461.23	0.52	-1.12
6	131.20	0.477	62.62	522.73	13.356%	0.471	61.84	13.356%	0.471	61.84	523.07	0.78	-0.34
7	131.20	0.422	55.36	578.09	13.388%	0.415	54.45	13.388%	0.415	54.45	577.52	0.91	0.57
8	131.20	0.373	48.93	627.02	12.629%	0.386	50.67	12.629%	0.386	50.67	628.19	-1.73	-1.17
9	131.20	0.330	43.26	670.28	13.386%	0.323	42.35	13.386%	0.323	42.35	670.54	0.90	-0.26
10	131.20	0.291	38.24	708.52	13.373%	0.285	37.40	13.373%	0.285	37.40	707.94	0.84	0.58
11	131.20	0.258	33.81	742.33	13.240%	0.255	33.41	13.240%	0.255	33.41	741.35	0.39	0.97
12	1,131.20	0.228	257.67	1,003.00	0.000%	0.000	0.000	13.064%	0.229	258.65	1,000.00	-0.97	0.00

TREASURY BOND: Theoretical Spot Rate Calculation: 17 years

TREASURY BOND

1,000.00 = Par Value
13.28% = Yield to Maturity or IRR
17 = No. of years of analysis

spot rates	no. of years to maturity
12.26%	1
12.82%	2
13.04%	3
13.11%	4
13.29%	5
13.36%	6
13.35%	7
12.63%	8
13.39%	9
13.37%	10
13.24%	11
13.08%	12
13.08%	13
13.08%	14
13.08%	15
13.08%	16
13.08%	17

THEORETICAL SPOT RATE CURVE CALCULATION

estimated

Year	Bond Cash flow	Discount factor	Present value-treasury	Cumulative present value	given spot rate	rate discount factor given	present value spot	calculated late spot rate	discount factor spot rate	present value @ spot	cumulative pres value spot	difference present value treasury less spot	cumulative difference treasury less spot
1	132.80	0.883	117.23	117.23	12.26%	0.891	118.30	12.26%	0.891	118.30	118.30	-1.07	-1.07
2	132.80	0.779	103.49	220.72	12.82%	0.786	104.33	12.824%	0.786	104.33	222.62	-0.84	-1.90
3	132.80	0.688	91.36	312.08	13.04%	0.692	91.94	13.040%	0.692	91.94	314.56	-0.58	-2.48
4	132.80	0.607	80.65	392.72	13.11%	0.611	81.12	13.113%	0.611	81.12	395.69	-0.48	-2.96
5	132.80	0.536	71.19	463.91	13.29%	0.536	71.17	13.286%	0.536	71.17	466.86	0.02	-2.94
6	132.80	0.473	62.85	526.76	13.36%	0.471	62.59	13.356%	0.471	62.59	529.45	0.25	-2.69
7	132.80	0.418	55.48	582.24	13.35%	0.415	55.11	13.388%	0.415	55.11	584.56	0.37	-2.32
8	132.80	0.369	48.97	631.21	12.63%	0.386	51.29	12.629%	0.386	51.29	635.85	-2.31	-4.63
9	132.80	0.326	43.23	674.45	13.39%	0.323	42.87	13.386%	0.323	42.87	678.72	0.36	-4.27
10	132.80	0.287	38.17	712.61	13.37%	0.285	37.85	13.373%	0.285	37.85	716.57	0.31	-3.96
11	132.80	0.254	33.69	746.30	13.24%	0.255	33.82	13.240%	0.255	33.82	750.40	-0.13	-4.09
12	132.80	0.224	29.74	776.04	13.08%	0.229	30.37	13.084%	0.229	30.37	780.76	-0.62	-4.72
13	132.80	0.198	26.25	802.30	13.08%	0.202	26.86	13.080%	0.202	26.86	807.63	-0.61	-5.33
14	132.80	0.175	23.18	825.48	13.08%	0.179	23.76	13.080%	0.179	23.76	831.38	-0.58	-5.91
15	132.80	0.154	20.46	845.94	13.08%	0.158	21.01	13.080%	0.158	21.01	852.39	-0.55	-6.46
16	132.80	0.136	18.06	864.00	13.08%	0.140	18.58	13.080%	0.140	18.58	870.97	-0.52	-6.97
17	1,132.80	0.120	136.00	1,000.00	0.000%	0.114	129.03	13.631%	0.114	129.03	1,000.00	6.97	0.00

139

Table 11-14. Theoretical Spot Rate Calculation: 18 years

TREASURY BOND

1,000.00 = Par Value
13.32% = Yield to Maturity or IRR
18 = No. of years of analysis

spot no. of rates years to maturity	
12.26%	1
12.82%	2
13.04%	3
13.11%	4
13.29%	5
13.36%	6
13.39%	7
12.63%	8
13.39%	9
13.37%	10
13.24%	11
13.08%	12
13.08%	13 estimated
13.08%	14 estimated
13.08%	15 estimated
13.08%	16 estimated
13.63%	17
	18
	19
	20

THEORETICAL SPOT
RATE CURVE CALCU-
LATION!

Year	Bond Cash flow	Dis-count factor	Present value treas-ury	Cumula-tive present value	Spot given spot rate	Spot rate discount factor	present value spot	calcu-lated spot rate	dis-count latefactor-spot	pres-ent value @ spot	cumula-tive pres value @ spot	differ-ence present value treasury less pv spot	cumula-tive differ-ence spot
1	133.20	0.882	117.54	117.54	12.260%	0.891	118.65	12.260%	0.891	118.65	118.65	-1.11	-1.11
2	133.20	0.779	103.73	221.27	12.824%	0.786	104.64	12.824%	0.786	104.64	223.29	-0.91	-2.02
3	133.20	0.687	91.53	312.80	13.040%	0.692	92.22	13.040%	0.692	92.22	315.51	-0.68	-2.71
4	133.20	0.606	80.78	393.58	13.113%	0.611	81.37	13.113%	0.611	81.37	396.88	-0.59	-3.30
5	133.20	0.535	71.28	464.86	13.286%	0.536	71.39	13.286%	0.536	71.39	468.27	-0.11	-3.41
6	133.20	0.472	62.90	527.76	13.356%	0.471	62.78	13.356%	0.471	62.78	531.05	0.12	-3.29
7	133.20	0.417	55.51	583.27	13.388%	0.415	55.28	13.388%	0.415	55.28	586.32	0.23	-3.05
8	133.20	0.368	48.98	632.25	12.629%	0.386	51.44	12.629%	0.386	51.44	637.76	-2.46	-5.51
9	133.20	0.325	43.23	675.48	13.386%	0.323	43.00	13.386%	0.323	43.00	680.76	0.23	-5.28
10	133.20	0.286	38.15	713.63	13.373%	0.285	37.97	13.373%	0.285	37.97	718.73	0.18	-5.11
11	133.20	0.253	33.66	747.29	13.240%	0.255	33.92	13.240%	0.255	33.92	752.66	-0.26	-5.37
12	133.20	0.223	29.70	776.99	13.084%	0.229	30.46	13.084%	0.229	30.46	783.11	-0.75	-6.12
13	133.20	0.197	26.21	803.20	13.080%	0.202	26.95	13.080%	0.202	26.95	810.06	-0.73	-6.85
14	133.20	0.174	23.13	826.34	13.080%	0.179	23.83	13.080%	0.179	23.83	833.89	-0.70	-7.55
15	133.20	0.153	20.41	846.75	13.080%	0.158	21.07	13.080%	0.158	21.07	854.96	-0.66	-8.21
16	133.20	0.135	18.01	864.76	13.080%	0.140	18.64	13.080%	0.140	18.64	873.59	-0.62	-8.83
17	133.20	0.119	15.90	880.66	13.631%	0.114	15.17	13.631%	0.114	15.17	888.77	0.72	-8.11
					13.764%	0.098		13.764%	0.098	111.23	1,000.00	8.11	0.00

10 TREASURY BOND
11
12 1,000.00 = Par Value
13 13.31% = Yield to Maturity or IRR
14 19 = No. of years of analysis
15
16 spot   no. of
17 rates   years to
18   maturity

THEORETICAL SPOT
RATE CURVE CALCU-
LATION

	spot rates	years to maturity
19	12.26%	1
20	12.82%	2
21	13.04%	3
22	13.11%	4
23	13.29%	5
24	13.36%	6
25	13.39%	7
26	12.63%	8
27	13.39%	9
28	13.37%	10
29	13.24%	11
30	13.08%	12
31	13.08%	13
32	13.08%	14
33	13.08%	15
34	13.08%	16
35	13.63%	17
36	13.76%	18
37		19
38		20

41 Years   19
42 Bond YTM 13.310%

	Year	Bond Cash flow	Discount factor	Present value treasury	Cumulative present value treasury	Spot rate given	discount factor given spot rate	present value spot	calculated spot rate	discount factor spot rate	present value @ spot	cumulative present value @ spot	difference present value treasury less pv spot	cumulative difference treasury spot
47	1	133.10	0.883	117.47	117.47	12.26%	0.891	118.56	12.260	0.891	118.56	118.56	-1.10	-1.10
48	2	133.10	0.775	103.67	221.13	12.824%	0.786	104.56	12.824	0.786	104.56	223.13	-0.90	-1.99
49	3	133.10	0.687	91.49	312.62	13.040%	0.692	92.15	13.040	0.692	92.15	315.27	-0.66	-2.65
50	4	133.10	0.607	80.74	393.37	13.113%	0.611	81.31	13.113	0.611	81.31	396.58	-0.56	-3.21
51	5	133.10	0.535	71.26	464.62	13.286%	0.536	71.33	13.286	0.536	71.33	467.91	-0.08	-3.29
52	6	133.10	0.472	62.89	527.51	13.356%	0.471	62.74	13.356	0.471	62.74	530.65	0.15	-3.14
53	7	133.10	0.417	55.50	583.01	13.388%	0.415	55.23	13.388	0.415	55.23	585.88	0.27	-2.87
54	8	133.10	0.368	48.96	631.99	12.629%	0.386	51.40	12.629	0.386	51.40	637.29	-2.42	-5.29
55	9	133.10	0.325	43.23	675.22	13.386%	0.323	42.97	13.386	0.323	42.97	684.25	0.26	-5.03
56	10	133.10	0.287	38.15	713.37	13.373%	0.285	37.94	13.373	0.285	37.94	718.19	0.21	-4.82
57	11	133.10	0.253	33.67	747.04	13.240%	0.255	33.96	13.240	0.255	33.96	752.49	-0.23	-5.05
58	12	133.10	0.223	29.71	776.76	13.084%	0.229	30.43	13.084	0.229	30.43	782.52	-0.72	-5.77
59	13	133.10	0.197	26.22	802.98	13.080%	0.202	26.53	13.080	0.202	26.53	809.45	-0.76	-6.47
60	14	133.10	0.174	23.14	826.12	13.080%	0.179	23.81	13.080	0.179	23.81	833.26	-0.67	-7.14
61	15	133.10	0.153	20.42	846.55	13.080%	0.158	21.06	13.080	0.158	21.06	854.32	-0.63	-7.77
62	16	133.10	0.135	18.03	864.57	13.080%	0.140	18.62	13.080	0.140	18.62	872.94	-0.60	-7.62
63	17	133.10	0.120	15.91	880.48	13.631%	0.114	15.16	13.631	0.114	15.16	888.10	0.75	-8.37
64	18	133.10	0.105	14.04	894.52	13.764%	0.098	13.06	13.764	0.098	13.06	901.16	0.98	-7.62
65	19	1,133.10	0.093	105.48	1,000.00	13.699%	0.087	98.84	13.699	0.087	98.84	1,000.00	6.64	0.02

Table 11-16. Theoretical Spot Rate Calculation: 20 years

```
10 TREASURY BOND
11
12  1,000.00 = Par Value
13   13.28% = Yield to Maturity or IRR
14      20  = No. of years of analysis
15
16  spot   no. of
17  rates  years to
18         maturity
```

┌┐┌┐┌┐┌┐┌┐┌┐┌┐┌┐┌┐┌┐┌┐┌┐ ┌┐
└┘└┘└┘└┘└┘└┘└┘└┘└┘└┘└┘└┘ └┘
┌┐   ┌┐
└┘   THEORETICAL SPOT   └┘
┌┐   RATE CURVE CALCU-   ┌┐
└┘   LATION   └┘
┌┐   ┌┐
└┘└┘└┘└┘└┘└┘└┘└┘└┘└┘└┘└┘ └┘

spot no. of rates years to maturity	spot rate
1	12.26%
2	12.82%
3	13.04%
4	13.11%
5	13.29%
6	13.36%
7	13.39%
8	12.63%
9	13.39%
10	13.37%
11	13.24%
12	13.08%
13	13.08%
14	13.08%
15	13.08%
16	13.08%
17	13.63%
18	13.76%
19	13.70%
20	

```
41 Years     20
42 TBond YTM  13.28%
```

Year	Bond Cash flow	Discount factor	Present value-treasury	Cumulative present value	Spot rate given spot rate	discount factor given	present value spot	Cumulative present value spot	calculated spot rate	discount factor spot rate	present value @ spot	cumulative present value @ spot	difference present value treasury less pv spot	cumulative difference
1	132.80	0.883	117.23	117.23	12.260%	0.891	118.30	118.30	12.260%	0.891	118.30	118.30	-1.07	-1.07
2	132.80	0.779	103.49	220.72	12.824%	0.786	104.33	222.62	12.824%	0.786	104.33	222.62	-0.84	-1.90
3	132.80	0.688	91.36	312.08	13.040%	0.692	91.94	314.56	13.040%	0.692	91.94	314.56	-0.58	-2.49
4	132.80	0.607	80.65	392.72	13.113%	0.611	81.12	395.69	13.113%	0.611	81.12	395.69	-0.48	-2.96
5	132.80	0.536	71.19	463.91	13.286%	0.536	71.17	466.86	13.286%	0.536	71.17	466.86	0.02	-2.94
6	132.80	0.473	62.85	526.76	13.356%	0.471	62.59	529.45	13.356%	0.471	62.59	529.45	0.25	-2.69
7	132.80	0.418	55.48	582.24	13.388%	0.415	55.11	584.56	13.388%	0.415	55.11	584.56	0.37	-2.32
8	132.80	0.369	48.97	631.21	12.629%	0.386	51.29	635.85	12.629%	0.386	51.29	635.85	-2.31	-4.63
9	132.80	0.326	43.23	674.45	13.386%	0.323	42.87	678.72	13.386%	0.323	42.87	678.72	0.36	-4.27
10	132.80	0.287	38.17	712.61	13.373%	0.285	37.85	716.57	13.373%	0.285	37.85	716.57	0.31	-3.96
11	132.80	0.254	33.69	746.30	13.240%	0.255	33.82	750.40	13.240%	0.255	33.82	750.40	-0.13	-4.09
12	132.80	0.224	29.74	776.04	13.080%	0.229	30.37	780.76	13.080%	0.229	30.37	780.76	-0.62	-4.72
13	132.80	0.198	26.25	802.30	13.080%	0.202	26.86	807.63	13.080%	0.202	26.86	807.63	-0.61	-5.33
14	132.80	0.175	23.18	825.48	13.080%	0.179	23.76	831.38	13.080%	0.179	23.76	831.38	-0.58	-5.91
15	132.80	0.154	20.46	845.94	13.080%	0.158	21.01	852.39	13.080%	0.158	21.01	852.39	-0.55	-6.46
16	132.80	0.136	18.06	864.00	13.080%	0.140	18.58	870.97	13.080%	0.140	18.58	870.97	-0.52	-6.97
17	132.80	0.120	15.94	879.94	13.631%	0.114	15.13	886.10	13.631%	0.114	15.13	886.10	0.82	-6.16
18	132.80	0.106	14.07	894.02	13.764%	0.098	13.03	899.13	13.764%	0.098	13.03	899.13	1.04	-5.12
19	132.80	0.094	12.42	906.44	13.699%	0.087	11.58	910.72	13.699%	0.087	11.58	910.72	0.84	-4.28

Table 11-17. CATS Prices Offered by Broker, July 18, 1984

Maturity	Yield	Price per $100	Maturity	Yield	Price per $100
2-15-85	$11^{60}\%$	93.992	8-15-95	$12^{75}\%$	25.519
8-15-85	12	88.488	2-15-96	12^{75}	23.990
2-15-86	12^{15}	83.296	8-15-96	12^{75}	22.552
8-15-86	12^{30}	78.299	2-15-97	12^{75}	21.200
2-15-87	12^{60}	73.233	8-15-97	12^{75}	19.930
8-15-87	12^{65}	68.794	2-15-98	12^{75}	18.736
2-15-88	12^{70}	64.594	8-15-98	12^{75}	17.613
8-15-88	12^{75}	60.621	2-15-99	12^{75}	16.557
2-15-89	12^{80}	56.867	8-15-99	12^{75}	15.565
8-15-89	12^{85}	53.319	2-15-00	12^{75}	14.632
2-15-90	12^{85}	50.100	8-15-00	12^{75}	13.755
8-15-90	12^{85}	47.076	2-15-01	12^{75}	12.931
2-15-91	12^{85}	44.234	8-15-01	12^{75}	12.156
8-15-91	12^{85}	41.563	2-15-02	12^{75}	11.427
2-15-92	12^{90}	38.916	8-15-02	12^{70}	10.834
8-15-92	12^{90}	36.558	2-15-03	12^{65}	10.276
2-15-93	12^{85}	34.481	8-15-03	12^{60}	9.752
8-15-93	12^{85}	32.399	2-15-04	12^{50}	9.344
2-15-94	12^{80}	30.580	8-15-04	12^{45}	8.878
8-15-94	12^{80}	28.741	2-15-05	12^{40}	8.439
2-15-95	12^{75}	27.146	8-15-05	12^{40}	7.946

Table 11-18. Comparison of Spot Rates to Broker's Offering

Theoretical Spot Rates	Number of Years to Maturity	Zero Coupon Offered by Broker	YTM or IRR of Treasury Bonds	Broker Rates Less Spot Rates	% Difference Broker vs. Spot
12.26%	1	12.00%	12.26%	-0.26%	-2.12%
12.82	2	12.30	12.79	-0.52	-4.09
13.04	3	12.65	12.99	-0.39	-2.99
13.11	4	12.75	13.06	-0.36	-2.77
13.29	5	12.85	13.20	-0.44	-3.28
13.36	6	12.85	13.26	-0.51	-3.79
13.39	7	12.85	13.29	-0.54	-4.02
12.63	8	12.90	12.82	0.27	2.15
13.39	9	12.85	13.25	-0.54	-4.00
13.37	10	12.80	13.25	-0.57	-4.28
13.24	11	12.75	13.19	-0.49	-3.70
13.08	12	12.75	13.12	-0.33	-2.55
13.08	13	12.75		-0.33	-2.52
13.08	14	12.75		-0.33	-2.52
13.08	15	12.75		-0.33	-2.52
13.08	16	12.75		-0.33	-2.52
13.63	17	12.75	13.28	-0.88	-6.46
13.76	18	12.70	13.32	-1.06	-7.73
13.699	19	12.60	13.31	-1.10	-8.03
13.545	20	12.45	13.28	-1.10	-8.11

Table 11-19. Comparison of Spot Rates to Treasury Bond Yield Curve

Theoretical Spot Rates	Number of Years to Maturity	Zero Coupon Offered by Broker	YTM or IRR of Treasury Bonds	YTM or IRR of Treasury Bonds Less Theoretical Spot Rates	% Difference YTM or IRR vs. Spot
12.26%	1	12.00%	12.26%	0.00%	0.00%
12.82	2	12.30	12.79	-0.03	-0.27
13.04	3	12.65	12.99	-0.05	-0.38
13.11	4	12.75	13.06	-0.05	-0.40
13.29	5	12.85	13.20	-0.09	-0.65
13.36	6	12.85	13.26	-0.10	-0.72
13.39	7	12.85	13.29	-0.10	-0.73
12.63	8	12.90	12.82	0.19	1.51
13.39	9	12.85	13.25	-0.14	-1.02
13.37	10	12.80	13.25	-0.12	-0.92
13.24	11	12.75	13.19	-0.05	-0.38
13.08	12	12.75	13.12	0.04	0.28
13.08	13	12.75			
13.08	14	12.75			
13.08	15	12.75			
13.08	16	12.75			
13.63	17	12.75	13.28	-0.35	-2.58
13.76	18	12.70	13.32	-0.44	-3.23
13.699	19	12.60	13.31	-0.39	-2.85
13.545	20	12.45	13.28	-0.27	-2.00

Table 11-20. Comparison of Treasury Bond Yield Curve to Broker's Offering

Theoretical Spot Rates	Number of Years to Maturity	Zero Coupon Offered by Broker	YTM or IRR of Treasury Bonds	YTM or IRR of Treasury Bonds less Zero Coupon Rates—Broker	% Difference YTM or IRR vs. Zero
12.26%	1	12.00%	12.26%	0.26%	2.17%
12.82	2	12.30	12.79	0.49	3.98
13.04	3	12.65	12.99	0.34	2.69
13.11	4	12.75	13.06	0.31	2.43
13.29	5	12.85	13.20	0.35	2.72
13.36	6	12.85	13.26	0.41	3.19
13.39	7	12.85	13.29	0.44	3.42
12.63	8	12.90	12.82	-0.08	-0.62
13.39	9	12.85	13.25	0.40	3.11
13.37	10	12.80	13.25	0.45	3.52
13.24	11	12.75	13.19	0.44	3.45
13.08	12	12.75	13.12	0.37	2.90
13.08	13	12.75			
13.08	14	12.75			
13.08	15	12.75			
13.08	16	12.75			
13.63	17	12.75	13.28	0.53	4.16
13.76	18	12.70	13.32	0.62	4.88
13.699	19	12.60	13.31	0.71	5.63
13.545	20	12.45	13.28	0.83	6.67

The Treasury bond yield curve compared to the yields offered by the broker is shown in Table 11-20. Notice that there is a fairly close correlation between the yields offered by the broker and the Treasury bond yields for the same maturity. Thus it seems the zeros were mostly offered at between 0.3 percent and 0.5 (absolute values, not relative) percent below the Treasury bond yields for the same maturity.

YIELD CURVE SLOPE

To further analyze the relationship between Treasury bond yields and theoretical spot rates let us consider both an **upward-sloping yield curve** and then a **downward-sloping curve.**

For the hypothetical upward-sloping curve, we shall start with a one-year Treasury bill yield of 8 percent, with yields increasing at the rate of 0.25 percent for each subsequent year, until in the twentieth year, the yield is 12.75 percent. Chart 11-2 shows such a Treasury bond yield curve and the theoretical spot rate curve. The theoretical spot rate curve was developed from Tables 11-21 through 11-39. The chart shows a classic pattern or relationship between the spot rates and the Treasury bond yield curve for a positive or upward-sloping yield curve.

For a downward-sloping yield curve, Chart 11-3 compares the Treasury bond yield curve and its derivative, the theoretical spot rate curve. The spot rates were determined by the procedures and calculations shown in Tables 11-40 through 11-58.

As may be expected, the relationship of spot rates to Treasury bonds is classic for a downward-sloping yield curve.

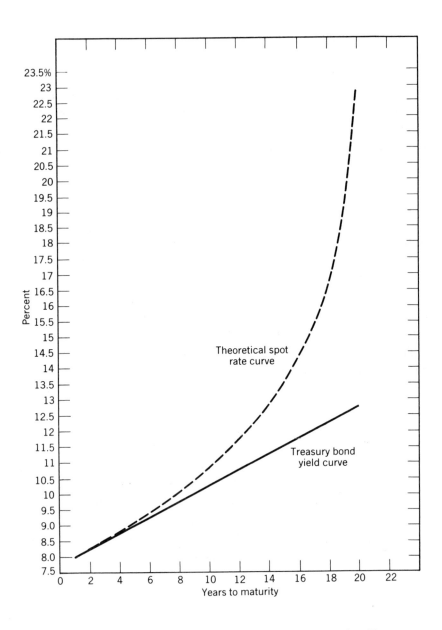

Chart 11-2. Theoretical Spot Rates with Upward-sloping Treasury Bond Yield Curve.

Table 11-21. Upward-sloping Treasury Bond Yield Curve: Theoretical Spot Rate Calculation

Years 2
Bond YTM: 8.250%

Year	Bond Cash Flow	Disc. Factor	PV Treas.	Cum. PV	Spot Rate Given	From Given Spot Rates Disc. Factor	PV	Calc. Spot Rate	Disc. Factor Spot Rate	PV @ Spot	Cum. PV @ Spot	Difference PV Treas. Less PV Spot	Cum. Difference
1	82.50	0.924	76.21	76.21	8.000%	0.926	76.39	8.000%	0.926	76.39	76.39	-0.18	-0.18
2	1,082.50	0.853	923.79	1,000.00	0.000%	0.000	0.00	8.26%	0.853	923.61	1,000.00	0.18	0.00

Table 11-22. Upward-sloping Treasury Bond Yield Curve: Theoretical Spot Rate Calculation

Years 3
Bond YTM: 8.500%

Year	Bond Cash Flow	Disc. Factor	PV Treas.	Cum. PV	Spot Rate Given	From Given Spot Rates Disc. Factor	PV	Calc. Spot Rate	Disc. Factor Spot Rate	PV @ Spot	Cum. PV @ Spot	Difference PV Treas. Less PV Spot	Cum. Difference
1	85.00	0.922	78.34	78.34	8.000%	0.926	78.70	8.000%	0.926	78.70	78.70	-0.36	-0.36
2	85.00	0.849	72.20	150.54	8.263%	0.853	72.52	8.260%	0.853	72.52	151.23	-0.32	-0.68
3	1,085.00	0.783	849.46	1,000.00	0.000%	0.000	0.00	8.529%	0.782	848.77	1,000.00	0.68	0.00

Table 11-23. Upward-sloping Treasury Bond Yield Curve: Theoretical Spot Rate Calculation

Years 4
TBond YTM 8.750%

Year	Bond Cash Flow	Disc. Factor	PV Treas.	Cum. PV	Spot Rate Given	From Given Spot Rates		Calc. Spot Rate	Disc. Factor Spot Rate	PV @ Spot	Cum. PV @ Spot	Difference PV Treas. Less PV Spot	Cum. Difference
						Disc. Factor	PV						
1	87.50	0.920	80.46	80.46	8.000%	0.926	81.02	8.000%	0.926	81.02	81.02	-0.56	-0.56
2	87.50	0.846	73.99	154.45	8.260%	0.853	74.66	8.260%	0.853	74.66	155.68	-0.67	-1.23
3	87.50	0.778	68.03	222.48	8.529%	0.782	68.45	8.529%	0.782	68.45	224.13	-0.42	-1.65
4	1,087.50	0.715	777.52	1,000.00	0.000%	0.000	0.00	8.808%	0.713	775.87	1,000.00	1.65	0.00

Table 11-24. Upward-sloping Treasury Bond Yield Curve: Theoretical Spot Rate Calculation

Years 5
TBond YTM 9.000%

Year	Bond Cash Flow	Disc. Factor	PV Treas.	Cum. PV	Spot Rate Given	From Given Spot Rates		Calc. Spot Rate	Disc. Factor Spot Rate	PV @ Spot	Cum. PV @ Spot	Difference PV Treas. Less PV Spot	Cum. Difference
						Disc. Factor	PV						
1	90.00	0.917	82.57	82.57	8.000%	0.926	83.33	8.000%	0.926	83.33	83.33	-0.76	-0.76
2	90.00	0.842	75.75	158.32	8.260%	0.853	76.79	8.260%	0.853	76.79	160.12	-1.04	-1.80
3	90.00	0.772	69.50	227.82	8.529%	0.782	70.41	8.529%	0.782	70.41	230.53	-0.91	-2.71
4	90.00	0.708	63.76	291.57	8.808%	0.713	64.21	8.808%	0.713	64.21	294.74	-0.45	-3.16
5	1,090.00	0.650	708.43	1,000.00	0.000%	0.000	0.00	9.098%	0.647	705.26	1,000.00	3.16	0.00

Table 11-25. Upward-sloping Treasury Bond Yield Curve: Theoretical Spot Rate Calculation

Years 6
TBond YTM 9.250%

Year	Bond Cash Flow	Disc. Factor	PV Treas.	Cum. PV	Spot Rate Given	From Given Spot Rates Disc. Factor	PV	Calc. Spot Rate	Disc. Factor Spot Rate	PV @ Spot	Cum. PV @ Spot	Difference PV Treas. Less PV Spot	Cum. Difference
1	92.50	0.915	84.67	84.67	8.000%	0.926	85.65	8.000%	0.926	85.65	85.65	-0.98	-0.98
2	92.50	0.838	77.50	162.17	8.260%	0.853	78.92	8.260%	0.853	78.92	164.57	-1.42	-2.40
3	92.50	0.767	70.94	233.11	8.529%	0.782	72.36	8.529%	0.782	72.36	236.93	-1.42	-3.83
4	92.50	0.702	64.93	298.04	8.808%	0.713	65.99	8.808%	0.713	65.99	302.93	-1.06	-4.89
5	92.50	0.643	59.43	357.47	9.098%	0.647	59.85	9.098%	0.647	59.85	362.77	-0.42	-5.30
6	1,092.50	0.588	642.53	1,000.00	0.000%	0.000	0.00	9.401%	0.583	637.23	1,000.00	5.30	0.00

Table 11-26. Upward-sloping Treasury Bond Yield Curve: Theoretical Spot Rate Calculation

Years 7
TBond YTM 9.500%

Year	Bond Cash Flow	Disc. Factor	PV Treas.	Cum. PV	Spot Rate Given	From Given Spot Rates Disc. Factor	PV	Calc. Spot Rate	Disc. Factor Spot Rate	PV @ Spot	Cum. PV @ Spot	Difference PV Treas. Less PV Spot	Cum. Difference
1	95.00	0.913	86.76	86.76	8.000%	0.926	87.96	8.000%	0.926	87.96	87.96	-1.20	-1.20
2	95.00	0.834	79.23	165.99	8.260%	0.853	81.06	8.260%	0.853	81.06	169.02	-1.83	-3.03
3	95.00	0.762	72.36	238.35	8.529%	0.782	74.32	8.529%	0.782	74.32	243.34	-1.96	-4.99
4	95.00	0.696	66.08	304.43	8.808%	0.713	67.78	8.808%	0.713	67.78	311.11	-1.70	-6.69
5	95.00	0.635	60.35	364.77	9.098%	0.647	61.47	9.098%	0.647	61.47	372.58	-1.12	-7.81
6	95.00	0.580	55.11	419.88	9.401%	0.583	55.41	9.401%	0.583	55.41	427.99	-0.30	-8.11
7	1,095.00	0.530	580.12	1,000.00	0.000%	0.000	0.00	9.720%	0.522	572.01	1,000.00	8.11	0.00

151

Table 11-27. Upward-sloping Treasury Bond Yield Curve: Theoretical Spot Rate Calculation

Years 8
TBond YTM 9.750%

Year	Bond Cash Flow	Disc. Factor	PV Treas.	Cum. PV	Spot Rate Given	From Given Spot Rates		Calc. Spot Rate	Disc. Factor Spot Rate	PV @ Spot	Cum. PV @ Spot	Difference PV Treas. Less PV Spot	Cum. Difference
						Disc. Factor	PV						
1	97.50	0.911	88.84	88.84	8.000%	0.926	90.28	8.000%	0.926	90.28	90.28	-1.44	-1.44
2	97.50	0.836	80.95	169.78	8.260%	0.853	83.19	8.260%	0.853	83.19	173.47	-2.24	-3.68
3	97.50	0.756	73.75	243.54	8.529%	0.782	76.27	8.529%	0.782	76.27	249.74	-2.52	-6.20
4	97.50	0.689	67.20	310.74	8.808%	0.713	69.56	8.808%	0.713	69.56	319.30	-2.36	-8.56
5	97.50	0.628	61.23	371.97	9.098%	0.647	63.08	9.098%	0.647	63.08	382.38	-1.85	-10.41
6	97.50	0.572	55.79	427.77	9.401%	0.583	56.87	9.401%	0.583	56.87	439.25	-1.08	-11.49
7	97.50	0.521	50.84	478.60	9.720%	0.522	50.93	9.720%	0.522	50.93	490.19	-0.10	-11.58
8	1,097.50	0.475	521.40	1,000.00	0.000%	0.000	0.00	10.059%	0.465	509.81	1,000.00	11.58	0.00

Table 11-28. Upward-sloping Treasury Bond Yield Curve: Theoretical Spot Rate Calculation

Years 9
TBond YTM 10.000%

Year	Bond Cash Flow	Disc. Factor	PV Treas.	Cum. PV	Spot Rate Given	From Given Spot Rates		Calc. Spot Rate	Disc. Factor Spot Rate	PV @ Spot	Cum. PV @ Spot	Difference PV Treas. Less PV Spot	Cum. Difference
						Disc. Factor	PV						
1	100.00	0.909	90.91	90.91	8.000%	0.926	92.59	8.000%	0.926	92.59	92.59	-1.68	-1.68
2	100.00	0.826	82.64	173.55	8.260%	0.853	85.32	8.260%	0.853	85.32	177.92	-2.68	-4.36
3	100.00	0.751	75.13	248.69	8.529%	0.782	78.23	8.529%	0.782	78.23	256.14	-3.10	-7.46
4	100.00	0.683	68.30	316.99	8.808%	0.713	71.34	8.808%	0.713	71.34	327.49	-3.04	-10.50
5	100.00	0.621	62.09	379.08	9.098%	0.647	64.70	9.098%	0.647	64.70	392.19	-2.61	-13.11
6	100.00	0.564	56.45	435.53	9.401%	0.583	58.33	9.401%	0.583	58.33	450.52	-1.88	-14.99
7	100.00	0.513	51.32	486.84	9.720%	0.522	52.24	9.720%	0.522	52.24	502.76	-0.92	-15.91
8	100.00	0.467	46.65	533.49	10.059%	0.465	46.45	10.059%	0.465	46.45	549.21	0.20	-15.71
9	1,100.00	0.424	466.51	1,000.00	0.000%	0.000	0.00	10.420%	0.410	450.79	1,000.00	15.71	0.00

Table 11-29. Upward-sloping Treasury Bond Yield Curve: Theoretical Spot Rate Calculation

Years 10
TBond YTM 10.250%

Year	Bond Cash Flow	Disc. Factor	PV Treas.	Cum. PV	Spot Rate Given	From Given Spot Rates Disc. Factor	PV	Calc. Spot Rate	Disc. Factor Spot Rate	PV @ Spot	Cum. PV @ Spot	Difference PV Treas. Less PV Spot	Cum. Difference
1	102.50	0.907	92.97	92.97	8.000%	0.926	94.91	8.000%	0.926	94.91	94.91	-1.94	-1.94
2	102.50	0.823	84.33	177.30	8.260%	0.853	87.46	8.260%	0.853	87.46	182.36	-3.13	-5.07
3	102.50	0.746	76.49	253.78	8.529%	0.782	80.18	8.529%	0.782	80.18	262.55	-3.70	-8.76
4	102.50	0.677	69.38	323.16	8.808%	0.713	73.13	8.808%	0.713	73.13	335.67	-3.75	-12.51
5	102.50	0.614	62.93	386.09	9.098%	0.647	66.32	9.098%	0.647	66.32	401.99	-3.39	-15.91
6	102.50	0.557	57.08	443.16	9.401%	0.583	59.79	9.401%	0.583	59.79	461.78	-2.71	-18.62
7	102.50	0.505	51.77	494.93	9.720%	0.522	53.55	9.720%	0.522	53.55	515.32	-1.78	-20.39
8	102.50	0.458	46.96	541.89	10.059%	0.465	47.61	10.059%	0.465	47.61	562.94	-0.66	-21.05
9	102.50	0.416	42.59	584.48	10.420%	0.410	42.00	10.420%	0.410	42.00	604.94	0.59	-20.46
10	1,102.50	0.377	415.52	1,000.00	0.000%	0.000	0.00	10.808%	0.358	395.06	1,000.00	20.46	0.00

153

Table 11-30. Upward-sloping Treasury Bond Yield Curve: Theoretical Spot Rate Calculation

Years 11
TBond YTM 10.500%

Year	Bond Cash Flow	Disc. Factor	PV Treas.	Cum. PV	Spot Rate Given	From Given Spot Rates Disc. Factor	PV	Calc. Spot Rate	Disc. Factor Spot Rate	PV @ Spot	Cum. PV @ Spot	Difference PV Treas. Less PV Spot	Cum. Difference
1	105.00	0.905	95.02	95.02	8.000%	0.926	97.22	8.000%	0.926	97.22	97.22	-2.20	-2.20
2	105.00	0.819	85.99	181.02	8.260%	0.853	89.59	8.260%	0.853	89.59	186.81	-3.60	-5.79
3	105.00	0.741	77.82	258.84	8.529%	0.782	82.14	8.529%	0.782	82.14	268.95	-4.32	-10.11
4	105.00	0.671	70.43	329.27	8.808%	0.713	74.91	8.808%	0.713	74.91	343.86	-4.48	-14.60
5	105.00	0.607	63.73	393.00	9.098%	0.647	67.94	9.098%	0.647	67.94	411.80	-4.20	-18.80
6	105.00	0.549	57.68	450.68	9.401%	0.583	61.24	9.401%	0.583	61.24	473.04	-3.56	-22.36
7	105.00	0.497	52.20	502.88	9.720%	0.522	54.85	9.720%	0.522	54.85	527.89	-2.65	-25.02
8	105.00	0.450	47.24	550.11	10.059%	0.465	48.77	10.059%	0.465	48.77	576.67	-1.54	-26.55
9	105.00	0.407	42.75	592.86	10.420%	0.410	43.03	10.420%	0.410	43.03	619.70	-0.28	-26.83
10	105.00	0.368	38.69	631.55	10.808%	0.358	37.63	10.808%	0.358	37.63	657.32	1.06	-25.77
11	1,105.00	0.333	368.45	1,000.00	0.000%	0.000	0.00	11.231%	0.310	342.68	1,000.00	25.77	0.00

Table 11-31. Upward-sloping Treasury Bond Yield Curve: Theoretical Spot Rate Calculation

Years 12
T-Bond YTM 10.75%

Year	Bond Cash Flow	Disc. Factor	PV Treas.	Cum. PV	Spot Rate Given	From Given Spot Rates Disc. Factor	PV	Calc. Spot Rate	Disc. Factor Spot Rate	PV @ Spot	Cum. PV @ Spot	Difference PV Treas. Less PV Spot	Cum. Differ- ence
1	107.50	0.903	97.07	97.07	8.000%	0.926	99.54	8.000%	0.926	99.54	99.54	-2.47	-2.47
2	107.50	0.815	87.64	184.71	8.260%	0.853	91.72	8.260%	0.853	91.72	191.26	-4.08	-6.55
3	107.50	0.736	79.14	263.85	8.529%	0.782	84.10	8.529%	0.782	84.10	275.35	-4.96	-11.51
4	107.50	0.665	71.46	335.30	8.808%	0.713	76.69	8.808%	0.713	76.69	352.05	-5.24	-16.75
5	107.50	0.600	64.52	399.82	9.098%	0.647	69.55	9.098%	0.647	69.55	421.60	-5.04	-21.78
6	107.50	0.542	58.26	458.08	9.401%	0.583	62.70	9.401%	0.583	62.70	484.30	-4.45	-26.23
7	107.50	0.489	52.60	510.68	9.720%	0.522	56.16	9.720%	0.522	56.16	540.46	-3.56	-29.78
8	107.50	0.442	47.50	558.18	10.059%	0.465	49.93	10.059%	0.465	49.93	590.40	-2.44	-32.22
9	107.50	0.399	42.89	601.06	10.420%	0.410	44.05	10.420%	0.410	44.05	634.45	-1.17	-33.39
10	107.50	0.360	38.72	639.78	10.808%	0.358	38.52	10.808%	0.358	38.52	672.97	0.20	-33.19
11	107.50	0.325	34.96	674.75	11.231%	0.310	33.34	11.231%	0.310	33.34	706.31	1.63	-31.56
12	1,107.50	0.294	325.25	1,000.00	0.000%	0.000	0.00	11.696%	0.265	293.69	1,000.00	31.56	0.00

155

Table 11-32. Upward-sloping Treasury Bond Yield Curve: Theoretical Spot Rate Calculation

Years 13
TBond YTM 11.000%

Year	Bond Cash Flow	Disc. Factor	PV Treas.	Cum. PV	Spot Rate Given	From Given Spot Rates Disc. Factor	From Given Spot Rates PV	Calc. Spot Rate	Disc. Factor Spot Rate	PV @ Spot	Cum. PV @ Spot	Difference PV Treas. Less PV Spot	Cum. Difference
1	110.00	0.901	99.10	99.10	8.000%	0.926	101.85	8.000%	0.926	101.85	101.85	-2.75	-2.75
2	110.00	0.812	89.28	188.38	8.260%	0.853	93.85	8.260%	0.853	93.85	195.71	-4.58	-7.33
3	110.00	0.731	80.43	268.81	8.529%	0.782	86.05	8.529%	0.782	86.05	281.76	-5.62	-12.95
4	110.00	0.659	72.46	341.27	8.808%	0.713	78.48	8.808%	0.713	78.48	360.24	-6.02	-18.97
5	110.00	0.593	65.28	406.55	9.098%	0.647	71.17	9.098%	0.647	71.17	431.41	-5.89	-24.86
6	110.00	0.535	58.81	465.36	9.401%	0.583	64.16	9.401%	0.583	64.16	495.57	-5.35	-30.21
7	110.00	0.482	52.98	518.34	9.720%	0.522	57.46	9.720%	0.522	57.46	553.03	-4.48	-34.69
8	110.00	0.434	47.73	566.07	10.059%	0.465	51.10	10.059%	0.465	51.10	604.13	-3.35	-38.05
9	110.00	0.391	43.00	609.08	10.420%	0.410	45.08	10.420%	0.410	45.08	649.21	-2.08	-40.13
10	110.00	0.352	38.74	647.82	10.808%	0.358	39.42	10.808%	0.358	39.42	688.62	-0.68	-40.81
11	110.00	0.317	34.90	682.72	11.231%	0.310	34.11	11.231%	0.310	34.11	722.73	0.79	-40.02
12	110.00	0.286	31.44	714.16	11.696%	0.265	29.17	11.696%	0.265	29.17	751.90	2.27	-37.75
13	1,110.00	0.258	285.84	1,000.00	0.000%	0.000	0.00	12.216%	0.224	248.10	1,000.00	37.75	0.00

Table 11-33. Upward-sloping Treasury Bond Yield Curve: Theoretical Spot Rate Calculation

Years 14
TBond YTM 11.250%

Year	Bond Cash Flow	Disc. Factor	PV Treas.	Cum. PV	Spot Rate Given	From Given Spot Rates Disc. Factor	PV	Calc. Spot Rate	Disc. Factor Spot Rate	PV @ Spot	Cum. PV @ Spot	Difference PV Treas. Less PV Spot	Cum. Difference
1	112.50	0.899	101.12	101.12	8.000%	0.926	104.17	8.000%	0.926	104.17	104.17	-3.04	-3.04
2	112.50	0.808	90.90	192.02	8.260%	0.853	95.99	8.260%	0.853	95.99	200.15	-5.09	-8.13
3	112.50	0.726	81.71	273.73	8.529%	0.782	88.01	8.529%	0.782	88.01	288.16	-6.30	-14.43
4	112.50	0.653	73.44	347.17	8.808%	0.713	80.26	8.808%	0.713	80.26	368.42	-6.82	-21.25
5	112.50	0.587	66.02	413.19	9.098%	0.647	72.79	9.098%	0.647	72.79	441.21	-6.77	-28.03
6	112.50	0.527	59.34	472.53	9.401%	0.583	65.62	9.401%	0.583	65.62	506.83	-6.28	-34.30
7	112.50	0.474	53.34	525.87	9.720%	0.522	58.77	9.720%	0.522	58.77	565.60	-5.43	-39.73
8	112.50	0.426	47.95	573.81	10.059%	0.465	52.26	10.059%	0.465	52.26	617.86	-4.31	-44.04
9	112.50	0.383	43.10	616.91	10.420%	0.410	46.10	10.420%	0.410	46.10	663.96	-3.00	-47.05
10	112.50	0.344	38.74	655.65	10.808%	0.358	40.31	10.808%	0.358	40.31	704.27	-1.57	-48.62
11	112.50	0.310	34.82	690.47	11.231%	0.310	34.89	11.231%	0.310	34.89	739.16	-0.07	-48.69
12	112.50	0.278	31.30	721.77	11.696%	0.265	29.83	11.696%	0.265	29.83	762.99	1.47	-47.22
13	112.50	0.250	28.14	749.91	12.216%	0.224	25.14	12.216%	0.224	25.14	794.14	2.99	-44.23
14	1,112.50	0.225	250.09	1,000.00	0.000%	0.000	0.00	12.897%	0.185	205.86	1,000.00	44.23	0.00

157

Table 11-34. Upward-sloping Treasury Bond Yield Curve: Theoretical Spot Rate Calculation

Years: 15
TBond YTM: 11.500%

Year	Bond Cash Flow	Disc. Factor	PV Treas.	Cum. PV	Spot Rate Given	From Given Spot Rates Disc. Factor	PV	Calc. Spot Rate	Disc. Factor Spot Rate	PV @ Spot	Cum. PV @ Spot	Difference PV Treas. Less PV Spot	Cum. Difference
1	115.00	0.897	103.14	103.14	3.000%	0.926	106.48	8.000%	0.926	106.48	106.48	-3.34	-3.34
2	115.00	0.804	92.50	195.64	8.260%	0.853	98.12	8.260%	0.853	98.12	204.60	-5.62	-8.96
3	115.00	0.721	82.96	278.60	8.529%	0.782	89.96	8.529%	0.782	89.96	294.56	-7.00	-15.96
4	115.00	0.647	74.40	353.01	8.808%	0.713	82.05	8.808%	0.713	82.05	376.61	-7.64	-23.60
5	115.00	0.580	66.73	419.74	9.098%	0.647	74.41	9.098%	0.647	74.41	451.02	-7.68	-31.28
6	115.00	0.520	59.85	479.58	9.401%	0.583	67.08	9.401%	0.583	67.08	518.09	-7.23	-38.51
7	115.00	0.467	53.68	533.26	9.720%	0.522	60.08	9.720%	0.522	60.08	578.17	-6.40	-44.91
8	115.00	0.419	48.14	581.40	10.059%	0.465	53.42	10.059%	0.465	53.42	631.59	-5.28	-50.19
9	115.00	0.375	43.17	624.57	10.420%	0.410	47.13	10.420%	0.410	47.13	678.71	-3.95	-54.14
10	115.00	0.337	38.72	663.29	10.808%	0.358	41.21	10.808%	0.358	41.21	719.92	-2.49	-56.63
11	115.00	0.302	34.73	698.02	11.231%	0.310	35.66	11.231%	0.310	35.66	755.59	-0.94	-57.56
12	115.00	0.271	31.15	729.17	11.696%	0.265	30.50	11.696%	0.265	30.50	786.08	0.65	-56.92
13	115.00	0.243	27.93	757.10	12.216%	0.224	25.70	12.216%	0.224	25.70	811.79	2.23	-54.68
14	115.00	0.218	25.05	782.15	12.807%	0.185	21.28	12.807%	0.185	21.28	833.07	3.77	-50.91
15	1,115.00	0.195	217.85	1,000.00	0.000%	0.000	0.00	13.496%	0.150	166.93	1,000.00	50.91	0.00

Table 11-35. Upward-sloping Treasury Bond Yield Curve: Theoretical Spot Rate Calculation

Years 16
TBond YTM 11.750%

Year	Bond Cash Flow	Disc. Factor	PV Treas.	Cum. PV	Spot Rate Given	From Given Spot Rates Disc. Factor	PV	Calc. Spot Rate	Disc. Factor Spot Rate	PV @ Spot	Cum. PV @ Spot	Difference PV Treas. Less PV Spot	Cum. Difference
1	117.50	0.895	105.15	105.15	8.000%	0.926	108.80	8.000%	0.926	108.80	108.80	-3.65	-3.65
2	117.50	0.801	94.09	199.24	8.260%	0.853	100.25	8.260%	0.853	100.25	209.05	-6.16	-9.82
3	117.50	0.717	84.20	283.43	8.529%	0.782	91.92	8.529%	0.782	91.92	300.97	-7.72	-17.54
4	117.50	0.641	75.34	358.78	8.808%	0.713	83.83	8.808%	0.713	83.83	384.80	-8.49	-26.02
5	117.50	0.574	67.42	426.20	9.098%	0.647	76.02	9.098%	0.647	76.02	460.82	-8.60	-34.62
6	117.50	0.513	60.33	486.53	9.401%	0.583	68.53	9.401%	0.583	68.53	529.36	-8.20	-42.83
7	117.50	0.459	53.99	540.52	9.720%	0.522	61.38	9.720%	0.522	61.38	590.74	-7.39	-50.22
8	117.50	0.411	48.31	588.83	10.059%	0.465	54.58	10.059%	0.465	54.58	645.32	-6.27	-56.49
9	117.50	0.368	43.23	632.05	10.420%	0.410	48.15	10.420%	0.410	43.15	693.47	-4.92	-61.41
10	117.50	0.329	38.69	670.75	10.808%	0.358	42.10	10.808%	0.358	42.10	735.57	-3.42	-64.82
11	117.50	0.295	34.62	705.37	11.231%	0.310	36.44	11.231%	0.310	36.44	772.01	-1.82	-66.64
12	117.50	0.264	30.98	736.35	11.696%	0.265	31.16	11.696%	0.265	31.16	803.17	-0.18	-66.82
13	117.50	0.236	27.72	764.67	12.216%	0.224	26.26	12.216%	0.224	26.26	829.43	1.46	-65.36
14	117.50	0.211	24.81	788.88	12.807%	0.185	21.74	12.807%	0.185	21.74	851.18	3.06	-62.30
15	117.50	0.189	22.20	811.08	13.496%	0.150	17.59	13.496%	0.150	17.59	868.77	4.61	-57.69
16	1,117.50	0.169	188.92	1,000.00	0.000%	0.000	0.00	14.324%	0.117	131.23	1,000.00	57.69	0.00

Table 11-36. Upward-sloping Treasury Bond Yield Curve: Theoretical Spot Rate Calculation

Years 17
TBond YTM 12.000%

Year	Bond Cash Flow	Disc. Factor	PV Treas.	Cum. PV	Spot Rate Given	From Given Spot Rates		Calc. Spot Rate	Disc. Factor Spot Rate	PV @ Spot	Cum. PV @ Spot	Difference PV Treas. Less PV Spot	Cum. Difference
						Disc. Factor	PV						
1	120.00	0.893	107.14	107.14	8.000%	0.926	111.11	8.000%	0.926	111.11	111.11	-3.97	-3.97
2	120.00	0.797	95.66	202.81	8.260%	0.853	102.39	8.260%	0.853	102.39	213.50	-6.72	-10.69
3	120.00	0.712	85.41	288.22	8.529%	0.782	93.87	8.529%	0.782	93.87	307.37	-8.46	-19.15
4	120.00	0.636	76.26	364.48	8.808%	0.713	85.61	8.808%	0.713	85.61	392.98	-9.35	-28.50
5	120.00	0.567	68.09	432.57	9.098%	0.647	77.64	9.098%	0.647	77.64	470.63	-9.55	-38.05
6	120.00	0.507	60.80	493.37	9.401%	0.583	69.99	9.401%	0.583	69.99	540.62	-9.20	-47.25
7	120.00	0.452	54.28	547.65	9.720%	0.522	62.69	9.720%	0.522	62.69	603.31	-8.41	-55.66
8	120.00	0.404	48.47	596.12	10.059%	0.465	55.74	10.059%	0.465	55.74	659.05	-7.28	-62.93
9	120.00	0.361	43.27	639.39	10.420%	0.410	49.18	10.420%	0.410	49.18	708.22	-5.90	-68.83
10	120.00	0.322	38.64	678.03	10.808%	0.358	43.00	10.808%	0.358	43.00	751.22	-4.36	-73.20
11	120.00	0.287	34.50	712.52	11.231%	0.310	37.21	11.231%	0.310	37.21	786.44	-2.72	-75.91
12	120.00	0.257	30.86	743.32	11.696%	0.265	31.82	11.696%	0.265	31.82	820.26	-1.02	-76.93
13	120.00	0.229	27.50	770.83	12.216%	0.224	26.82	12.216%	0.224	26.82	847.08	0.68	-76.25
14	120.00	0.205	24.55	795.38	12.807%	0.185	22.21	12.807%	0.185	22.21	869.29	2.35	-73.91
15	120.00	0.183	21.92	817.30	13.496%	0.150	17.97	13.496%	0.150	17.97	887.25	3.96	-69.95
16	120.00	0.163	19.57	836.88	14.324%	0.117	14.09	14.324%	0.117	14.09	901.35	5.48	-64.47
17	1,120.00	0.146	163.12	1,000.00	0.000%	0.000	0.00	15.363%	0.088	98.65	1,000.00	64.47	0.00

Table 11-37. Upward-sloping Treasury Bond Yield Curve: Theoretical Spot Rate Calculation

Years 18
TBond YTM 12.250%

Year	Bond Cash Flow	Disc. Factor	PV Treas.	Cum. PV	Spot Rate Given	From Given Spot Rates Disc. Factor	PV	Calc. Spot Rate	Disc. Factor Spot Rate	PV @ Spot	Cum. PV @ Spot	Difference PV Treas. Less PV Spot	Cum. Difference
1	122.50	0.891	109.13	109.13	8.000%	0.926	113.43	8.000%	0.926	113.43	113.43	-4.29	-4.29
2	122.50	0.794	97.22	206.35	8.260%	0.853	104.52	8.260%	0.853	104.52	217.95	-7.30	-11.59
3	122.50	0.707	86.61	292.96	8.529%	0.782	95.83	8.529%	0.782	95.83	313.78	-9.22	-20.81
4	122.50	0.630	77.16	370.12	8.808%	0.713	87.40	8.808%	0.713	87.40	401.17	-10.24	-31.05
5	122.50	0.561	68.74	438.86	9.098%	0.647	79.26	9.098%	0.647	79.26	480.43	-10.52	-41.57
6	122.50	0.500	61.24	500.10	9.401%	0.583	71.45	9.401%	0.583	71.45	551.88	-10.21	-51.78
7	122.50	0.445	54.55	554.66	9.720%	0.522	63.99	9.720%	0.522	63.99	615.88	-9.44	-61.22
8	122.50	0.397	48.60	603.26	10.059%	0.465	56.90	10.059%	0.465	56.90	672.78	-8.30	-69.52
9	122.50	0.353	43.30	646.55	10.420%	0.410	50.20	10.420%	0.410	50.20	722.98	-6.90	-76.42
10	122.50	0.315	38.57	685.13	10.808%	0.358	43.90	10.808%	0.358	43.90	766.87	-5.32	-81.75
11	122.50	0.281	34.36	719.49	11.231%	0.310	37.99	11.231%	0.310	37.99	804.86	-3.63	-85.37
12	122.50	0.250	30.61	750.10	11.696%	0.265	32.49	11.696%	0.265	32.49	837.35	-1.87	-87.25
13	122.50	0.223	27.27	777.37	12.216%	0.224	27.38	12.216%	0.224	27.38	864.73	-0.11	-87.35
14	122.50	0.198	24.30	801.67	12.807%	0.185	22.67	12.807%	0.185	22.67	887.40	1.63	-85.73
15	122.50	0.177	21.64	823.31	13.496%	0.150	18.34	13.496%	0.150	18.34	905.74	3.30	-82.42
16	122.50	0.157	19.28	842.60	14.324%	0.117	14.39	14.324%	0.117	14.39	920.12	4.90	-77.53
17	122.50	0.140	17.18	859.77	15.363%	0.088	10.79	15.363%	0.088	10.79	930.91	6.39	-71.14
18	1,122.50	0.125	140.23	1,000.00	0.000%	0.000	0.00	16.753%	0.062	69.09	1,000.00	71.14	0.00

Table 11-38. Upward-sloping Treasury Bond Yield Curve: Theoretical Spot Rate Calculation

Years 19
T-bond YTM 12.500%

Year	Bond Cash Flow	Disc. Factor	PV Treas.	Cum. PV	Spot Rate Given	From Given Spot Rates Disc. Factor	From Given Spot Rates PV	Calc. Spot Rate	Disc. Factor Spot Rate	PV @ Spot	Cum. PV @ Spot	Difference PV Treas. Less PV Spot	Cum. Difference
1	125.00	0.889	111.11	111.11	8.000%	0.926	115.74	8.000%	0.926	115.74	115.74	-4.63	-4.63
2	125.00	0.790	98.77	209.88	8.260%	0.853	106.65	8.260%	0.853	106.65	222.39	-7.89	-12.52
3	125.00	0.702	87.79	297.67	8.529%	0.782	97.79	8.529%	0.782	97.79	320.18	-9.99	-22.51
4	125.00	0.624	78.04	375.70	8.808%	0.713	89.18	8.808%	0.713	89.18	409.36	-11.14	-33.65
5	125.00	0.555	69.37	445.07	9.098%	0.647	80.88	9.098%	0.647	80.88	490.24	-11.51	-45.17
6	125.00	0.493	61.66	506.73	9.401%	0.583	72.91	9.401%	0.583	72.91	563.15	-11.25	-56.42
7	125.00	0.438	54.81	561.54	9.720%	0.522	65.30	9.720%	0.522	65.30	628.44	-10.49	-66.91
8	125.00	0.390	48.72	610.26	10.059%	0.465	58.06	10.059%	0.465	58.06	686.51	-9.35	-76.25
9	125.00	0.346	43.30	653.56	10.420%	0.410	51.22	10.420%	0.410	51.22	737.73	-7.92	-84.17
10	125.00	0.308	38.49	692.05	10.808%	0.358	44.79	10.808%	0.358	44.79	782.53	-6.30	-90.47
11	125.00	0.274	34.22	726.27	11.231%	0.310	38.76	11.231%	0.310	38.76	821.29	-4.55	-95.02
12	125.00	0.243	30.41	756.68	11.696%	0.265	33.15	11.696%	0.265	33.15	854.44	-2.73	-97.75
13	125.00	0.216	27.04	783.72	12.216%	0.224	27.94	12.216%	0.224	27.94	882.38	-0.90	-98.66
14	125.00	0.192	24.03	807.75	12.807%	0.185	23.13	12.807%	0.185	23.13	905.51	0.90	-97.76
15	125.00	0.171	21.36	829.11	13.496%	0.150	18.72	13.496%	0.150	18.72	924.22	2.65	-95.11
16	125.00	0.152	18.99	848.10	14.324%	0.117	14.68	14.324%	0.117	14.68	938.90	4.31	-90.80
17	125.00	0.135	16.88	864.98	15.363%	0.088	11.01	15.363%	0.088	11.01	949.91	5.87	-84.93
18	125.00	0.120	15.00	879.98	16.753%	0.062	7.69	16.753%	0.062	7.69	957.60	7.31	-77.62
19	1,125.00	0.107	120.02	1,000.00	0.000%	0.000	0.00	18.833%	0.038	42.40	1,000.00	77.62	0.00
			120.02	1,000.00									

Table 11-39. Upward-sloping Treasury Bond Yield Curve: Theoretical Spot Rate Calculation

Years 20
TBond YTM 12.750%

Year	Bond Cash Flow	Disc. Factor	PV Treas.	Cum. PV	Spot Rate Given	From Given Spot Rates Disc. Factor	PV	Calc. Spot Rate	Disc. Factor Spot Rate	PV @ Spot	Cum. PV @ Spot	Difference PV Treas. Less PV Spot	Cum. Difference
1	127.50	0.887	113.08	113.08	8.000%	0.926	118.06	8.000%	0.926	118.06	118.06	-4.97	-4.97
2	127.50	0.787	100.29	213.38	8.260%	0.853	108.79	8.260%	0.853	108.79	226.84	-8.49	-13.47
3	127.50	0.698	88.95	302.33	8.529%	0.782	99.74	8.529%	0.782	99.74	326.58	-10.79	-24.25
4	127.50	0.619	78.89	381.22	8.808%	0.713	90.96	8.808%	0.713	90.96	417.55	-12.07	-36.32
5	127.50	0.549	69.97	451.20	9.098%	0.647	82.49	9.098%	0.647	82.49	500.04	-12.52	-48.84
6	127.50	0.487	62.06	513.26	9.401%	0.583	74.37	9.401%	0.583	74.37	574.41	-12.31	-61.15
7	127.50	0.432	55.04	568.30	9.720%	0.522	66.61	9.720%	0.522	66.61	641.01	-11.56	-72.72
8	127.50	0.383	48.82	617.12	10.059%	0.465	59.23	10.059%	0.465	59.23	700.24	-10.41	-83.12
9	127.50	0.340	43.30	660.41	10.420%	0.410	52.25	10.420%	0.410	52.25	752.49	-8.95	-92.07
10	127.50	0.301	38.40	698.81	10.808%	0.358	45.69	10.808%	0.358	45.69	798.18	-7.29	-99.36
11	127.50	0.267	34.06	732.87	11.231%	0.310	39.54	11.231%	0.310	39.54	837.71	-5.48	-104.84
12	127.50	0.237	30.21	763.08	11.696%	0.265	33.81	11.696%	0.265	33.81	871.53	-3.60	-108.45
13	127.50	0.210	26.79	789.87	12.216%	0.224	28.50	12.216%	0.224	28.50	900.02	-1.71	-110.15
14	127.50	0.186	23.76	813.63	12.807%	0.185	23.59	12.807%	0.185	23.59	923.62	0.17	-109.98
15	127.50	0.165	21.07	834.71	13.496%	0.150	19.09	13.496%	0.150	19.09	942.71	1.98	-108.00
16	127.50	0.147	18.69	853.40	14.324%	0.117	14.97	14.324%	0.117	14.97	957.68	3.72	-104.28
17	127.50	0.130	16.58	869.98	15.363%	0.088	11.23	15.363%	0.088	11.23	968.91	5.35	-98.93
18	127.50	0.115	14.70	884.68	16.753%	0.062	7.85	16.753%	0.062	7.85	976.76	6.86	-92.08
19	127.50	0.102	13.04	897.72	18.833%	0.038	4.81	18.833%	0.038	4.81	981.56	8.24	-83.84
20	1,127.50	0.091	102.28	1,000.00	0.000%	0.000	0.00	22.834%	0.016	18.44	1,000.00	83.84	0.00

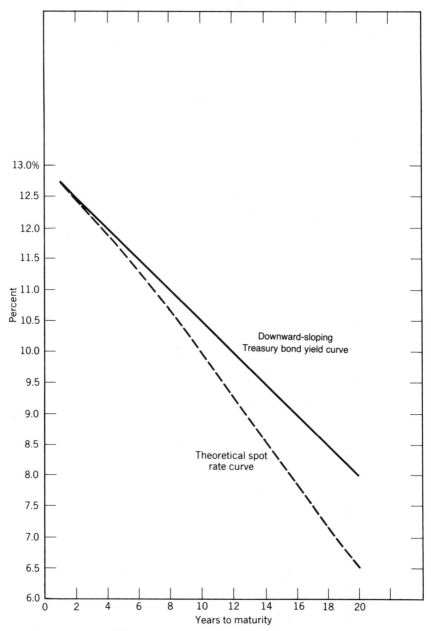

Chart 11-3. Theoretical Spot Rate Curve with Downward-sloping Treasury Bond Yield Curve.

Table 11-40. Downward-sloping Treasury Bond Yield Curve: Theoretical Spot Rate Calculation

Years 2
TBond YTM 12.500%

Year	Bond Cash Flow	Disc. Factor	PV Treas.	Cum. PV	Spot Rate Given	From Given Spot Rates Disc. Factor	PV	Calc. Spot Rate	Disc. Factor Spot Rate	PV @ Spot	Cum. PV @ Spot	Difference PV Treas. Less PV Spot	Cum. Difference
1	125.00	0.889	111.11	111.11	12.750%	0.887	110.86	12.750%	0.887	110.86	110.86	0.25	0.25
2	1,125.00	0.790	888.89	1,000.00	12.484%	0.000	0.00	12.484%	0.790	889.14	1,000.00	−0.25	0.00

Table 11-41. Downward-sloping Treasury Bond Yield Curve: Theoretical Spot Rate Calculation

Years 3
TBond YTM 12.250%

Year	Bond Cash Flow	Disc. Factor	PV Treas.	Cum. PV	Spot Rate Given	From Given Spot Rates Disc. Factor	PV	Calc. Spot Rate	Disc. Factor Spot Rate	PV @ Spot	Cum. PV @ Spot	Difference PV Treas. Less PV Spot	Cum. Difference
1	122.50	0.891	109.13	109.13	12.750%	0.887	108.65	12.750%	0.887	108.65	108.65	0.48	0.48
2	122.50	0.794	97.22	206.35	12.484%	0.790	96.82	12.484%	0.790	96.82	205.47	0.40	0.89
3	1,122.50	0.767	793.65	1,000.00	12.208%	0.000	0.00	12.208%	0.708	794.53	1,000.00	−0.89	0.00

Table 11-42. Downward-sloping Treasury Bond Yield Curve: Theoretical Spot Rate Calculation

Years 4
TBond YTM 12.000%

Year	Bond Cash Flow	Disc. Factor	PV Treas.	Cum. PV	Spot Rate Given	From Given Spot Rates		Calc. Spot Rate	Disc. Factor Spot Rate	PV @ Spot	Cum. PV @ Spot	Difference PV Treas. Less PV Spot	Cum. Difference
						Disc. Factor	PV						
1	120.00	0.893	107.14	107.14	12.750%	0.887	106.43	12.750%	0.887	106.43	106.43	0.71	0.71
2	120.00	0.797	95.66	202.81	12.484%	0.790	94.84	12.484%	0.790	94.84	201.27	0.82	1.53
3	120.00	0.712	85.41	288.22	12.208%	0.708	84.94	12.208%	0.708	84.94	286.21	0.47	2.01
4	1,120.00	0.636	711.78	1,000.00	0.000%	0.000	0.00	11.921%	0.637	713.79	1,000.00	-2.01	0.00

Table 11-43. Downward-sloping Treasury Bond Yield Curve: Theoretical Spot Rate Calculation

Years 5
TBond YTM 11.750%

Year	Bond Cash Flow	Disc. Factor	PV Treas.	Cum. PV	Spot Rate Given	From Given Spot Rates		Calc. Spot Rate	Disc. Factor Spot Rate	PV @ Spot	Cum. PV @ Spot	Difference PV Treas. Less PV Spot	Cum. Difference
						Disc. Factor	PV						
1	117.50	0.895	105.15	105.15	12.750%	0.887	104.21	12.750%	0.887	104.21	104.21	0.93	0.93
2	117.50	0.801	94.09	199.24	12.484%	0.790	92.87	12.484%	0.790	92.87	197.08	1.22	2.16
3	117.50	0.717	84.20	283.43	12.208%	0.708	83.17	12.208%	0.708	83.17	280.25	1.03	3.18
4	117.50	0.641	75.34	358.78	11.921%	0.637	74.88	11.921%	0.637	74.88	355.13	0.46	3.64
5	1,117.50	0.574	641.22	1,000.00	0.000%	0.000	0.00	11.623%	0.577	644.87	1,000.00	-3.64	0.00

Table 11-44. Downward-sloping Treasury Bond Yield Curve: Theoretical Spot Rate Calculation

Years 6
TBond YTM 11.500%

Year	Bond Cash Flow	Disc. Factor	PV Treas.	Cum. PV	Spot Rate Given	From Given Spot Rates Disc. Factor	PV	Calc. Spot Rate	Disc. Factor Spot Rate	PV @ Spot	Cum. PV @ Spot	Difference PV Treas. Less PV Spot	Cum. Difference
1	115.00	0.897	103.14	103.14	12.750%	0.887	102.00	12.750%	0.887	102.00	102.00	1.14	1.14
2	115.00	0.804	92.50	195.64	12.484%	0.790	90.89	12.484%	0.790	90.89	192.89	1.61	2.75
3	115.00	0.721	82.96	278.60	12.208%	0.708	81.40	12.208%	0.708	81.40	274.29	1.56	4.32
4	115.00	0.647	74.40	353.01	11.921%	0.637	73.29	11.921%	0.637	73.29	347.58	1.11	5.43
5	115.00	0.580	66.73	419.74	11.623%	0.577	66.36	11.623%	0.577	66.36	413.94	0.37	5.80
6	1,115.00	0.520	580.26	1,000.00	0.000%	0.000	0.00	11.315%	0.526	586.06	1,000.00	-5.80	0.00

Table 11-45. Downward-sloping Treasury Bond Yield Curve: Theoretical Spot Rate Calculation

Years 7
TBond YTM 11.250%

Year	Bond Cash Flow	Disc. Factor	PV Treas.	Cum. PV	Spot Rate Given	From Given Spot Rates Disc. Factor	PV	Calc. Spot Rate	Disc. Factor Spot Rate	PV @ Spot	Cum. PV @ Spot	Difference PV Treas. Less PV Spot	Cum. Difference
1	112.50	0.899	101.12	101.12	12.750%	0.887	99.78	12.750%	0.887	99.78	99.78	1.35	1.35
2	112.50	0.808	90.90	192.02	12.484%	0.790	88.91	12.484%	0.790	88.91	188.69	1.98	3.33
3	112.50	0.726	81.71	273.73	12.208%	0.708	79.63	12.208%	0.708	79.63	268.32	2.07	5.40
4	112.50	0.653	73.44	347.19	11.921%	0.637	71.70	11.921%	0.637	71.70	340.02	1.75	7.15
5	112.50	0.587	66.02	413.19	11.623%	0.577	64.92	11.623%	0.577	64.92	404.94	1.10	8.24
6	112.50	0.527	59.34	472.53	11.315%	0.526	59.13	11.315%	0.526	59.13	464.07	0.21	8.45
7	1,112.50	0.474	527.47	1,000.00	0.000%	0.000	0.00	10.998%	0.482	535.93	1,000.00	-8.45	0.00

167

Table 11-46. Downward-sloping Treasury Bond Yield Curve: Theoretical Spot Rate Calculation

Years 8
TBond YTM 11.000%

Year	Bond Cash Flow	Disc. Factor	PV Treas.	Cum. PV	Spot Rate Given	From Given Spot Rates Disc. Factor	From Given Spot Rates PV	Calc. Spot Rate	Disc. Factor Spot Rate	PV @ Spot	Cum. PV @ Spot	Difference PV Treas. Less PV Spot	Cum. Difference
1	110.00	0.901	99.10	99.10	12.750%	0.887	97.56	12.750%	0.887	97.56	97.56	1.54	1.54
2	110.00	0.812	89.28	188.38	12.484%	0.790	86.94	12.484%	0.790	86.94	184.50	2.34	3.88
3	110.00	0.731	80.43	268.81	12.208%	0.708	77.86	12.208%	0.708	77.86	262.36	2.57	6.45
4	110.00	0.659	72.46	341.27	11.921%	0.637	70.10	11.921%	0.637	70.10	332.47	2.36	8.80
5	110.00	0.593	65.28	406.55	11.623%	0.577	63.48	11.623%	0.577	63.48	395.94	1.80	10.61
6	110.00	0.535	58.81	465.36	11.315%	0.526	57.82	11.315%	0.526	57.82	453.76	0.99	11.60
7	110.00	0.482	52.98	518.34	10.998%	0.482	52.99	10.998%	0.482	52.99	506.75	-0.01	11.59
8	1,110.00	0.434	481.66	1,000.00	0.000%	0.000	0.00	10.671%	0.444	493.25	1,000.00	-11.59	0.00

Table 11-47. Downward-sloping Treasury Bond Yield Curve: Theoretical Spot Rate Calculation

Years 9
TBond YTM 10.750%

Year	Bond Cash Flow	Disc. Factor	PV Treas.	Cum. PV	Spot Rate Given	From Given Spot Rates Disc. Factor	From Given Spot Rates PV	Calc. Spot Rate	Disc. Factor Spot Rate	PV @ Spot	Cum. PV @ Spot	Difference PV Treas. Less PV Spot	Cum. Difference
1	107.50	0.903	97.07	97.07	12.750%	0.887	95.34	12.750%	0.887	95.34	95.34	1.72	1.72
2	107.50	0.815	87.64	184.71	12.484%	0.790	84.96	12.484%	0.790	84.96	180.31	2.68	4.40
3	107.50	0.736	79.14	263.85	12.208%	0.708	76.09	12.208%	0.708	76.09	256.40	3.04	7.45
4	107.50	0.665	71.46	335.30	11.921%	0.637	68.51	11.921%	0.637	68.51	324.91	2.94	10.39
5	107.50	0.600	64.52	399.82	11.623%	0.577	62.04	11.623%	0.577	62.04	386.94	2.48	12.88
6	107.50	0.542	58.26	458.08	11.315%	0.526	56.50	11.315%	0.526	56.50	443.45	1.75	14.63
7	107.50	0.489	52.60	510.68	10.998%	0.482	51.78	10.998%	0.482	51.78	495.23	0.82	15.44
8	107.50	0.442	47.50	558.18	10.671%	0.444	47.77	10.671%	0.444	47.77	543.00	-0.27	15.17
9	1,107.50	0.399	441.82	1,000.00	0.000%	0.000	0.00	10.335%	0.413	457.00	1,000.00	-15.17	0.00

Table 11-48. Downward-sloping Treasury Bond Yield Curve: Theoretical Spot Rate Calculation

Years 10
TBond YTM 10.500%

Year	Bond Cash Flow	Disc. Factor	PV Treas.	Cum. PV	Spot Rate Given	From Given Spot Rates Disc. Factor	PV	Calc. Spot Rate	Disc. Factor Spot Rate	PV @ Spot	Cum. PV @ Spot	Difference PV Treas. Less PV Spot	Cum. Difference
1	105.00	0.905	95.02	95.02	12.750%	0.887	93.13	12.750%	0.887	93.13	93.13	1.90	1.90
2	105.00	0.819	85.99	181.02	12.484%	0.790	82.99	12.484%	0.790	82.99	176.11	3.01	4.90
3	105.00	0.741	77.82	258.84	12.208%	0.708	74.32	12.208%	0.708	74.32	250.44	3.50	8.40
4	105.00	0.671	70.43	329.27	11.921%	0.637	66.92	11.921%	0.637	66.92	317.35	3.51	11.91
5	105.00	0.607	63.73	393.00	11.623%	0.577	60.59	11.623%	0.577	60.59	377.95	3.14	15.05
6	105.00	0.549	57.68	450.68	11.315%	0.526	55.19	11.315%	0.526	55.19	433.14	2.49	17.54
7	105.00	0.497	52.20	502.88	10.998%	0.482	50.58	10.998%	0.482	50.58	483.72	1.62	19.16
8	105.00	0.450	47.24	550.11	10.671%	0.444	46.66	10.671%	0.444	46.66	530.37	0.58	19.74
9	105.00	0.407	42.75	592.86	10.335%	0.413	43.33	10.335%	0.413	43.33	573.70	-0.58	19.16
10	1,105.00	0.368	407.14	1,000.00	0.000%	0.000	0.00	9.993%	0.386	426.30	1,000.00	-19.16	0.00

Table 11-49. Downward-sloping Treasury Bond Yield Curve: Theoretical Spot Rate Calculation

Years 11
TBond YTM 10.250%

Year	Bond Cash Flow	Disc. Factor	PV Treas.	Cum. PV	Spot Rate Given	From Given Spot Rates Disc. Factor	PV	Calc. Spot Rate	Disc. Factor Spot Rate	PV @ Spot	Cum. PV @ Spot	Difference PV Treas. Less PV Spot	Cum. Differ-ence
1	102.50	0.967	92.97	92.97	12.750%	0.887	90.91	12.750%	0.887	90.91	90.91	2.06	2.06
2	102.50	0.823	84.33	177.30	12.484%	0.790	81.01	12.484%	0.790	81.01	171.92	3.32	5.38
3	102.50	0.746	76.49	253.78	12.208%	0.708	72.55	12.208%	0.708	72.55	244.47	3.93	9.31
4	102.50	0.677	69.38	323.16	11.921%	0.637	65.32	11.921%	0.637	65.32	309.80	4.05	13.36
5	102.50	0.614	62.93	386.09	11.623%	0.577	59.15	11.623%	0.577	59.15	368.95	3.78	17.14
6	102.50	0.557	57.08	443.16	11.315%	0.526	53.88	11.315%	0.526	53.88	422.82	3.20	20.34
7	102.50	0.505	51.77	494.93	10.998%	0.482	49.38	10.998%	0.482	49.38	472.20	2.39	22.73
8	102.50	0.458	46.96	541.89	10.671%	0.444	45.55	10.671%	0.444	45.55	517.75	1.41	24.14
9	102.50	0.416	42.59	584.48	10.335%	0.413	42.30	10.335%	0.413	42.30	560.04	0.29	24.44
10	102.50	0.377	38.63	623.11	9.993%	0.386	39.54	9.993%	0.386	39.54	599.59	-0.91	23.52
11	1,102.50	0.342	376.89	1,000.00	0.000%	0.000	0.00	9.645%	0.363	400.41	1,000.00	-23.52	0.00

Table 11-50. Downward-sloping Treasury Bond Yield Curve: Theoretical Spot Rate Calculation

Years 12
TBond YTM 10.000%

Year	Bond Cash Flow	Disc. Factor	PV Treas.	Cum. PV	Spot Rate Given	From Given Spot Rates Disc. Factor	PV	Calc. Spot Rate	Disc. Factor Spot Rate	PV @ Spot	Cum. PV @ Spot	Difference PV Treas. Less PV Spot	Cum. Difference
1	100.00	0.909	90.91	90.91	12.750%	0.887	88.69	12.750%	0.887	88.69	88.69	2.22	2.22
2	100.00	0.826	82.64	173.55	12.484%	0.790	79.03	12.484%	0.790	79.03	167.73	3.61	5.83
3	100.00	0.751	75.13	248.69	12.208%	0.708	70.78	12.208%	0.708	70.78	238.51	4.35	10.18
4	100.00	0.683	68.30	316.99	11.921%	0.637	63.73	11.921%	0.637	63.73	302.24	4.57	14.75
5	100.00	0.621	62.09	379.08	11.623%	0.577	57.71	11.623%	0.577	57.71	359.95	4.38	19.13
6	100.00	0.564	56.45	435.53	11.315%	0.526	52.56	11.315%	0.526	52.56	412.51	3.88	23.01
7	100.00	0.513	51.32	486.84	10.996%	0.482	48.17	10.998%	0.482	48.17	460.68	3.14	26.16
8	100.00	0.467	46.65	533.49	10.671%	0.444	44.44	10.671%	0.444	44.44	505.12	2.22	28.37
9	100.00	0.424	42.41	575.90	10.335%	0.413	41.26	10.335%	0.413	41.26	546.38	1.14	29.52
10	100.00	0.386	38.55	614.46	9.993%	0.386	38.58	9.993%	0.386	38.58	584.96	-0.02	29.49
11	100.00	0.350	35.05	649.51	9.645%	0.363	36.32	9.645%	0.363	36.32	621.28	-1.27	28.23
12	1,100.00	0.319	350.49	1,000.00	0.000%	0.000	0.00	9.292%	0.344	378.72	1,000.00	-28.23	0.00

Table 11-51. Downward-sloping Treasury Bond Yield Curve: Theoretical Spot Rate Calculation

Years 13
TBond YTM 9.75%

Year	Bond Cash Flow	Disc. Factor	PV Treas.	Cum. PV	Spot Rate Given	From Given Spot Rates Disc. Factor	From Given Spot Rates PV	Calc. Spot Rate	Disc. Factor-Spot Rate	PV @ Spot	Cum. PV @ Spot	Difference PV Treas. Less PV Spot	Cum. Difference
1	97.50	0.911	88.84	88.84	12.750%	0.887	86.47	12.750%	0.887	86.47	86.47	2.36	2.36
2	97.50	0.830	80.95	169.78	12.484%	0.790	77.06	12.484%	0.790	77.06	163.53	3.89	6.25
3	97.50	0.756	73.75	243.54	12.208%	0.708	69.01	12.208%	0.708	69.01	232.55	4.74	10.99
4	97.50	0.689	67.20	310.74	11.921%	0.637	62.14	11.921%	0.637	62.14	294.68	5.06	16.06
5	97.50	0.628	61.23	371.97	11.623%	0.577	56.26	11.623%	0.577	56.26	350.95	4.97	21.02
6	97.50	0.572	55.79	427.77	11.315%	0.526	51.25	11.315%	0.526	51.25	402.20	4.54	25.57
7	97.50	0.521	50.84	478.60	10.996%	0.482	46.97	10.998%	0.482	46.97	449.17	3.87	29.44
8	97.50	0.475	46.32	524.92	10.671%	0.444	43.32	10.671%	0.444	43.32	492.49	3.00	32.43
9	97.50	0.433	42.20	567.13	10.335%	0.413	40.23	10.335%	0.413	40.23	532.72	1.97	34.40
10	97.50	0.394	38.46	605.58	9.993%	0.386	37.61	9.993%	0.386	37.61	570.34	0.84	35.25
11	97.50	0.359	35.04	640.62	9.645%	0.363	35.41	9.645%	0.363	35.41	605.75	-0.37	34.87
12	97.50	0.327	31.93	672.55	9.292%	0.344	33.57	9.292%	0.344	33.57	639.32	-1.64	33.23
13	1,097.50	0.298	327.45	1,000.00	0.000%	0.000	0.00	8.937%	0.329	360.68	1,000.00	-33.23	0.00

Table 11-52. Downward-sloping Treasury Bond Yield Curve: Theoretical Spot Rate Calculation

Years 14
TBond YTM 9.500%

Year	Bond Cash Flow	Disc. Factor	PV Treas.	Cum. PV	Spot Rate Given	From Given Spot Rates Disc. Factor	PV	Calc. Spot Rate	Disc. Factor Spot Rate	PV @ Spot	Cum. PV @ Spot	Difference PV Treas. Less PV Spot	Cum. Difference
1	95.00	0.913	86.76	86.76	12.750%	0.887	84.26	12.750%	0.887	84.26	84.26	2.50	2.50
2	95.00	0.834	79.23	165.99	12.484%	0.790	75.08	12.484%	0.790	75.08	159.34	4.15	6.65
3	95.00	0.762	72.36	238.35	12.208%	0.708	67.24	12.208%	0.708	67.24	226.58	5.11	11.76
4	95.00	0.696	66.08	304.43	11.921%	0.637	60.54	11.921%	0.637	60.54	287.13	5.53	17.30
5	95.00	0.635	60.35	364.77	11.623%	0.577	54.82	11.623%	0.577	54.82	341.95	5.52	22.82
6	95.00	0.580	55.11	419.88	11.315%	0.526	49.93	11.315%	0.526	49.93	391.89	5.18	28.00
7	95.00	0.530	50.33	470.21	10.998%	0.482	45.76	10.998%	0.482	45.76	437.65	4.57	32.56
8	95.00	0.484	45.96	516.18	10.671%	0.444	42.21	10.671%	0.444	42.21	479.86	3.75	36.31
9	95.00	0.442	41.98	558.15	10.335%	0.413	39.20	10.335%	0.413	39.20	519.06	2.77	39.09
10	95.00	0.404	38.33	596.49	9.993%	0.386	36.65	9.993%	0.386	36.65	555.71	1.68	40.77
11	95.00	0.369	35.01	631.49	9.645%	0.363	34.50	9.645%	0.363	34.50	590.22	0.51	41.28
12	95.00	0.337	31.97	663.46	9.292%	0.344	32.71	9.292%	0.344	32.71	622.92	-0.74	40.54
13	95.00	0.307	29.20	692.66	8.937%	0.329	31.22	8.937%	0.329	31.22	654.15	-2.02	38.52
14	1,095.00	0.281	307.34	1,000.00	0.000%	0.000	0.00	8.580%	0.316	345.85	1,000.00	-38.52	0.00

Table 11-53. Downward-sloping Treasury Bond Yield Curve: Theoretical Spot Rate Calculation

Years 15
TBond YTM 9.250%

Year	Bond Cash Flow	Disc. Factor	PV Treas.	Cum. PV	Spot Rate Given	From Given Spot Rates Disc. Factor	PV	Calc. Spot Rate	Disc. Factor Spot Rate	PV @ Spot	Cum. PV @ Spot	Difference PV Treas. Less PV Spot	Cum. Difference
1	92.50	0.915	84.67	84.67	12.750%	0.887	82.04	12.750%	0.887	82.04	82.04	2.63	2.63
2	92.50	0.838	77.50	162.17	12.484%	0.790	73.11	12.484%	0.790	73.11	155.15	4.39	7.02
3	92.50	0.767	70.94	233.11	12.208%	0.708	65.47	12.208%	0.708	65.47	220.62	5.46	12.48
4	92.50	0.702	64.93	298.04	11.921%	0.637	58.95	11.921%	0.637	58.95	279.57	5.98	18.46
5	92.50	0.643	59.43	357.47	11.623%	0.577	53.38	11.623%	0.577	53.38	332.95	6.05	24.52
6	92.50	0.588	54.40	411.87	11.315%	0.526	48.62	11.315%	0.526	48.62	381.57	5.78	30.30
7	92.50	0.538	49.80	461.67	10.998%	0.482	44.56	10.998%	0.482	44.56	426.13	5.24	35.54
8	92.50	0.493	45.58	507.25	10.671%	0.444	41.10	10.671%	0.444	41.10	467.23	4.48	40.01
9	92.50	0.451	41.72	548.97	10.335%	0.413	38.17	10.335%	0.413	38.17	505.40	3.55	43.56
10	92.50	0.413	38.19	587.16	9.993%	0.386	35.69	9.993%	0.386	35.69	541.09	2.50	46.07
11	92.50	0.378	34.95	622.11	9.645%	0.363	33.59	9.645%	0.363	33.59	574.68	1.36	47.43
12	92.50	0.346	32.00	654.11	9.292%	0.344	31.85	9.292%	0.344	31.85	606.53	0.15	47.57
13	92.50	0.317	29.29	683.39	8.937%	0.329	30.40	8.937%	0.329	30.40	636.93	-1.11	46.46
14	92.50	0.290	26.81	710.20	8.580%	0.316	29.22	8.580%	0.316	29.22	666.15	-2.41	44.05
15	1,092.50	0.265	289.80	1,000.00	0.000%	0.000	0.00	8.224%	0.306	333.85	1,000.00	-44.05	0.00

Table 11-54. Downward-sloping Treasury Bond Yield Curve: Theoretical Spot Rate Calculation

Years 16
TBond YTM 9.000%

Year	Bond Cash Flow	Disc. Factor	PV Treas.	Cum. PV	Spot Rate Given	From Given Spot Rates Disc. Factor	PV	Calc. Spot Rate	Disc. Factor-Spot Rate	PV @ Spot	Cum. PV @ Spot	Differ-ence PV Treas. Less PV Spot	Cum. Differ-ence
1	90.00	0.917	82.57	82.57	12.750%	0.887	79.82	12.750%	0.887	79.82	79.82	2.75	2.75
2	90.00	0.842	75.75	158.32	12.484%	0.790	71.13	12.484%	0.790	71.13	150.95	4.62	7.37
3	90.00	0.772	69.50	227.82	12.208%	0.708	63.70	12.208%	0.708	63.70	214.66	5.79	13.16
4	90.00	0.708	63.76	291.57	11.921%	0.637	57.36	11.921%	0.637	57.36	272.02	6.40	19.56
5	90.00	0.650	58.49	350.07	11.623%	0.577	51.94	11.623%	0.577	51.94	323.95	6.56	26.12
6	90.00	0.596	53.66	403.73	11.315%	0.526	47.31	11.315%	0.526	47.31	371.26	6.36	32.47
7	90.00	0.547	49.23	452.97	10.998%	0.482	43.35	10.998%	0.482	43.35	414.61	5.88	38.35
8	90.00	0.502	45.17	498.13	10.671%	0.444	39.99	10.671%	0.444	39.99	454.61	5.18	43.53
9	90.00	0.460	41.44	539.57	10.335%	0.413	37.14	10.335%	0.413	37.14	491.74	4.30	47.83
10	90.00	0.422	38.02	577.59	9.993%	0.386	34.72	9.993%	0.386	34.72	526.47	3.30	51.12
11	90.00	0.388	34.88	612.47	9.645%	0.363	32.69	9.645%	0.363	32.69	559.15	2.19	53.31
12	90.00	0.356	32.00	644.47	9.292%	0.344	30.99	9.292%	0.344	30.99	590.14	1.01	54.33
13	90.00	0.326	29.36	673.82	8.937%	0.329	29.58	8.937%	0.329	29.58	619.72	-0.22	54.10
14	90.00	0.299	26.93	700.75	8.580%	0.316	28.43	8.580%	0.316	28.43	648.14	-1.50	52.61
15	90.00	0.275	24.71	725.46	8.224%	0.306	27.50	8.224%	0.306	27.50	675.65	-2.80	49.81
16	1,090.00	0.252	274.54	1,000.00	0.000%	0.000	0.00	7.870%	0.298	324.35	1,000.00	-49.81	0.00

175

Table 11-55. Downward-sloping Treasury Bond Yield Curve: Theoretical Spot Rate Calculation

Years 17
TBond YTM 8.750%

Year	Bond Cash Flow	Disc. Factor	PV Treas.	Cum. PV	Spot Rate Given	From Given Spot Rates Disc. Factor	From Given Spot Rates PV	Calc. Spot Rate	Disc. Factor Spot Rate	PV @ Spot	Cum. PV @ Spot	Difference PV Treas. Less PV Spot	Cum. Difference
1	87.50	0.920	80.46	80.46	12.750%	0.887	77.61	12.750%	0.887	77.61	77.61	2.85	2.85
2	87.50	0.846	73.99	154.45	12.484%	0.790	69.16	12.484%	0.796	69.16	146.76	4.83	7.68
3	87.50	0.778	68.03	222.48	12.208%	0.708	61.94	12.208%	0.708	61.94	208.70	6.10	13.78
4	87.50	0.715	62.56	285.04	11.921%	0.637	55.77	11.921%	0.637	55.77	264.46	6.79	20.58
5	87.50	0.657	57.53	342.56	11.623%	0.577	50.49	11.623%	0.577	50.49	314.95	7.03	27.61
6	87.50	0.605	52.90	395.46	11.315%	0.526	45.99	11.315%	0.526	45.99	360.95	6.90	34.51
7	87.50	0.556	48.64	444.10	10.998%	0.482	42.15	10.998%	0.482	42.15	403.10	6.49	41.00
8	87.50	0.511	44.73	488.83	10.671%	0.444	38.88	10.671%	0.444	38.88	441.98	5.85	46.85
9	87.50	0.470	41.13	529.96	10.335%	0.413	36.11	10.335%	0.413	36.11	478.09	5.02	51.87
10	87.50	0.432	37.82	567.78	9.993%	0.386	33.76	9.993%	0.386	33.76	511.84	4.06	55.94
11	87.50	0.397	34.78	602.55	9.645%	0.363	31.78	9.645%	0.363	31.78	543.62	3.00	58.93
12	87.50	0.365	31.98	634.53	9.292%	0.344	30.13	9.292%	0.344	30.13	573.75	1.85	60.79
13	87.50	0.336	29.41	663.94	8.937%	0.329	28.76	8.937%	0.329	28.76	602.50	0.65	61.44
14	87.50	0.309	27.04	690.98	8.580%	0.316	27.64	8.580%	0.316	27.64	630.14	-0.60	60.84
15	87.50	0.284	24.86	715.84	8.224%	0.306	26.74	8.224%	0.306	26.74	656.88	-1.88	58.96
16	87.50	0.261	22.86	738.70	7.870%	0.298	26.04	7.870%	0.298	26.04	682.92	-3.17	55.79
17	1,087.50	0.240	261.30	1,000.00	0.000%	0.000	0.00	7.519%	0.292	317.08	1,000.00	-55.79	0.00

Table 11-56. Downward-sloping Treasury Bond Yield Curve: Theoretical Spot Rate Calculation

Years 18
TBond YTM 8.500%

Year	Bond Cash Flow	Disc. Factor	PV Treas.	Cum. PV	Spot Rate Given	From Given Spot Rates Disc. Factor	PV	Calc. Spot Rate	Disc. Factor-Spot Rate	PV @ Spot	Cum. PV @ Spot	Difference PV Treas. Less PV Spot	Cum. Difference
1	85.00	0.922	78.34	78.34	12.750%	0.887	75.39	12.750%	0.887	75.39	75.39	2.95	2.95
2	85.00	0.849	72.20	150.54	12.484%	0.790	67.18	12.484%	0.790	67.18	142.57	5.02	7.98
3	85.00	0.783	66.55	217.09	12.208%	0.708	60.17	12.208%	0.708	60.17	202.73	6.38	14.36
4	85.00	0.722	61.33	278.43	11.921%	0.637	54.17	11.921%	0.637	54.17	256.90	7.16	21.52
5	85.00	0.665	56.53	334.95	11.623%	0.577	49.05	11.623%	0.577	49.05	305.96	7.48	29.00
6	85.00	0.613	52.10	387.05	11.315%	0.526	44.68	11.315%	0.526	44.68	350.63	7.42	36.42
7	85.00	0.565	48.02	435.07	10.998%	0.482	40.95	10.998%	0.482	40.95	391.58	7.07	43.49
8	85.00	0.521	44.26	479.33	10.671%	0.444	37.77	10.671%	0.444	37.77	429.35	6.49	49.98
9	85.00	0.480	40.79	520.12	10.335%	0.413	35.08	10.335%	0.413	35.08	464.43	5.71	55.69
10	85.00	0.442	37.59	557.71	9.993%	0.386	32.79	9.993%	0.386	32.79	497.22	4.80	60.50
11	85.00	0.408	34.65	592.36	9.645%	0.363	30.87	9.645%	0.363	30.87	528.09	3.78	64.28
12	85.00	0.376	31.93	624.30	9.292%	0.344	29.27	9.292%	0.344	29.27	557.35	2.67	66.94
13	85.00	0.346	29.43	653.73	8.937%	0.329	27.93	8.937%	0.329	27.93	585.29	1.50	68.44
14	85.00	0.319	27.13	680.86	8.580%	0.316	26.85	8.580%	0.316	26.85	612.14	0.28	68.72
15	85.00	0.294	25.00	705.86	8.224%	0.306	25.98	8.224%	0.306	25.98	638.11	-0.97	67.75
16	85.00	0.271	23.04	728.90	7.870%	0.298	25.29	7.870%	0.298	25.29	663.41	-2.25	65.50
17	85.00	0.250	21.24	750.14	7.519%	0.292	24.78	7.519%	0.292	24.78	688.19	-3.55	61.95
18	1,085.00	0.230	249.86	1,000.00	0.000%	0.000	0.00	7.173%	0.287	311.81	1,000.00	-61.95	0.00

177

Table 11-57. Downward-sloping Treasury Bond Yield Curve: Theoretical Spot Rate Calculation

Years 19
TBond YTM 8.250%

Year	Bond Cash Flow	Disc. Factor	PV Treas.	Cum. PV	Spot Rate Given	From Given Spot Rates Disc. Factor	From Given Spot Rates PV	Calc. Spot Rate	Disc. Factor Spot Rate	PV @ Spot	Cum. PV @ Spot	Difference PV Treas. Less PV Spot	Cum. Difference
1	82.50	0.924	76.21	76.21	12.750%	0.887	73.17	12.750%	0.887	73.17	73.17	3.04	3.04
2	82.50	0.853	70.40	146.62	12.484%	0.796	65.20	12.484%	0.796	65.20	138.37	5.20	8.24
3	82.50	0.788	65.04	211.66	12.208%	0.708	58.40	12.208%	0.708	58.40	196.77	6.64	14.88
4	82.50	0.728	60.08	271.74	11.921%	0.637	52.58	11.921%	0.637	52.58	249.35	7.50	22.39
5	82.50	0.673	55.50	327.24	11.623%	0.577	47.61	11.623%	0.577	47.61	296.96	7.89	30.28
6	82.50	0.621	51.27	378.51	11.315%	0.526	43.36	11.315%	0.526	43.36	340.32	7.91	38.19
7	82.50	0.574	47.37	425.88	10.998%	0.482	39.74	10.998%	0.482	39.74	380.06	7.62	45.81
8	82.50	0.530	43.76	469.63	10.671%	0.444	36.66	10.671%	0.444	36.66	416.72	7.10	52.91
9	82.50	0.490	40.42	510.05	10.335%	0.413	34.04	10.335%	0.413	34.04	450.77	6.38	59.29
10	82.50	0.453	37.34	547.39	9.993%	0.386	31.83	9.993%	0.386	31.83	482.59	5.51	64.80
11	82.50	0.418	34.49	581.89	9.645%	0.363	29.96	9.645%	0.363	29.96	512.56	4.53	69.33
12	82.50	0.386	31.87	613.75	9.292%	0.344	28.40	9.292%	0.344	28.40	540.96	3.46	72.79
13	82.50	0.357	29.44	643.19	8.937%	0.329	27.11	8.937%	0.329	27.11	568.07	2.32	75.12
14	82.50	0.330	27.19	670.38	8.580%	0.316	26.06	8.580%	0.316	26.06	594.13	1.13	76.25
15	82.50	0.304	25.12	695.50	8.224%	0.306	25.21	8.224%	0.306	25.21	619.34	-0.09	76.16
16	82.50	0.281	23.21	718.71	7.870%	0.298	24.55	7.870%	0.298	24.55	643.89	-1.34	74.82
17	82.50	0.260	21.44	740.15	7.519%	0.292	24.05	7.519%	0.292	24.05	667.95	-2.62	72.20
18	82.50	0.240	19.80	759.95	7.173%	0.287	23.71	7.173%	0.287	23.71	691.66	-3.91	68.29
19	1,082.50	0.222	240.05	1,000.00	0.000%	0.000	0.00	6.833%	0.285	308.34	1,000.00	-68.29	0.00

Table 11-58. Downward-sloping Treasury Bond Yield Curve: Theoretical Spot Rate Calculation

Years 20
TBond YTM 8.000%

Year	Bond Cash Flow	Disc. Factor	PV Treas.	Cum. PV	Spot Rate Given	From Given Spot Rates Disc. Factor	PV	Calc. Spot Rate	D-sc. Factor-Spot Rate	PV @ Spot	Cum. PV @ Spot	Difference PV Treas. Less PV Spot	Cum. Difference
1	80.00	0.926	74.07	74.07	12.750%	0.887	70.95	12.750%	0.887	70.95	70.95	3.12	3.12
2	80.00	0.857	68.59	142.66	12.484%	0.790	63.23	12.484%	0.790	63.23	134.18	5.36	8.48
3	80.00	0.794	63.51	206.17	12.208%	0.708	56.63	12.208%	0.708	56.63	190.81	6.88	15.36
4	80.00	0.735	58.80	264.97	11.921%	0.637	50.99	11.921%	0.637	50.99	241.79	7.82	23.18
5	80.00	0.681	54.45	319.42	11.623%	0.577	46.17	11.623%	0.577	46.17	287.96	8.28	31.46
6	80.00	0.630	50.41	369.83	11.315%	0.526	42.05	11.315%	0.526	42.05	330.01	8.36	39.82
7	80.00	0.583	46.68	416.51	10.998%	0.482	38.54	10.998%	0.482	38.54	368.55	8.14	47.96
8	80.00	0.540	43.22	459.73	10.671%	0.444	35.55	10.671%	0.444	35.55	404.09	7.67	55.64
9	80.00	0.500	40.02	499.75	10.335%	0.413	33.01	10.335%	0.413	33.01	437.11	7.01	62.64
10	80.00	0.463	37.06	536.81	9.993%	0.386	30.86	9.993%	0.386	30.86	467.97	6.19	68.84
11	80.00	0.429	34.31	571.12	9.645%	0.363	29.05	9.645%	0.363	29.05	497.02	5.26	74.09
12	80.00	0.397	31.77	602.89	9.292%	0.344	27.54	9.292%	0.344	27.54	524.57	4.22	78.32
13	80.00	0.368	29.42	632.30	8.937%	0.329	26.29	8.937%	0.329	26.29	550.86	3.12	81.44
14	80.00	0.340	27.24	659.54	8.580%	0.316	25.27	8.580%	0.316	25.27	576.13	1.97	83.41
15	80.00	0.315	25.22	684.76	8.224%	0.306	24.45	8.224%	0.306	24.45	600.58	0.77	84.18
16	80.00	0.292	23.35	708.11	7.870%	0.298	23.81	7.870%	0.298	23.81	624.38	-0.45	83.73
17	80.00	0.270	21.62	729.73	7.519%	0.292	23.33	7.519%	0.292	23.33	647.71	-1.70	82.02
18	80.00	0.250	20.02	749.75	7.173%	0.287	22.99	7.173%	0.287	22.99	670.70	-2.97	79.05
19	80.00	0.232	18.54	768.29	6.833%	0.285	22.79	6.833%	0.285	22.79	693.49	-4.25	74.80
20	1,080.00	0.215	231.71	1,000.00	0.000%	0.000	0.00	6.500%	0.284	306.51	1,000.00	-74.80	0.00

179

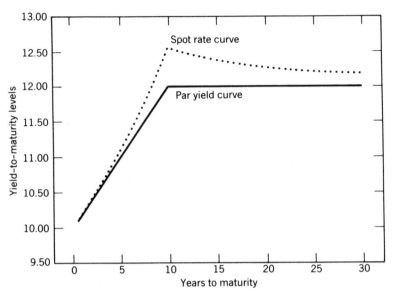

Chart 11-4. "Positive" Yield Curve and Theoretical Spot Rate Curve (in Percent) (*Source:* Thomas E. Klaffky, *Coupon Stripping: The Theoretical Spot Rate Curve,* Salomon Brothers, Inc., October 1982).

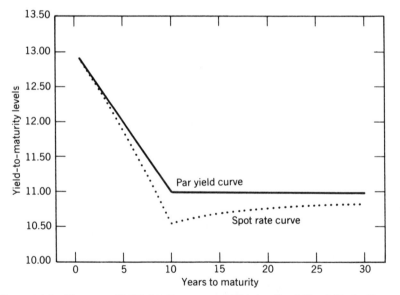

Chart 11-5. "Inverted" Yield Curve and Theoretical Spot Rate Curve (in Percent) (*Source:* Thomas E. Klaffky, *Coupon Stripping: The Theoretical Spot Rate Curve,* Salomon Brothers, Inc., October 1982).

SPOT RATE RELATION TO TREASURY BOND YIELD CURVE

If you intend to invest in zero coupon bonds at any time, an *understanding is paramount* of the relationship between the spot rate yields (which you should expect to receive) and the corresponding Treasury bond yield curve.

With an *upward*-sloping yield curve, the more distant the maturity of the zero coupon bond, the higher (as compared to Treasury bonds of the same maturity) the zero coupon bond's yield should be.

With a *downward*-sloping yield curve, the more distant the maturity of the zero coupon bond, the less its yield should be as compared to Treasury bonds of the same maturity. Charts 11-4 and 11-5 show the relationship that spot rates have to Treasury yields for "positive" yield curves and for "inverted" curves.

12

How to Pay
a Fair Price
for a Zero

And Avoid
Being Gouged!

To accurately determine the yield at which a zero coupon security should be priced requires the type of analysis described in the preceding chapters. Such calculations involve a rather painstaking exercise. However, one may estimate the reasonableness of the yields offered by broker–dealers to buyers rather simply.

COMPARE ZEROS TO CONVENTIONAL TREASURY BONDS

First, consider the number of years until maturity of the zero coupon bond and compare its yield to that of a Treasury bond of the same duration. Such comparison may show the yield of the zero security to be either above or below that of the Treasury. (Either may be fair, as was described in Chapter 10, Pricing Surprises.)

Second, make a rough sketch of the Treasury bond yield curve. If it is upward sloping, then you know that the yield of the zero should be *higher* than that of a Treasury bond of the same maturity.

If the yield curve is downward sloping, then the yield of the zero should be *less* than that of the Treasury bond of the same duration. If the yield curve has a positive slope, the yield of the zero bond should be *greater* than that of the Treasury bond.

And if the yield curve is inverted, one may expect the yield of the zero bond to be *less* than that of the Treasury bond.

CATs Traded on New York Exchange

Above all, don't judge the reasonableness of price and yield by what you see on the New York Stock Exchange (NYSE). An extraordinary aspect of the zero coupon pricing situation involves certain zero coupon bonds in the form of CATS that are listed and traded on the New York Stock Exchange. The trading activity on the exchange has taken place at incredibly high prices and amazingly low yields. The explanation, as reported in *Forbes*, October 22, 1984, page 247 is:

> Almost all of them (zero coupon bonds) trade over-the-counter— except for a handful of Salomon Brothers' so-called certificates of accrual on Treasury securities, which are on the New York Stock Exchange.
>
> Salomon figured that a Big Board listing would help its certificates of accrual gain respectability, but it turned out that CATs sold beautifully without going through the red tape of a Big Board listing application. Those listed CATs still exist, however, and trade several hundred thousand dollars' worth daily at prices that are just plain ridiculous—as much as 30% more than identical o-t-c (over-the-counter) CATs.
>
> That's a hefty premium for the privilege of looking up your bond's quote in the newspaper—the only difference between the two securities. Says Adrian Massie, a managing director of Salomon Brothers: "A rational buyer should never buy them, and those that have them should sell and replace them." Massie is being kind. What he means is that recent buyers of these listed CATs are just plain stupid. The market is rational.

The simple guidelines expressed will help, but they are not a panacea because the rules of thumb do not indicate how much higher or how much lower the yield should be of the zero compared to the Treasury bond of the same maturity. An accurate determination of the yield at which the zero security should be purchased (the spot rates) may be accomplished by the method described in the preceding two chapters.[1]

---

[1]A computer program to determine spot rates for IBM PCs, Apples, and compatibles is available from Larry Rosen Co.

CHECK THE MARKET BEFORE TRADING

Another safeguard, before buying a zero, is to check at least three active dealers, including a bank, to obtain competitive quotes. This is no guarantee that all three are not charging too high a price (or too low if you are selling), but it is certainly better than not checking the market at all.

13

STRIPS

U.S. TREASURY PROMOTES ZEROS

The STRIPS program was established in early 1985 by the U.S. Treasury. STRIPS means "Separate Trading of Registered Interest and Principal of Securities." Since 1982, the U.S. Treasury has realized significant savings in financing costs from the zero-coupon initiatives of the private market. The strong marketing of zeros created a demand for U.S. Treasury securities to back the zero coupon bonds. Increased demand, to the extent that it results in a shift in the demand curve in the traditional supply and demand sense, means the Treasury is able to sell its debt at a lower interest cost.

In announcing the STRIPS program the secretary of the Treasury stated that STRIPS would greatly reduce market transaction and financing costs, stimulate competition, and facilitate further expansion of the zero coupon market. The savings made possible by STRIPS is reflected in the competitive bidding for Treasury securities.[1] However, in spite of the Treasury propaganda, the introduction of STRIPS has not had much impact on the market. The Treasury does not itself issue zero coupon securities. It continues to auction its securities in the same manner as before. However, for selected Treasury issues, depository financial institutions (i.e., most banks, savings and loans, credit unions, and savings banks) that maintain a book-entry account at a Federal Reserve Bank can have the Treasury securities separated into their component parts, principal and interest. Each component can be traded separately and be separately owned. In other words, the STRIPS program allows banks and other financial institutions to join the zero coupon bandwagon by buying Treasury bonds and reselling custodial certificates to the public in the form of safekeeping certificates for zero coupon

---

[1]"Treasury Announces New STRIPS Program," *Treasury News,* Department of the Treasury, Washington, D.C., January 15, 1985.

instruments in $1000 maturity denominations or multiples thereof.

Choice of Maturities

STRIPS offer a range of 120 maturities, every three months, covering a period of from 1 to 30 years. Investors thus are able to choose a maturity (or a series of maturities) to suit specific future demands for cash flows.

Maturity Values Constant

All STRIPS mature for an even $1000.

SOME CALL PROVISIONS ELIMINATED

One major benefit of the STRIPS program is that some bond issues of the Treasury have eliminated their call provision. Prior to the STRIPS program, 30-year bond issues were callable by the Treasury after 25 years. As a result separate trading of the callable interest components (the final 5 years) was not possible. The Treasury spokesperson stated that the call feature was eliminated to accommodate market demand for the separate trading of longer-term interest components.[2]

Non-U.S. STRIPS Investors

STRIPS, like other Treasury instruments issued after July 18, 1984, may be purchased by foreign investors, who will not be subject to U.S. withholding tax (provided the foreign beneficial owner is identified by name).

[2]*Ibid.*

Price Information

The Treasury expects the Federal Reserve Bank of New York to eventually (after a liquid market develops) collect from government security dealers price and yield information on the most active maturities.

Heightened Competition from Banks

Perhaps the most important aspect of the STRIPS program is the addition of the banks (to the brokers) as the marketers of zeros. This will have a positive effect on the pricing practices of the investment brokerage industry. The same caveats that have been discussed are equally applicable to buying zeros from banks. Banks are in business to make a profit just like the brokers, and it is incumbent on investors to properly do their homework, to improve their chances of buying or selling zeros at a fair and reasonable price.

Banks' Markup or Commission Policy on Zeros   One large bank that has been active in STRIPS confidentially disclosed that its markup policy in a riskless transaction (where the bank buys to fill a specific customer order) is to charge 20 basis points (2/10 of 1 percent). This works as follows in the case of a 10-year maturity which the bank buys at a 10.0 percent yield. The cost to the bank for $100,000 face amount at maturity is $38,554. The bank then resells to its customer at a 9.80 percent yield (the bank's cost less 20 basis points). Thus the price to the customer is $39,262. The dollar markup is thus $708. The cited markup as a percentage of the customer investment is 1.8 percent. The markup as a percentage of the face amount of the bonds is 7/10 of 1 percent.

How reasonable is this markup policy? Traditionally, costs to buy or sell bonds have approximated $5 per bond. Assuming a market value of $1000 per bond, this amounts to 5/10 of 1 percent. Thus the bank's markup policy is not too far out of line. The entry of banks into the retail marketing of zeros introduces a strong competitive force that should help alleviate price gouging of consumers.

Two-tiered Marketing by Banks The STRIPS program has developed into a two-tier marketing arrangement whereby local and regional banks do not normally acquire the bonds they market from the Federal Reserve or Treasury directly. Such institutions probably buy the STRIPS from money center banks like Citicorp, Chase Manhattan, Manufacturer's Hanover, and so forth. The reason is the Federal Reserve–Treasury program does not allow the financial institutions to buy the specific maturity the institution (or its customer) desires. The bank, in turn, must buy the entire bond with all its interest coupons, and that entire bond then may be coverted into its parts. Thus to get one coupon, say 20 years distant, the bank would have to buy 19 coupons (if interest were paid annually) and the principal or corpus for which it had no need. Rather than do that the bank buys the specific maturity desired from another money center bank, which in effect functions as a wholesaler with its own markup added to the ultimate cost paid by the consumer. Of course, if the customer buys directly from the money center bank, then the second local stage in the marketing process is eliminated.

Pledging STRIPS as Collateral

Starting in July 1986, all new government bonds are issued only in book-entry form by the Federal Reserve.[3] No definitive or bearer government bonds have been issued since December 1982. The issuance of definitive registered bonds ceased with the July

---

[3]See Appendix C, Bureau of the Public Debt: The Safety of Book-Entry Treasury Securities.

1986 book-entry start-up. Even though no negotiable physical certificate exists, facilities do exist for recording pledges (as, for example, collateral for a loan).

WHERE CAN STRIPS BE PURCHASED?

Stockbrokers, insurance companies, investment advisors, and so forth, cannot buy STRIPS directly from the Federal Reserve. STRIPS can only be bought from the Federal Reserve by such financial institutions as banks, savings banks, credit unions, and savings and loan associations. It may be wise to keep this in mind when deciding how best to buy zeros.

Is it Better to Buy STRIPS from a Bank or Zeros from a Broker?

This is like asking someone to answer yes or no to the question "Have you stopped beating your wife?" There is no correct answer. The logical procedure is to check several sources in both markets. In addition, the methods described in Chapters 10, 11, and 12 should be used to form an independent judgment about fair prices. Even though brokers can't buy STRIPS from the Federal Reserve, they can and do trade them with their customers.

Book Entry

STRIPS are not issued with a physical certificate to serve as proof of ownership. Investors receive only a safekeeping receipt issued by the financial institution from which they were purchased. They are held in book entry form through the Federal Reserve, registered in the name of the financial institution from which they were bought. This contrasts with some "physicals" (actual certificates)—that is, actual stripped coupons or remaining corpus (the bond from which the coupons were stripped) that are traded in bearer form, and which originate from debt obligations originally issued prior to December 1982. For further information on book entry, please refer to Appendix C, Bureau of the Public Debt: The Safety of Book-Entry Treasury Securities.

14

Frequent Mistakes about YTM and Reinvestment of Interest

ERRORS IN *THE WASHINGTON POST,* NEW YORK TIMES NEWS SERVICE, *THE COURIER JOURNAL,* BARRON'S, INC., AND DOW JONES-IRWIN

The financial press, on the whole, does a fairly creditable job. However, many inaccuracies and outright errors creep into respected newspapers and magazines. Particularly prevalent are errors concerning whether reinvestment is required in order to achieve the yield to maturity (YTM) at which a bond is purchased. Consider the following excerpts.

The yield to maturity for regular notes and bonds, however, is based on a standardized formula and is seldom realized by the small investor.

For example, the 11 7/8 percent Treasury bonds due in 2003 were recently offered at a price of $101 per $1000, with a yield to maturity of 11.77 percent. That yield to maturity, however, assumes that each of the 40 interest payments received during the next 20 years will be reinvested at 11.77 percent. Obviously that is not likely, especially in the case of small investors whose best alternative might be to reinvest the interest payments in a money market fund paying considerably less than 11.77.

The effect of the reinvestment assumption can be staggering. According to Ronald J. Ryan, president of the Ryan Financial Strategy Group, the 11 7/8 percent bond will produce a true yield to maturity of only 8.13 percent assuming the semiannual interest payments are reinvested at 5 percent. And if the reinvestment rate is 10 percent, the yield will reach 10.73 percent—but still more than a percentage point below the 11.77 percent yield-to-maturity formula.

Source: The Courier-Journal, February 26, 1984, by Michael Quint, New York Times News Service.

Any investor, small or large, who buys a bond at a stated YTM or internal rate of return (IRR), who holds the bond to maturity, realizes that stated return (assuming there is no default by the issuer). For example, Steve Blank buys a bond maturing in the year 2000 at a YTM or IRR of 12 percent. He realizes that yield. Period! Steve doesn't have to reinvest a dime. It doesn't matter what happens to future interest rates. He can spend his interest each year on cashews, whipped cream, and pistachios.

In other words, the first two paragraphs of the New York Times News Service story are absolutely erroneous. The writer and Ryan have mixed up a concept called "total realized compound yield," popularized by Sidney Homer and Martin Leibowitz in their *Inside the Yield Book,* with the conventional term "yield to maturity" or "internal rate of return." The terms are in no way synonymous. This subject is explored in detail in *The Dow Jones-Irwin Guide to Calculating Yields—Quick Solutions for Investment Selection Using Computer Generated Internal Rate of Return Analysis.*

> Zeros also let you lock in today's interest rates. The yield to maturity quoted on ordinary bonds assumes that you reinvest the bonds' coupons at the same rate as when you bought the bonds. But if maturity is some years away, it is hard to know how much you will wind up with. . . .
>
> Source: "Your Money," *Inc.,* Lisa R. Sheeran, July 1984

The same comments apply to the foregoing. The yield to maturity does not assume one yen or sou of reinvestment of income.

The errors are not confined to the press, as evidenced by the following four quotations from books published by Dow Jones-Irwin, Inc.

Marcia Stigum's *Money Market Calculations—Yields, Break-Evens, and Arbitrage,* page 113, says:

> The yield to maturity that any note or bond offers is a function of three key variables:
>
> 1. The known (or assumed) cash flows the security will generate.
> 2. The frequency of compounding.
> 3. The reinvestment rate.

Frank J. Fabozzi's *The Handbook of Fixed Income Securities,*
page 67, erroneously states:

Yield-to-Maturity   Unlike the current yield, the yield-to-maturity does take into account any capital gain or loss. The yield-
to-maturity does consider the reinvestment of the contracted
periodic payments; however, it implicitly *assumes that these payments are reinvested at the yield-to-maturity.*

As explained in Chapter 4, the quoted yield-to-maturity is a prom-
ised yield. It reflects the yield to the investor if the security is
held to maturity and if coupon interest payments are reinvested
at the yield-to-maturity.[1]

When using the yield-to-maturity as a measure of investment
return, it is assumed that the coupon interest can be reinvested
at a rate equal to the yield-to-maturity. That is, if the yield-to-
maturity is 12 percent, it is assumed that the coupon interest
payments can be reinvested to yield 12 percent.[2]

The stated yield to maturity on a bond assumes that each coupon
is clipped every six months and reinvested at that yield. That
sounds like a small technicality, but it's a big deal long-term, and
long-term, after all, is how you invest for retirement.

Source: Barron's, Randall W. Forsyth, April 2, 1984.

Again, Forsyth has missed the same boat. No interest reinvestment is required to realize the yield to maturity at purchase.

The yield-to-maturity on other bonds assumes that you'll always
invest the interest income at the same rate paid by the underlying
bond, which is not always possible.

Source: The Courier-Journal, 1985; Jane Bryant Quinn, *The Washington
Post,* February 14, 1985.

---

[1]Frank J. Fabozzi and Irving M. Pollack, eds.; *Handbook of Fixed Income Securities,
U.S. Treasury Obligations,* by Marcia Stigum, Ph.D and Frank J. Fabozzi, Ph.D., C.F.A.,
C.P.A., p. 257: Dow Jones-Irwin, Inc. Homewood, IL, 1983
[2]*Ibid.* "Bond Yield Measures and Price Volatility Properties," by Frank J. Fabozzi,
Ph.D, C.F.A., C.P.A., p. 75.

Once again, it's the same old trap that Quinn has fallen into. No reinvestment is required to realize the "yield-to-maturity" at purchase.

> That eliminates reinvestment risk, an important matter because a bond's yield-to-maturity calculation assumes that each interest coupon is reinvested at the same yield. For example, a 20-year bond with a 12 percent stated yield to maturity will yield only 11.2 percent if the coupons are reinvested at 10 percent instead of 12 percent, according to calculations by Sharmin Mossavar-Rahmani of Ryan Strategy Group.
>
> *Source:* "Current Yield," *Barron's,* Randall W. Forsyth, September 24, 1984.

Again and again the same misconceptions and incorrect statements abound in the press.

Once and for all, let's set the record straight. **No reinvestment is required, at all, for an investor to achieve the "yield to maturity" or "internal rate of return" at purchase.**

PROOF THAT NO REINVESTMENT REQUIRED TO EARN IRR OR YTM

Assume a three-year bond is purchased for $901.66. The bond pays $80 annual interest ($40 semiannually) and matures for $1000. The yield to maturity (YTM) or internal rate of return (IRR) at purchase is 12 percent, as shown in Table 14-1. The question is whether the semiannual interest must be reinvested at 12 percent for the purchaser to realize the expected 12 percent yield to maturity. It is the author's contention that no reinvestment whatsoever is needed in order to realize a 12 percent YTM or IRR.

If the periodic interest is reinvested at an annual rate of 12 percent, then the terminal value of the bond (the value of all cash flows at maturity including the proceeds of reinvestment)

Table 14-1. Three-Year Bond with/without Reinvestment—Cash Flows

Tax bracket	0.00%
Number of semiannual periods	6
Maturity value	$1000
Semiannual percent earned on reinvestment	6.00%
Purchase price of bond	$901.66
Semiannual coupon interest	$40
Portion of long-term capital gain untaxed	60.00%

Semi-annual Period	Cash Flow Tax Exempt	Cash Flow Pre-reinvestment	Cumulative Balance Pre-reinvestment	Interest Reinvestment			Total Cash Flow
				Original Balance	Semi-Annual Interest[a]	Ending Balance	
0	-902	-901.66	0	0.00	0.00	0.00	-901.66
1	40	40	40	0.00	0.00	40.00	40.00
2	40	40	80	40.00	2.40	82.40	42.40
3	40	40	120	82.40	4.94	127.34	44.94
4	40	40	160	127.34	7.64	174.98	47.64
5	40	40	200	174.98	10.50	225.48	50.50
6	1040	1040	1240	225.48	13.53	1279.01	1053.53
Totals		338.34			39.01		337.36

With reinvestment at 12% per year (6% semiannually) the Revised IRR is 13.3%

Without reinvestment the IRR or YTM is 12%

Source: Lawrence R. Rosen, "Investment Analysis—After Tax IRR for Stocks, Bonds and Real Estate," Copyright 1984 by L. R. Rosen, 7008 Springdale Road, Louisville, KY. Unauthorized reproduction is prohibited.

[a]This semi-annual interest is the "interest-on-interest," or interest earned from the reinvesting of interest.

is $1279. The realized compound yield (see following discussion) which by definition is the rate which equates the purchase price (901.69) to the terminal value ($1279) is 12 percent.

But with reinvestment the IRR is no longer 12 percent, as the cash flows now include the proceeds of reinvestment. The revised cash flows with reinvestment are shown in Table 14-1 under the caption "Total Cash Flow" and in Table 14-2 under the caption "Cash Flow with Reinvestment at 6 Percent semiannually." The IRR with reinvestment (the Revised IRR) is 13.30 percent as compared to 12 percent without reinvestment.

The **indisputable proof** of the foregoing is shown in Table 14-2. If in fact the revised cash flows which include the proceeds of reinvestment are discounted at the revised IRR of 13.30 percent, and if the net or discounted present value of such cash flows is equal to the initial investment of $901.66, then it is axiomatic that the YTM or IRR *with reinvestment* (at 6 percent semiannually) is 13.30 percent. The discounted present values of same are shown in the second column of Table 14-2 under the caption "With Reinvestment Discounted Present Value of Total Cash Flow at 6.65 Percent" (per semiannual period, that is, 13.30 percent on an annual basis). The sum of the discounted present values is $901.21. (The difference between $901.21 and $901.66 is due to rounding—if 6.65 percent is carried out to more decimal places the sum is $901.66.)

This proves that the IRR with reinvestment is 13.30 percent—not the original 12 percent, which is the IRR with no reinvestment. Revised IRR is a term describing the return with reinvestment, e.g., The Revised IRR is 13.3 percent.

Additional proof that the IRR of 12 percent is correct without reinvestment at all: If the discounted present value of the cash flows without reinvestment, at a discount rate of 12 percent per year (6 percent semiannually), is equal to the $901.66 initial investment, then it is definitively proved that the IRR without reinvestment of the interest is 12 percent.

Table 14-2 contains the proof, as follows: The cash flows with

Table 14-2. Three-Year Bond with/without Reinvestment— Discounted Present Values

Cash Flow with Reinvestment at six Percent Semi- annually	With Reinvestment Discounted Present Value of Total Cash Flow at 6.65 Percent	Cash Flow with No Reinvestment	No Reinvestment Discounted Present Value of Total Cash Flow at 6 Percent	Semi- annual Period
−901.66	0.00	−901.66	0.00	
40.00	37.51	40.00	37.74	1
42.40	37.28	40.00	35.60	2
44.94	37.05	40.00	33.58	3
47.64	36.82	40.00	31.68	4
50.50	36.60	40.00	29.89	5
1053.53	715.95	1040.00	733.16	6
$ 337.36	$901.21		$901.65	

Initial investment $901.66
Coupon interest without reinvestment $240
Interest-on-interest from reinvestment $39.01
Maturity value $1000
Terminal value (240.00 + 39.01 + 1000) $1279.01
Note: Terminal value includes interest-on-interest from reinvestment at an annual rate of 12%.

Compound realized yield which equates the initial investment of $901.66 to the terminal value of $1279.01 is 12 percent

1.419 is the compound interest factor for 6% for 6 semiannual periods.

1.419 times $901.66 is $1279.01.

no reinvestment are shown under the column captioned "Cash Flow with No Reinvestment." The discounted values at a 12 percent (6 percent semiannually) rate are shown under the column entitled "No Reinvestment Discounted Present Value of Total Cash Flow at 6 Percent." As shown in Table 14-2, the sum of such present values (discounted at the IRR of 12 percent) is $901.65. **Thus, it is proved that no reinvestment of cash flows is needed to actually earn the YTM or IRR at which a bond is purchased.**

On the other hand, $1279.12 is the terminal value, which includes interest reinvestment at 12 percent per year (6 percent semiannually). And the cash flows implicit in arriving at $1279.12 ending or terminal balance are shown in Tables 14-1 and 14-2.

The compound rate that equates the purchase price to the terminal value is 12 percent. Since the terminal value includes interest reinvestment at 12 percent, and the IRR at purchase is 12 percent, the realized compound yield is 12 percent. And, under the same reinvestment circumstances, the Revised IRR is 13.3 percent.

REALIZED COMPOUND YIELDS

The rate that equates the purchase price (e.g., $901.69) to the future value ($1279.01, which includes interest-on-interest) is called realized compound yield (or compound realized yield). This term, which was coined by Homer and Leibowitz in their *Inside the Yield Book,* is by definition the compound rate that equates the purchase price to the terminal value, where the terminal value includes reinvestment of the periodic interest.

If you include the proceeds of interest-on-interest at a reinvestment rate equal to the IRR or YTM at purchase in the terminal value, the compound realized yield will be equal to the

YTM or IRR at purchase. However, this does not demonstrate that to achieve the YTM or IRR a purchaser must reinvest.

If and only if the percentage rate on reinvestment is equal to the IRR, then the realized compound yield is equal to the IRR.

But the realized compound yield is not—repeat, not—the same as IRR or yield to maturity. IRR and yield to maturity are synonymous. YTM and IRR both mean the discount rate, which equates future cash flows to the initial investment. Realized compound yield is a totally different concept. Realized compound yield is the compound rate that equates the purchase price to the terminal value, when the terminal value includes interest reinvestment. The only time the realized compound yield (12 percent in this case) is equal to the IRR at purchase (also 12 percent in this case) is when the rate earned on reinvestment (12 percent in this case) is equal to the IRR at purchase.

At any other rate earned on reinvestment, the realized compound yield will not be equal to the IRR at purchase. At reinvestment rates higher than the IRR at purchase, the realized compound yield will be higher; conversely, at reinvestment rates lower than the IRR at purchase, the realized compound yield will be less than the IRR at purchase.

To summarize, Table 14-1 shows that the IRR or YTM at purchase is 12 percent (6 percent semiannually) and that if interest is reinvested at 12 percent, the IRR increases to 13.3 percent (6.65 percent semiannually). To achieve the 12 percent IRR no reinvestment was required.

Table 14-2 proves that the 12 percent IRR without reinvestment is accurate, and that 13.3 percent is the revised IRR when reinvestment takes place at 12 percent.

Thus all the articles and texts quoted earlier in this chapter are incorrect when they state that it is necessary to reinvest to achieve the YTM at purchase. The errors apparently stem from a misinterpretation of the excellent book by Homer and Leibowitz, who coined a new term, "realized compound yield" or "compound realized yield." But their new term has its own unique definition and it is not the same as YTM or IRR.

It is important to understand both what is correct and why the errors are wrong. IRR or YTM can be viewed like a bank interest rate. You don't need to reinvest at all to earn what you think you are going to earn.

15

Callable Zero Coupon Bonds

Callable "Tails"

Historically, long-term Treasury bond issues have been callable five years before maturity. For example, 30-year bonds are callable after 25 years and 25-year bonds are callable after 20 years. Thus separation of the interest payments from the maturity payments of the bond is impossible for those five-year periods of time when the bonds are subject to call by the Treasury. Such a five-year period is frequently called the "callable tail" of the bonds.

CALLABLE TAILS

There is important significance to the callable tails of U.S. Treasury bonds. For example, consider the U.S. 12.5 percent of August 15, 2014, which are first callable on August 15, 2009. If the U.S. Treasury does not redeem the bonds on August 15, 2009, the owner of the callable tail will receive semiannual interest payments at a rate of 12.5 percent of the face amount starting February 15, 2010, and lasting until the first to occur of either the maturity date of the bonds (2014) or until the Treasury subsequently exercises its right to call the bonds prior to maturity.

An investor who owns $10,000 principal amount of the callable tail does not know with precision the ultimate amount that will be realized. At a minimum, if the bonds are called on August 15, 2009, $10,000 principal amount and no interest coupons will be received. At a maximum, if the bonds are not called, interest coupons of $625 will be received 10 times, starting February 15, 2010, and the principal payment on August 15, 2014, will be $10,000—a total of $6250 interest and $10,000 principal, a grand total of $16,250.

PAR VALUE REFERENCES

Securities brokers frequently speak of the price of the bonds as a percentage of par value. In evaluating callable zero coupon bonds, it is important to distinguish what par value the broker is referring to. That is, in the foregoing example, does a price of 10 percent mean 10 percent of $10,000 or 10 percent of $16,250? This is of utmost importance in comparing offerings of various brokers. If one broker is referring to $10,000 par and quotes a price of 10 percent and a second broker is referring to the par value of the tail as $16,250 and quotes a price of only 9 percent, the first broker's offer is much better. In other words, 10 percent of $10,000 means a **purchase price** of $1000 from the first broker versus 9 percent of $16,250, or $1462.50, from the second broker. Both brokers are offering the same callable tail; only the prices at which they are offered to you are different.

Quoted Yields

Another problem that arises in connection with callable tails is the determination of the yield, as quoted by brokers. The two most frequently used methods are (1) yield to first call and (2) yield to maturity. Sometimes a third method, yield to average life, is used, but we will not discuss that method here.

The appropriate yield for a bond broker to quote is the lowest one. Sometimes it may be "yield to first call." At other times it may be "yield to maturity." For example, the callable tail of the Treasury 2014 issue should be quoted at 11.58 percent yield to call, which yield is less than the yield to maturity of 11.70 percent. But if the price of the bond were lower, the bonds should be quoted at the yield to maturity of 13.19 percent, which is less than the yield to first call of 13.3 percent.

CALLABLE BONDS PROVIDE A FREE "PUT OPTION" TO THE ISSUER

Callable tails should trade at yields that are more than the yields for the closest maturing noncallable zero coupon bonds. This is because the callable tail can really be regarded as having two parts: (1) a value equal to that of the closest maturity of non-callable bonds, less (2) the value of a theoretical put option given to the government to sell the last 10 coupon payments to the investor. (A put option gives the holder the right to sell a security to another person under predetermined conditions of time and price.) If the Treasury bond has a coupon rate of 12 percent per year, and at the time of first call prevailing interest rates are at 15 percent, then the Treasury is not going to call the issue, and the investor is stuck with earning less than a market rate. Thus the Treasury has exercised its imputed option to put the callable tail to the investor. If interest rate levels were only 8 percent, however, then the Treasury would exercise its right to call the bonds at first call, and refinance the issue by borrowing at 8 percent to eliminate the 12 percent debt.

To summarize the important considerations concerning callable tails: (1) know whether the price quote refers to par as just the principal or whether it includes coupon interest as well as principal; (2) know whether the lowest quotation is yield to maturity or yield to first call; and (3) be sure that you pay less (i.e., obtain a higher yield) for a callable tail than for the closest maturity of a noncallable zero coupon to compensate for the free put option you are giving the government.

16

Convertible Zeros and Other Tidbits

CUSTODIANSHIP AND PHYSICALS VERSUS REGISTERED ZEROS

Zero coupon Treasury securities are available in two forms: U.S. Treasury bills issued directly by the U.S. Treasury and U.S. Treasury notes and bonds and their unmatured interest coupons which have been separated (stripped) by their holder, typically a custodian bank or investment brokerage firm. Merrill Lynch and Salomon Brothers popularized the process of separating the interest coupons from the underlying principal ("corpus") of the Treasury security. The certificates or custodial receipts evidencing ownership of the corpus or stripped interest coupons in the case of Merrill Lynch are called TIGRs (Treasury Income Growth Receipts) and for Salomon, CATS (Certificates of Accrual on Treasury Securities). A number of other firms have similarly stripped the interest coupons from Treasury bonds and resold them in custodial receipt programs with feline and other names. These include TBR's (E.F. Hutton's Treasury Bond Receipts), LIONs (Lehman Investment Opportunity Notes sponsored by Shearson/Lehman) and the generic TRs (Treasury Receipts).

The underlying Treasury bonds and notes are actually held in book-entry form at the Federal Reserve Bank (registered bonds) or, in the case of bearer securities (unregistered) in trust on behalf of the owners.

Through STRIPS (Separate Trading of Registered Interest and Principal of Securities), the Federal Reserve program, the beneficial ownership of the particular interest coupon or corpus is accounted for directly through the Federal Reserve book-entry recordkeeping system as described in Chapter 13, STRIPS. Under the STRIPS program, the need for the trust or custody arrangements via a bank is eliminated.

Where a bank acts as the custodian of the underlying stripped debt obligation, which may be held by it either in physical (e.g., bearer), or book-entry (e.g., registered) form, the terms of custody or trust generally provide that the underlying debt obligations will be held separate from the general assets of the custodian and will not be subject to any right, charge, security interest, lien, or claim of any kind in favor of the custodian or any person claiming through the custodian, and that the custodian will be responsible for applying all payments received on the underlying debt to the related certificates without making any deductions (other than any applicable tax withholding). The custodian may be required to maintain insurance to protect the holders of the receipts or certificates against losses which may occur in connection with the deposit of Treasury securities under the terms of the custody agreement.

Typically, a TIGR or CATS may be exchanged for the actual underlying Treasury security by the custodian. This would be another certificate indicating ownership of the Treasury security in book-entry form. This would be the same evidence of ownership that an investor would receive in buying any Treasury security in book-entry form directly from the Federal Reserve. Thus except for the small market where physical (bearer) trading of the actual stripped coupons or corpus takes place, the investor never takes possession of the actual Treasury instrument itself. The trading system involving custodianship is similar to the custodial bookkeeping system employed for decades by mutual fund investment programs.

HYBRIDS OR CONVERTIBLE ZEROS

A variant of the zero coupon bond is a hybrid that is a debt instrument which has the characteristics for a number of years (usually 10 to 15) of that of a zero coupon bond until a conversion point from which time until maturity it is like a conventional interest-paying bond, paying a predetermined at issuance rate of interest on the accreted value at the conversion point. Conversion is mandatory, not optional. For example, the Colorado Housing Finance Authority has a 10 1/2 percent convertible zero issue which accretes from an issuance price of $33 per bond to $100, 11 years later, at which point it begins to pay interest in cash at the rate of 10 1/2 percent of the $100 until maturity 20 years after the conversion date. Such bonds may be referred to as "convertible zeros." They combine the features of both zeros and conventional bonds. This type of bond is structured to appeal to the investor who wants maximum growth now, maximum income later.

The Turnpike Authority of Kentucky has an issue of similar nature called "bond income growth securities." And Massachusetts Housing Finance Agency issued a "FIGS" (Future Income Growth Security) convertible zero. Other convertible zeros have been issued by the Ohio Housing Finance Agency and by the Maryland Health and Higher Education Facilities Authority.

Among the multitude of catchy names ascribed to convertible zeros are: GAINS (growth and income series), PACS (principal appreciation conversion securities), FIGS (future income growth securities), TEDIS (tax-exempt discount and income securities), BIGS (bond income and growth securities), CADIS (capital appreciation and deferred income securities), PROFITS (postponed revenue on future income tax-exempt securities), CCABs (convertible capital appreciation bonds), CAFIS (capital appreciation and future income securities), STAIRS (stepped tax-exempt appreciation and income realization securities), and, finally, LIMOs (limited interest municipal obligations).

The hybrids lend themselves to the same type of scrutiny discussed throughout this book. Duration will be shorter than for a conventional zero coupon bond due to the conversion feature. Accordingly, volatility will be less. In particular, attention should be directed to both call features of the issue (typically, convertible zeros tend to have 15-year call protection, compared to a normal 10-year call protection on conventional zero coupon tax-exempts). Finally, the credit risk is very important, more than ever for zero coupon issues of any type, and as a result many zero municipals are insured or guaranteed in one form or another.[1]

Underwriters have favored using zero coupons or convertible zeros as financing tools because they dramatically reduce an issuer's debt service requirements in the early years of an issue. With no interest to pay on the zeros, an issuer is able to retire more debt in the early years of an issue. That makes it possible for the underwriters to structure an issue with shorter maturities and (with an upward-sloping yield curve) lower interest costs. The savings achieved by the issuer from the shorter maturity bonds compensates for the higher rate paid on zeros.

It seems that acquiring a "convertible zero" like the Colorado issue described previously is tantamount to buying an 11-year zero and giving the issuer a put option to sell you a 20-year bond paying 10 1/2 percent while at the same time receiving a call option to acquire the same 20-year bond. With our history of rising interest rates over time, it may well be that the put option accorded to the issuer has a lot more value than the call option received. Hence the yield on the initial 11-year period should be substantially higher than a straight zero of the same 11-year maturity.

Another variant, issued by Waste Management, Inc., is a "liq-

[1]Such external insurance, collateralization, or guaranty lends additional security to the investor. However, the strength of the guaranty or insurer must be evaluated. All insurers are by no means equal. Among the insurers of municipal bonds (with the largest amounts of municipal insurance in force) are: Municipal Bond Insurance Association (MBIA), American Municipal Bond Assurance Corp. (AMBAC), Financial Guaranty Insurance Corp. (FGIC), and Bond Investors Guaranty Group (BIG). Other insurers include: U.S. Fidelity and Guaranty Insurance Co., Industrial Indemnity Corp., Continental Casualty Corp., and Industrial Development Bond Insurance. The precise nature of the guaranty should also be determined: is it unconditional for both principal and interest, or otherwise? Some forms of bank "liquidity facilities" may not protect investors if the issuer becomes insolvent. They guarantee marketability but not credit.

uid yield option note," which is a zero coupon subordinated note exchangeable into the issuer's common stock at the option of the holder. In addition, the holder has the right to "put" the security to the issuer under certain circumstances and the issuer has the right to call the issue for redemption at its option under certain conditions.

17

The Summing Up

Institutional and private investors have acquired tens of billions of dollars of zero coupon bonds since their introduction in the early 1980s. What accounts for such stupendous popularity? Is the wide acclaim accorded to zeros deserved—are they a good investment?

FACTORS IN THE POPULARITY OF ZEROS

For institutions such as pension plans and insurance companies, zeros offer a distinct advantage in allowing the organization to match its future liabilities to assets which will mature in the appropriate year. The use of zero coupon bonds facilitates matching the cash inflows from a portfolio to the liability outflows as described in Chapter 3, Beware of Zero Coupon Volatility. Such matching of liabilities to assets can be accomplished without subjecting the portfolio to the unknown variable, the rate at which income will be able to be reinvested from the present until the time of the occurrence of the future liability.

In addition, certain zero coupon bonds may also free the portfolio from the risk of premature call (prior to maturity) and from the risk of default (as in the case of zeros founded on Treasury bonds). Zero coupon bonds may help reduce pension funding requirements, and enhance the sponsoring company's earnings and market value per share.

POSSIBLE DANGERS OF ZEROS

On the other hand, there are various pitfalls of which investors must be aware. First, there is the volatility risk. Zeros are the most volatile of bonds. As seen in Chapter 3, for a 20-year bond, in a rising interest rate environment, where yields to maturity increase from 6 percent to 9 percent, a 6 percent coupon bond will fall in price by 27.4 percent at the same time as a zero coupon bond plummets by 42.8 percent.

Such volatility can be either a curse or a blessing. If you are fortunate enough to buy at a time of peak interest rates, the volatility of a zero bond (compared to a conventional coupon bond) will maximize your capital gain. But should the reverse be true, and interest rates rise after your purchase, your unrealized losses due to decreased market value of the zero coupon bond will exceed (greatly in the case of longer maturities) the loss from a conventional bond. Investing in shorter-term maturities lessens the volatility risk. The nature of volatility is described in detail in Chapter 3, Beware of Zero Coupon Volatility.

Second, taxable purchasers should rarely buy a taxable zero coupon bond because of the highly adverse effect of taxation on after-tax return. The negative aspects of taxation are described in Chapter 4, Beware of Taxation with Conventional Zeros.

An alternative form of zero for a taxable purchaser is the tax-free or municipal zero coupon bond, as described in Chapter 6, Taxability of Municipal Zero Coupons. However, other potential pitfalls exist, such as the dangers of a prior to maturity call or forced redemption. The problems are discussed in Chapter 5.

LOCKING IN A REINVESTMENT RATE, GOOD OR BAD?

Inherent in the question of whether zero coupon bonds are a good investment is the notion of mandatory reinvestment of imputed income at a fixed, irrevocable rate. Brokers like to talk about "locking in today's high rates." But consider Chart 17-1, "Long- and Short-Term Interest Rates." It is evident that since the late

LONG- AND SHORT-TERM INTEREST RATES

ANNUALLY

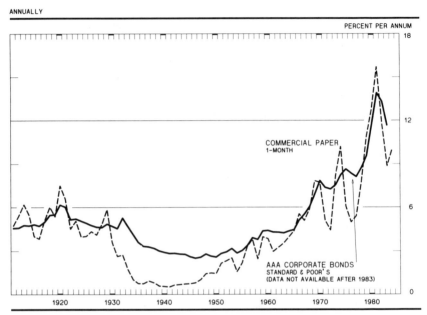

Chart 17-1. **Long- and Short-Term Interest Rates** (*Source: Historical Chart Book*, Board of Governors of Federal Reserve System, 1985).

1940s interest rates generally have been increasing steadily year by year. If you had purchased a zero coupon bond in 1950 and locked yourself into "today's high rates" of about 3 percent, how would you have felt when both long- and short-term rates exceeded 12 percent in the early 1980s?

What would be the effect if, for example, the reinvestment rate on a bond with 30 years until maturity turned out to merely double the yield to maturity (YTM) of a zero coupon bond? Let's assume the zero coupon bond was purchased to yield 10 percent, and that the average reinvestment rate on the coupon bond was 20 percent. (This is a much less extreme difference than has prevailed during the period since 1950.) Let's say $1000 is invested in both the zero coupon bond and a par bond with a $100 coupon. Both are purchased at 10 percent YTM. Without doubt, the coupon bond will produce superior results, as reinvestment at only 10 percent would cause its total value at maturity (pretax) to be equal to the zero coupon's maturity value. (This principle is described in detail in Chapters 8 and 9.)

The maturity value of the zero coupon bond is determinable by Graph 2-4. Enter the graph on the bottom axis at the 30-year mark, proceed vertically to the intersection with the 10 percent curve, then horizontally to the left axis, where the maturity value is seen to be about $17,450. By formula, the maturity value S is

$$S = P (1 + i)^{30}$$
$$= 1000 (1.1)^{30}$$
$$= 1000 (17.449)$$
$$= \underline{17,449}$$

Table 17-1 shows a 30-year, $100 coupon bond, with interest reinvested annually at 20 percent (in a zero tax bracket). In this case, the total value at maturity is $119,188, which is considerably more than the $17,449 produced by the zero coupon bond. The terminal value $119,188 is predominantly interest-on-interest, which represents all but $4000 of the total.

Let's give further consideration to the merits of "locking in" an interest rate. Tables 17-2 through 17-6 show a historical comparison of the purchase of a zero coupon bond (had they then existed) to the purchase of a par bond at the same yield. However, the reinvestment percentage rate for the par bonds is changed each year to reflect the actual trend of such historical interest rates. The methodology is described as follows:

Table 17-1. Bonds After Tax with Reinvestment

0%	Tax bracket of investor
30	Number of years until maturity of bond
$1,000	Maturity Value
20%	Reinvestment % rate earned before tax
$1,000	Purchase price of bond
$100	Coupon rate in dollars

Year	Cash Flows Each Year Before Reinvestment of Earnings	Balance Before Reinvestment	Interest Reinvestment		Ending Balance with Reinvestment	Cash Flow per Year with Reinvestment
			Original Balance	Annual Interest on Interest		
0	−1,000	0	0	0	0	−1,000
1	100	100	0	0.00	100	100
2	100	200	100	20.00	220	120
3	100	300	220	44.00	364	144
4	100	400	364	72.80	537	173
5	100	500	537	107.36	744	207
6	100	600	744	148.83	993	249
7	100	700	993	198.60	1,292	299
8	100	800	1,292	258.32	1,650	358
9	100	900	1,650	329.98	2,080	430
10	100	1,000	2,080	415.98	2,596	516
11	100	1,100	2,596	519.17	3,215	619
12	100	1,200	3,215	643.01	3,958	743
13	100	1,300	3,958	791.61	4,850	892
14	100	1,400	4,850	969.93	5,920	1,070

Year						
15	100	1,500	5,920	1,183.92	7,204	1,284
16	100	1,600	7,204	1,440.70	8,744	1,541
17	100	1,700	8,744	1,748.84	10,593	1,849
18	100	1,800	10,593	2,118.61	12,812	2,219
19	100	1,900	12,812	2,562.33	15,474	2,662
20	100	2,000	15,474	3,094.80	18,669	3,195
21	100	2,100	18,669	3,733.76	22,503	3,834
22	100	2,200	22,503	4,500.51	27,103	4,601
23	100	2,300	27,103	5,420.61	32,624	5,521
24	100	2,400	32,624	6,524.74	39,248	6,625
25	100	2,500	39,248	7,849.68	47,198	7,950
26	100	2,600	47,198	9,439.62	56,738	9,540
27	100	2,700	56,738	11,347.55	68,185	11,448
28	100	2,800	68,185	13,637.06	81,922	13,737
29	100	2,900	81,922	16,384.47	98,407	16,484
30	1,100	4,000	98,407	19,681.36	119,188	20,781
	4,000	4,000		115,188.00	119,188	119,188

Without reinvestment, the result is   Regular   IRR   10.00%
With reinvestment, the result is   Revised   IRR   28.81%

0%	Tax bracket of investor
30	Number of years until maturity of bond
$1,000	Maturity value
20%	Reinvestment % rate earned before tax
$1,000	Purchase price of bond
$100	Coupon rate in dollars

Table 17-2. Bonds, After Tax with Reinvestment at Increasing Rates

0%	Tax bracket of investor
34	Number of years until maturity of bond
$1000	Maturity value
3.0%	Reinvestment percent rate earned before tax, increasing by 0.28% per year
$1,000	Purchase price of bond
$30	Coupon rate in dollars
2,732	Maturity value of zero coupon bond

	Cash Flows Each Year Before Reinvestment of Earnings	Interest Reinvestment				Cash Flow per Year with Reinvestment	Reinvestment Rate (%)
		Balance Before Reinvestment	Original Balance	Annual Interest on Interest	Ending Balance with Reinvestment		
Year							
0	-1,000	0	0	0	0	-1,000	3.00%
1	30	30	0	0	30	30	3.28
2	30	60	30	1	61	31	3.56
3	30	90	61	2	93	32	3.84
4	30	120	93	4	127	34	4.12
5	30	150	127	5	162	35	4.40
6	30	180	162	7	199	37	4.68
7	30	210	199	9	238	39	4.96
8	30	240	238	12	280	42	5.24
9	30	270	280	15	325	45	5.51
10	30	300	325	18	373	48	5.79
11	30	330	373	22	424	52	6.07
12	30	360	424	26	480	56	6.35
13	30	390	480	31	541	61	

14	30	420	541	36	607	66	6.63
15	30	450	607	42	678	72	6.91
16	30	480	678	49	757	79	7.19
17	30	510	757	57	844	87	7.47
18	30	540	844	65	939	95	7.75
19	30	570	939	75	1,045	105	8.03
20	30	600	1,045	87	1,161	117	8.31
21	30	630	1,161	100	1,291	130	8.59
22	30	660	1,291	114	1,436	144	8.87
23	30	690	1,436	131	1,597	161	9.15
24	30	720	1,597	151	1,777	181	9.43
25	30	750	1,777	173	1,980	203	9.71
26	30	780	1,980	198	2,208	228	9.99
27	30	810	2,208	227	2,464	257	10.26
28	30	840	2,464	260	2,754	290	10.54
29	30	870	2,754	298	3,082	328	10.82
30	30	900	3,082	342	3,454	372	11.10
31	30	930	3,454	393	3,878	423	11.38
32	30	960	3,878	452	4,360	482	11.66
33	30	990	4,360	521	4,910	551	11.94
34	1,030	2,020	4,910	600	6,541	1,630	12.22
	2,020			4,521		3,454	

Without reinvestment the result is   Regular   IRR   3.00%

With reinvestment the result is   Revised   IRR   8.12%

Maturity value of zero bond   2,732

Maturity value of coupon with reinvestment   3,454

Difference   −723

225

Source: Lawrence K. Rosen, "Investment Analysis—After Tax IRR for Stocks, Bonds and Real Estate," Copyright 1984 by L. R. Rosen, 4008 Springdale Road, Louisville, KY. Unauthorized reproduction is prohibited.

Table 17-3. Bonds, After Tax with Reinvestment at Increasing Rates

0%	Tax bracket of investor (decimal form)
25	Number of years until maturity of bond
$1,000	Maturity value
4.0%	Reinvestment percent rate earned before tax, increasing by 0.34% per year
$1,000	Purchase price of bond
$40	Coupon rate in dollars
2,666	Maturity value of zero coupon bond

			Interest Reinvestment				
Year	Cash Flows Each Year Before Reinvestment of Earnings	Balance Before Reinvestment	Original Balance	Annual Interest on Interest	Ending Balance with Reinvestment	Cash Flow per Year with Reinvestment	Reinvestment Rate (%)
0	-1,000	0	0	0	0	-1,000	4.00%
1	40	40	0	0	40	40	4.34
2	40	80	40	2	82	42	4.68
3	40	120	82	4	126	44	5.02
4	40	160	126	6	172	46	5.36
5	40	200	172	9	221	49	5.70
6	40	240	221	13	274	53	6.04
7	40	280	274	17	330	57	6.38
8	40	320	330	21	391	61	6.72
9	40	360	391	26	458	66	

10	40	400	458	32	530	72	7.06
11	40	440	530	39	609	79	7.40
12	40	480	609	47	696	87	7.74
13	40	520	696	56	792	96	8.08
14	40	560	792	67	899	107	8.42
15	40	600	899	79	1,018	119	8.76
16	40	640	1,018	93	–,151	133	9.10
17	40	680	1,151	109	1,299	149	9.44
18	40	720	1,299	127	1,466	167	9.78
19	40	760	1,466	148	1,655	188	10.12
20	40	800	1,655	173	1,868	213	10.46
21	40	840	1,868	202	2,109	242	10.80
22	40	880	2,109	235	2,384	275	11.14
23	40	920	2,384	274	2,698	314	11.48
24	40	960	2,698	319	3,057	359	11.82
25	1,040	2,000	3,057	372	4,469	1,412	12.16
	2,000			2,469		4,469	

Without reinvestment, the result is   Regular   IRR   4.00%

With reinvestment, the result is   Revised   IRR   8.95%

Maturity value of zero bond   2,666

Maturity value of coupon with reinvestment   4,469

Difference   −1,803

Table 17-4. Bonds, After Tax with Reinvestment at Increasing Rates

0%	Tax bracket of investor
16	Number of years until maturity of bond
$1,000	Maturity value 60.00% of long-term gain untaxed
6.0%	Reinvestment percent rate earned before tax, increasing by 0.41% per year
$1,000	Purchase price of bond
$60	Coupon rate in dollars
2,540	Maturity value of zero coupon bond

			Interest Reinvestment				
Year	Cash Flows Each Year Before Reinvestment of Earnings	Balance Before Reinvestment	Original Balance	Annual Interest on Interest	Ending Balance with Reinvestment	Cash Flow per Year with Reinvestment	Reinvestment Rate (%)
0	−1,000	0	0	0	0	−1,000	6.00%
1	60	60	0	0	60	60	6.41
2	60	120	60	4	124	64	6.81
3	60	180	124	8	192	68	7.22
4	60	240	192	14	266	74	

Year							
5	60	300	266	20	346	80	7.63
6	60	360	346	28	434	88	8.03
7	60	420	434	37	531	97	8.44
8	60	480	531	47	638	107	8.84
9	60	540	638	59	757	119	9.25
10	60	600	757	73	890	133	9.66
11	60	660	890	90	1,040	150	10.06
12	60	720	1,040	109	1,208	169	10.47
13	60	780	1,208	131	1,400	191	10.88
14	60	840	1,400	158	1,618	218	11.28
15	60	900	1,618	189	1,867	249	11.69
16	1,060	1,960	1,867	226	3,152	1,286	12.09
	1,960			1,192		3,152	

Without reinvestment, the result is Regular IRR 6.00%
With reinvestment, the result is Revised IRR 10.72%

Maturity value of zero bond   2,540
Maturity value of coupon with reinvestment 3,152
Difference   −612

Source: Lawrence R. Rosen, "Investment Analysis—After Tax IRR for Stocks, Bonds and Real Estate," Copyright 1984 by L. R. Rosen, 7008 Springdale Road, Louisville, KY. Unauthorized reproduction is prohibited.

Table 17-5. Bonds, After Tax with Reinvestment at Increasing Rates

0%	Tax bracket of investor (decimal form)
10	Number of years until maturity of bond
$1,000	Maturity value
6.74%	Reinvestment percent rate earned before tax, increasing by 0.58% per year
$1,000	Purchase price of bond
$67.4	Coupon rate in dollars
1,920	Maturity value of zero coupon bond

Interest Reinvestment

Year	Cash Flows Each Year Before Reinvestment of Earnings	Balance Before Reinvestment	Original Balance	Annual Interest on Interest	Ending Balance with Reinvestment	Cash Flow per Year with Reinvestment	Reinvestment Rate (%)
0	-1,000	0	0	0	0	-1,000	
1	67	67	0	0	67	67	6.74%
2	67	135	67	5	140	72	7.32

3	67	202	140	11	218	78	7.89
4	67	270	218	18	304	86	8.47
5	67	337	304	27	399	95	9.04
6	67	404	399	38	505	106	9.62
7	67	472	505	51	624	119	10.20
8	67	539	624	67	758	135	10.77
9	67	607	758	86	912	153	11.35
10	1,067	1,674	912	109	2,088	1,176	11.92
	1,674			414		2,088	

Without reinvestment, the result is   Regular   IRR   6.74%

With reinvestment, the result is   Revised   IRR   9.99%

Maturity value of zero bond   1,920

Maturity value of coupon with reinvestment   2,088

Difference   −168

231

Table 17-6. Bonds, After Tax with Reinvestment at Increasing Rates

0%	Tax bracket of investor (decimal form)
5	Number of years until maturity of bond
$1,000	Maturity value
10.00%	Reinvestment percent rate earned before tax, increasing by 0.5% per year
$1,000	Purchase price of bond
$100	Coupon rate in dollars
1,611	Maturity value of zero coupon bond

Year	Cash Flows Each Year Before Reinvestment of Earnings	Balance Before Reinvestment	Interest Reinvestment			Cash Flow per Year with Reinvestment	Reinvestment Rate (%)
			Original Balance	Annual Interest on Interest	Ending Balance with Reinvestment		
0	−1,000	0	0	0	0	−1,000	10.00%
1	100	100	0	0	100	100	10.50
2	100	200	100	11	211	111	11.00
3	100	300	211	23	334	123	11.50
4	100	400	334	38	472	138	12.00
5	1,100	1,500	472	57	1,629	1,157	
	1,500			129		1,629	

Without reinvestment, the result is   Regular IRR   10.00%

With reinvestment, the result is   Revised IRR   12.25%

Maturity value of zero bond	1,611
Maturity value of coupon with reinvestment	1,629
Difference	−18

Source: Lawrence R. Rosen, "Investment Analysis—After Tax IRR for Stocks, Bonds and Real Estate," Copyright 1984 by L. R. Rosen, 7008 Springdale Road, Louisville, KY. Unauthorized reproduction is prohibited.

Interest Rates at Purchase[a,g]	Interest Rate at Maturity	Time Period	Increase in Rates during the Period	Average Increase in Rates per Year	For Further Reference see Table
3.0%	12.5%	34 years[b]	9.5%	0.28%	17-2
4.0	12.5	25[c]	8.5	0.34	17-3
6.0	12.5	16[d]	6.5	0.41	17-4
6.74	12.5	10[e]	5.76	0.58	17-5
10.0	12.5	5[f]	2.5	0.50	17-6

[a]Long-term government bond yields.
[b]1951–1984.
[c]1960–1984.
[d]1969–1984.
[e]1975–1984.
[f]1980–1984.
[g]Sources of government bond interest rates: *Federal Reserve Bulletin,* July 1975, p. A-28; *First Boston 1984 Handbook of Securities of the United States Government and Federal Agencies,* p. 65; *Federal Reserve Bulletin,* October 1983, p. A-28; *Board of Governors of the Federal Reserve System 1983 Historical Chart Book,* pp. 96–97.

Thus in the 34-year analysis (Table 17-2), the percentage rate at which reinvestment occurs is:

34 years ago	3.00%
33 years ago	3.28%
32 years ago	3.56%
31 years ago	3.84%
1 year ago	12.22%

Such percentage rates give a fairly accurate picture of the effects of not locking in an interest reinvestment rate, but simply reinvesting at the approximate prevailing rate each time that interest income is received.

A comparison (between a zero coupon bond and conventional bond) of the terminal results—that is, the final sum at maturity

after reinvesting all income during the period of ownership—
shows for an initial $1000 investment:

| | Terminal Values | | Difference in Favor of | Value in |
Years	Zero Bond	Coupon Bond	Zero Bond	Coupon Bond
34	$2,732	$3,454		$ 723
25	2,666	4,469		1,803
16	2,540	3,152		612
10	1,920	2,088		168
5	1,611	1,629		18

Clearly, the foregoing cases represent time periods of generally increasing interest rates. In such an environment, "locking
in" a rate, as with zeros, can be quite harmful.

On the other hand, if future interest rates decline, then "locking in" such rates would be advantageous. Thus locking in today's yields should not necessarily be high on one's priority list.
The risks of doing so much be evaluated, as shown previously,
against the possible benefits.

ZEROS OFFER TREMENDOUS PROFIT POSSIBILITIES—
174 PERCENT PRE-TAX IN 14 MONTHS

Even the most adventuresome investor should stand in awe of
the enormous potential profitability of investing in zeros—under
auspicious circumstances. The profit potential on a short-term
basis, from a few weeks to a few years, is principally a function
of two elements: (1) a decline in interest rates and (2) borrowing
part of the purchase price through a margin purchase.

Twenty-five-year CATS were priced at about 13 percent yield
at the end of June 1984. By the end of August 1985 the yields

had declined to about 10.8 percent—a yield decline of about 17 percent.

Let's analyze the approximate results of an investment over this time frame, with a fortuitous yield decline, with an investment made at the beginning of the 14-month period that consisted of 30 percent cash and 70 percent borrowed funds. The details are shown in Table 17-7. For a cash investment of $14,000 and change, around $1 million of maturity value in zeros was acquired. The gross sales proceeds from selling out 14 months later amounted to just over $77,000. The net after-tax cash flow (profit) was $16,584.66 after deducting the following:

Loan repayment	$32,971.40
Interest on loan	5,193.00
Tax at ordinary income tax rates on accretion in value	3,571.90
Tax at long-term capital gains rates on gain	4,551.44
Original cash investment	14,130.60

And the net after-tax cash flow of $16,584.66 divided by the cash investment of $14,130.60 is the return on cash investment, after tax, for 14 months, that is, 117.37 percent, which on an annual basis (12/14) is 100.6 percent.

A 100 percent after-tax return on investment certainly is not to be sneezed at. It's the result of the combination of leverage from borrowed funds and the rapid fall in yields that took place over the 14-month period.

Buying on Margin or Credit

Incidentally, the regulation of credit extended to purchase securities is regulated by the Federal Reserve Board through the provisions of Regulations T and U. The Board regards CATS, STRIPS, and so on, as exempt securities and does not limit the amount of loan a broker or bank can extend to a percentage (less

Table 17-7. Leveraged Zero Investment with Declining Yields

Date of purchase	June 29, 84	
Date of sale	Aug 31, 85	
Maturity value of zeros purchased		1,000,000
Yield to maturity at purchase		13.00%
Cost of zeros purchased		47,102.00
Portion of cost borrowed	70.00%	32,971.40
Cash investment		**14,130.60**
Yield to maturity at sale		10.80%
Sales proceeds, gross		77,003.00
Interest on borrowed funds at		
13.5% per year for 14 months		5,193.00
Sales proceeds, after interest and loan		
repayment		38,838.60
Sales proceeds less cash investment		24,708.00
Pre-tax return on cash investment		
24,708.00 divided by 14,130.60		__174.85%__
After tax analysis:		
Sales proceeds after interest and loan		
repayment		38,838.60
Less: ordinary income tax on accretion		
in value in 50% tax bracket		
Cost	47,102.00	
Rate of accretion	13.00%	
Time (years)	1.167	
Accretion in value	7,143.80	
Tax at 50% of accretion in value		3,571.90
Adjusted tax basis:		
Original cost	47,102.00	
Accretion	7,143.80	
Adjusted basis	54,245.80	
Long-term capital gain:		
Sales proceeds	77,003.00	
Less: adjusted tax basis	54,245.80	
Long-term capital gain	22,757.20	
Portion of gain not taxed (60%)	13,654.32	
Taxable portion of capital gain	9,102.88	
Tax resulting from gain (50%)		4,551.44

(*Continued*)

236

Table 17-7. Leveraged Zero Investment with Declining Yields
(Continued)

After tax sales proceeds, net	30,715.26
Net after-tax profit ($30,715.26 less cash investment of $14,130.60)	16,584.66
Net after-tax return on cash investment	<u>117.37%</u>

The 174.85% pre-tax return is for 14 months; annualized, it is about 150%.

The 117.37% after-tax return is for 14 months; annualized, it is about 100%.

than 100 percent) of the market value. So, if your bank or broker is willing, you can borrow even more than the 70 percent illustrated in Table 17-7. Additionally, however, the stock exchanges regulate credit and it appears that the present New York Stock Exchange policy is to allow a maximum of 70 percent loans. So, whether you desire to buy on credit may influence whether to buy through a bank or a broker.

This illustration is not a recommendation to buy zeros on credit. Leverage is a two-way street: Had interest rates risen, the adverse effects of borrowing would have been magnified in the opposite (unprofitable) direction. Before investing on margin, investors should be completely familiar with the margin loan practices of their lender, including the lender's policy on demanding additional collateral, marking to the market, and so forth.

BUYING AT A FAIR PRICE

Finally, aside from the potential problems just described, there is the question of how to buy zero coupon bonds at a fair and reasonable price. As seen in detail in Chapters 10 through 12, the fair price (yield) of a zero coupon bond is dependent on the shape of the conventional Treasury bond yield curve, and the theoretical spot rate yield for a zero coupon bond can be calculated arithmetically. So, if your evaluation indicates that the purchase of a zero coupon bond is desirable, be guided by Chapter 12, How to Pay a Fair Price for a Zero and Avoid Being Gouged.

STRIPS FUTURES

The Chicago Mercantile Exchange as well as The Chicago Board of Trade offer futures trading in STRIPS. A futures contract involves a commitment by an investor or speculator to make or accept delivery at a specified price and at a certain time. The face value of a single contract is $200,000. Futures trading may be engaged in by speculators (seeking extreme volatility) or by owners of STRIPS who desire to hedge or protect their position against certain price fluctuations during specific periods of time.

MUTUAL FUND OF ZEROS

Most investments with any following seem to inspire a mutual fund. Zeros are no exception. The Benham Target Maturities Trust (755 Page Mill Road, Palo Alto, CA. 94304-1018) offers a choice of zero coupon bond portfolios with varying maturity dates.

Zeros, an innovative creation of the 1980s, are here to stay. Their many features, intricacies, and ramifications make understanding them a virtual necessity for most investors. Providing such understanding has been the purpose of this book. If you are able to improve your investment's performance and reduce your risks as the result of reading this book, then the author's purpose will have been achieved.

Appendix A

Treasury receipts prospectus

$395,687,500
Treasury Receipts

$243,812,500 Coupon TRs due Semiannually
November 15, 1984—November 15, 2007
$151,875,000 Callable TRs due November 15, 2012

Treasury Receipts ("TRs") evidence ownership of future interest and principal payments on $100,000,000 United States Treasury 10⅜% Bonds due November 15, 2012 (the "Treasury Securities") to be held by State Street Bank and Trust Company (the "Custodian") for the benefit of TR owners pursuant to a custody agreement (the "Custody Agreement").

The semiannual interest payments due on the Treasury Securities up to and including November 15, 2007, the date on which the Treasury Securities initially become subject to call for redemption by the United States, are being offered in the form of TRs with separate maturities (the "Coupon TRs"). There will not be any payments on Coupon TRs prior to their maturities. The semiannual interest payments on and the principal of the Treasury Securities are being offered together as single units (collectively, the "Callable TRs"). The Coupon TRs have 47 separate maturities due semiannually from November 15, 1984 to November 15, 2007 with aggregate face amounts of $5,187,500 per maturity. The Callable TRs are due November 15, 2012. There will be ten semiannual interest payments, each aggregating $5,187,500, commencing May 15, 2008 on Callable TRs and payments aggregating $100,000,000 thereon at maturity. Callable TRs will be redeemed, in whole or in part, on or after November 15, 2007 if and when the Treasury Securities are redeemed at the option of the United States. See "General—Redemption of Treasury Securities Underlying Callable TRs" in the accompanying Descriptive Memorandum dated January 9, 1984 (the "Descriptive Memorandum"), of which this Descriptive Memorandum Supplement forms a part.

The obligor with respect to the interest and principal payments on the Treasury Securities underlying the TRs is The United States of America.

The face amount of each TR will be the payment to be received thereon. The TRs are being offered at substantial discounts from their face amounts. See "Income Tax Consequences" in the accompanying Descriptive Memorandum for a discussion of the United States tax treatment of TRs, including the implications of original issue discount.

Moseley, Hallgarten, Estabrook & Weeden Inc. intends to maintain a market for TRs but is not obligated to do so. See "General—Secondary Market" in the accompanying Descriptive Memorandum.

TRs are being offered to the public by Moseley, Hallgarten, Estabrook & Weeden Inc. in negotiated transactions at varying prices which will be determined at the time of sale and will be based upon market conditions at such time. TRs may also be sold to certain dealers at prices to be determined. The TRs are offered when, as and if delivered and subject to the right to reject orders in whole or in part. Moseley, Hallgarten, Estabrook & Weeden Inc. will deposit the Treasury Securities underlying such TRs with the Custodian. It is expected that the TRs will be ready for delivery against payment therefor on July 11, 1984.

Moseley, Hallgarten, Estabrook & Weeden Inc.
The date of this Descriptive Memorandum Supplement is June 25, 1984

Treasury Receipts

Treasury Receipts ("TRs") evidence ownership of future interest and principal payments on certain United States Treasury Notes or Bonds ("Treasury Securities"). **Such interest and principal payments are direct obligations of The United States of America.** The Treasury Securities will be held in custody by State Street Bank and Trust Company ("Custodian") on behalf of the holders of the related TRs.

TRs evidencing ownership of the semiannual interest payments due on the Treasury Securities will be offered from time to time as **Coupon TRs.** TRs evidencing ownership of the principal payments due on the Treasury Securities will be offered from time to time as **Principal TRs.** TRs evidencing ownership of both the principal payments due on redeemable Treasury Securities and any interest payments due thereon following the earliest redemption date will be offered from time to time as **Callable TRs.**

No payments will be made on TRs prior to the maturity of the corresponding interest or principal payments on the underlying Treasury Securities. In addition, in the event Treasury Securities underlying any Callable TRs are redeemed, no payments will be made on such Callable TRs with respect to interest payments due after such redemption. The face amount of each TR will be equal to the payment or payments to be received thereon, except that the face amount of Callable TRs will include interest payments on the underlying Treasury Securities which may not be made if such Treasury Securities are redeemed prior to maturity.

TRs will be offered at a discount from their face amounts. See "Income Tax Consequences" for a discussion of certain United States income tax considerations, including implications of original issue discount and possible tax withholding.

Any depositor of Treasury Securities who is acceptable to the Custodian ("Depositor") may offer the related TRs from time to time. Depositors intend to make a market in all TRs irrespective of which Depositor initially offered such TRs, but are not obligated to do so.

TRs will be offered in registered form and in denominations and at prices negotiated between the purchaser and the Depositor at the time of sale. TRs are offered when, as and if delivered and subject to the right of the Depositor to reject orders in whole or in part. Delivery will be made by the Depositor in New York against payments therefor in Federal or other immediately available funds at such time as is negotiated between the purchaser and the Depositor at the time of sale.

January 9, 1984

Coupon TRs	Custodial receipts issued in respect of individual semiannual interest payments on specific Treasury Securities. Holders of Coupon TRs will receive such interest payments at maturity of the underlying coupons and will receive no payments prior to such time.
Principal TRs	Custodial receipts issued in respect of principal payments on specific Treasury Securities. Holders of Principal TRs will receive such principal payments at maturity of the underlying Treasury Securities and will receive no payments prior to such time.
Callable TRs	Custodial receipts issued in respect of principal payments on specific redeemable Treasury Securities and any interest payments due thereon following the earliest redemption date. Holders of Callable TRs will receive such principal payments upon redemption or maturity of the underlying Treasury Securities and will receive such interest payments to the extent the underlying Treasury Securities are not redeemed prior to maturity.
Place of Payment	The designated office of the Custodian in New York City and London and the main office of J. Vontobel and Company in Zurich.
Tax Consequences	TRs will be treated as debt obligations issued with "original issue discount" and holders other than tax exempt investors will be required to include original issue discount in gross income over the life of the TRs. For additional information, including tax treatment of TRs and the payment of withholding taxes under certain circumstances, see "Income Tax Consequences".
Custodian and Custody Agreement	State Street Bank and Trust Company, Boston, Massachusetts, acts as the Custodian pursuant to a Custody Agreement dated January 9, 1984, a copy of which may be inspected at the designated office of the Custodian, 50 Broadway, New York City.

2

242

GENERAL

TRs are custodial receipts issued pursuant to the Custody Agreement and evidence ownership of future interest and principal payments on Treasury Securities deposited with the Custodian. The interest and principal payments on the Treasury Securities underlying TRs are direct obligations of The United States of America.

The Treasury Securities underlying TRs will be delivered to the Custodian by the Depositors and retained by the Custodian pursuant to the Custody Agreement until maturity or redemption, except as provided below. The statements below are summaries of certain provisions of the Custody Agreement, do not purport to be complete and are subject to and are qualified in their entirety by reference to the Custody Agreement. All parenthetical references contained herein are to sections in the Custody Agreement. A copy of the Custody Agreement may be inspected at the designated office of the Custodian, 50 Broadway, New York City.

Holders of TRs are the beneficial owners of the underlying Treasury Securities entitled to the rights and privileges evidenced thereby. Holders of TRs, as the real parties in interest, have the right upon default of the United States in making required interest or principal payments on the underlying Treasury Securities to proceed individually against the United States as they deem appropriate and will not be required by the Custody Agreement to act in concert with other holders of TRs or as directed by the Custodian. The Custodian will not be authorized to assert the rights and privileges of the holders of TRs upon a default and will have no duty to do so by reason of its status as the nominal holder of the Treasury Securities or otherwise.

Neither the Custodian nor the Depositors will be responsible for the payments due on TRs, except that the Custodian is obligated to apply all payments received in respect of Treasury Securities held in custody to the TRs to which such payments relate without making any deductions, other than any applicable tax withholding. See "Income Tax Consequences".

Redemption of Treasury Securities Underlying Callable TRs

The Treasury Securities underlying Callable TRs may be redeemed, in whole or in part, beginning on a date specified on the Callable TRs, on four months' notice given in such manner as the Secretary of the Treasury shall prescribe. In the event of a partial redemption, the Treasury Securities to be redeemed will be determined by such method as may be prescribed by the Secretary of the Treasury.

If the Treasury Securities underlying Callable TRs are called for redemption prior to maturity, notice of such call shall be given by the Custodian to holders of such Callable TRs within 30 days by publication in a financial journal of general circulation published on each business day in the City of New York and in a newspaper in each other city where such Callable TRs are payable or by mail to each holder of a Callable TR called for redemption at such holder's registered address. (Sections 7.03, 8.04)

If the Treasury Securities underlying any Callable TRs are redeemed, the holders of such Callable TRs will receive a payment equal to the principal portion of the face amount of such Callable TRs. Such holder will have no right to receive interest payments on the underlying Treasury Securities due after the redemption of such Treasury Securities. (Section 7.01)

Callable TRs may also be paid in part in the event of a partial redemption of the underlying Treasury Securities. In the event of a partial redemption of such Treasury Securities, the Custodian is directed in the Custody Agreement to select Callable TRs, or portions thereof, for redemption in such manner as the Custodian deems fair and appropriate and in a manner which will result in redemption of portions of Callable TRs no smaller than the smallest authorized denomination of the underlying Treasury Securities. (Section 7.02)

3

243

Withdrawal of Underlying Treasury Securities

Upon presentation of a TR at the designated office of the Custodian, the holder thereof may withdraw the underlying Treasury Securities, coupons or principal portion if available in certificate form, provided such withdrawal would not require the Custodian to strip or cut coupons from the certificate for any Treasury Security. In the event of a default by the Government in making any payment due on the underlying Treasury Securities, the Custodian will be obligated upon request to strip or cut coupons from any such Treasury Security held in custody in certificate form to facilitate withdrawals. In addition, upon the request of any holder of TRs evidencing the principal portion and all unmatured coupons pertaining to any Treasury Security, the Custodian will deliver such Treasury Security to such holder in book-entry form in exchange for such TRs. Any withdrawal of Treasury Securities, coupons or principal portions is, however, subject to the terms of the Custody Agreement, including the ability of the Custodian to obtain possession of Treasury Securities in certificate form and the right of the Custodian to suspend withdrawals in certain circumstances. (Sections 2.04, 2.05)

In connection with any such withdrawal, the related TRs must be surrendered to the Custodian and cancelled. The Custodian shall require payment of any tax or governmental charge that may be imposed, but will make no other service charges. Upon withdrawal, the holder of such Treasury Securities, coupons or principal portions will no longer be entitled to the benefits of the Custody Agreement. Treasury Securities, coupons or principal portions withdrawn from custody may not be replaced in custody with the Custodian unless subsequently deposited by a Depositor. (Sections 2.04, 2.05)

Delivery, Transfer and Exchange of TRs

Each Depositor will deliver TRs in denominations negotiated between the purchaser and the Depositor against payment in Federal or other immediately available funds. Delivery will be made at the specified offices of the Depositor or to an office (specified by the purchaser) of a bank that is a member of the Federal Reserve System or a member firm of the New York Stock Exchange, in each case located in the Borough of Manhattan, City of New York, or as otherwise agreed upon between the purchaser and the Depositor.

TRs will be issued in registered form and in authorized denominations equal to integral multiples of the smallest authorized denomination of the underlying Treasury Securities or interest payment thereon, as the case may be. TRs will be transferable only on the books of the Custodian upon presentation at its designated office in the City of New York and upon payment of the service charge then in effect. (Section 2.03)

At the option of the holder, TRs may be exchanged for TRs of a like aggregate face amount and maturities in different authorized denominations upon surrender of the TRs to be exchanged at the designated office of the Custodian in the City of New York and upon payment of the service charge then in effect. (Section 2.03)

All TRs delivered upon any exchange will evidence the same obligations and will be entitled to the same rights and privileges as the TRs surrendered.

Upon any transfer or exchange, the Custodian may require payment of a sum sufficient to cover any tax or governmental charge that may be imposed in connection with such transfer or exchange.

The Custodian and the Custody Agreement

The Treasury Securities will be held by the Custodian on behalf of the holders of the related TRs pursuant to a Custody Agreement dated January 9, 1984. The Custodian will establish a separate custody account for each issue of Treasury Securities underlying TRs and three subaccounts within each

4

separate account: first, for coupons underlying Coupon TRs; second, for principal portions underlying Principal TRs; and third, for all coupons and principal portions underlying Callable TRs. The Treasury Securities will be held by the Custodian in certificate form or in book-entry form at the Federal Reserve Bank of New York or of Boston. (Section 2.01)

The only responsibility of the Custodian with respect to payment on TRs will be to apply all payments received in respect of the Treasury Securities to the related TRs without making any deductions other than applicable tax withholding. (Section 4.01) See "Income Tax Consequences".

Custody accounts established for TRs will be special accounts separate from the general assets of the Custodian and the coupons, principal portions and money therein will not be subject to any right, charge, security interest, lien or claim of any kind in favor of the Custodian or any person claiming through it. The Custodian will not have the power or authority to assign, transfer, pledge or otherwise dispose of any of the assets of the custody accounts to any person except as otherwise permitted by the Custody Agreement. (Section 2.04)

The Custodian will maintain insurance for the protection of holders of TRs in customary amounts against losses resulting from the custody arrangement due to dishonest or fraudulent action by its employees. (Section 5.03)

The Custody Agreement provides that neither the Custodian nor the Depositors shall be subject to any liabilities to holders of TRs other than by reason of willful misconduct, bad faith or gross negligence in the performance of duties set forth in the Custody Agreement and that none of them shall be liable to such holders if any law, government regulation or other circumstance prevents or delays the performance of duties set forth in the Custody Agreement. (Section 5.04) The Majority Depositors (as defined in the Custody Agreement) and the Custodian may amend the Custody Agreement except that no amendment may be made which defers or alters the maturity of a TR or in any manner adversely affects the rights of a holder of a TR to the coupon or principal portion evidenced thereby or otherwise materially prejudices any substantial existing right of TR holders. (Section 6.01)

The Custodian may be removed only in the event of its becoming incapable of acting or upon its bankruptcy or insolvency, by court action instituted by any holder of a TR who has been a holder for six months or by holders of 10% of the face amount of TRs outstanding at such time. (Section 5.05)

Offices for Transfer, Payment and Exchange

TRs may be presented for transfer, payment and exchange at the designated office of the Custodian in New York City and may be presented for payment at the designated office of the Custodian in London and the main office of J. Vontobel and Company in Zurich.

Secondary Market

Depositors intend to make a market in all TRs subject to any applicable provision of Federal and state securities laws or regulatory requirements. No Depositor is obligated to make such a market.

5

245

INCOME TAX CONSEQUENCES

Federal Taxes

The following discussion of the Federal income tax consequences to purchasers of Coupon TRs, Principal TRs and Callable TRs represents the advice of Sullivan & Cromwell, counsel to certain of the Depositors.

Holders of TRs will be treated for Federal income tax purposes as owners of the rights to receive principal and interest on the Treasury Securities.

Under the Internal Revenue Code of 1954, as amended by the Tax Equity and Fiscal Responsibility Act of 1982 ("TEFRA"), an investor who purchases a Principal TR or a Coupon TR, either initially or in the secondary market, will be treated as purchasing an obligation issued on the purchase date with an original issue discount equal to the excess of the amount payable on the TR at maturity over the purchase price. Such a purchaser, whether on the cash or accrual method of accounting, will be required to take into income each year as ordinary income the portion of such discount determined by the "constant yield" method. Such income will increase the holder's tax basis for the TR for the purpose of determining gain or loss on a later sale or other disposition of the TR, and gain or loss recognized on sale or other disposition of the TR will be capital gain or loss if the TR is held as a capital asset.

An investor who purchases a Callable TR, either initially or in the secondary market, will likewise be treated as purchasing one or more obligations issued on the purchase date with original issue discount, but it is unclear in the absence of Treasury regulations whether (a) the purchase price will be allocated entirely to the right to receive principal, in which case the purchaser would be taxable on the constant yield method (as set forth above) over the period to the earliest date on which the underlying Treasury Securities may be called on the excess over such purchase price of the amount payable at such date and thereafter on interest, if any, received or accrued or (b) the purchase price must be allocated among the rights to principal and interest, in which case the purchaser would be taxable on a constant yield method on the excess over the allocable parts of such purchase price of the amounts payable as interest or at final maturity and would be entitled to deduct as a loss any amount of the purchase price allocable to interest that was not paid.

A purchaser of a TR who is a nonresident alien individual or a foreign corporation and has no U.S. trade or business, will not be subject to Federal income tax on the discount on the TR prior to sale or payment at maturity. The tax consequences to such a holder of a sale or payment at maturity are not entirely clear, but it is possible that Federal income tax will be imposed upon sale or at maturity at the rate of 30% (or such lower rate as may be provided for interest by an applicable tax treaty) on the excess of the payment received over the cost of the TR and that payments of interest on a Callable TR may also be subject to tax at such rates. The tax may be collected by withholding.

The foregoing does not consider tax considerations that may be applicable to insurance companies and other specially treated taxpayers. In addition, in the absence of regulations the treatment of TRs under TEFRA is not altogether clear and potential purchasers are therefore advised to consult their own tax advisors prior to purchasing TRs.

State and Local Taxes

Under Federal law, Treasury Securities are exempt from state and local taxes in the United States, other than certain corporate franchise taxes and estate and inheritance taxes. Under this law and a recent Supreme Court decision, income arising on the sale or maturity of TRs and annual accruals of discount on TRs should be exempt from state and local taxation. Because certain states may possibly take a contrary position, however, purchasers should consult their own tax advisors concerning state and local taxes.

$395,687,500

Treasury Receipts

$243,812,500 Coupon TRs
Due Semiannually
November 15, 1984-November 15, 2007

$151,875,000 Callable TRs
Due November 15, 2012

No person has been authorized to give any information or to make any representation not contained in this Descriptive Memorandum Supplement and the accompanying Descriptive Memorandum in connection with the offering made hereby
and, if given or made, such information or representation must not be relied upon. This Descriptive
Memorandum Supplement and the accompanying
Descriptive Memorandum do not constitute an offer to sell or a solicitation of an offer to buy any of
the TRs offered hereby in any jurisdiction to any
person to whom it is unlawful to make such offer or
solicitation in such jurisdiction. Neither the delivery of this Descriptive Memorandum Supplement
and the accompanying Descriptive Memorandum
nor any sale hereunder shall under any circumstances create any implication that there has been
no change since the date hereof.

DESCRIPTIVE MEMORANDUM
SUPPLEMENT
Dated June 25, 1984

247

Appendix B

How to get back your money if you've been deceived by a broker

INVESTORS ARE PROTECTED

If you think you have been victimized by a broker–dealer in purchasing or selling a security, you are not without means to obtain redress. Not only are you protected by the Federal Securities laws such as the Securities Act of 1933, the Securities Exchange Act of 1934, and the Investment Company Act of 1940, you are also protected by the rules and regulations of the National Association of Securities Dealers, Inc. (NASD), in particular by the NASD Rules of Fair Practice, as well as the rules and regulations of the New York (and other) Stock Exchanges. Last, but not necessarily least, you are protected by the securities laws of the state in which you reside. The stock exchanges, as well as the NASD, have arbitration procedures, so as you attempt to obtain justice you need not suffer through the expense and tribulations of a courtroom trial.

How many investors have read carefully the "Customer's Agreement" or "Joint Account Agreement" that is signed when a brokerage account is established? Not many. Typically, there is a clause along the following lines:

> This agreement and its enforcement shall be governed by the laws of the State of (state where broker's home office is located), its provisions shall be continuous and shall inure to the benefit of your present corporation and its successors and it shall inure to the benefit of, and shall be binding upon, the estate, executors, administrators and assigns of the undersigned. Any controversy arising out of or relating to my account, to transactions with you for me or to this agreement or the breach, shall be settled by arbitration in accordance with the rules, then in effect, of the American Stock Exchange, the New York Stock Exchange, Inc., or the National Association of Securities Dealers, Inc., as I may elect. If I do not make such election by registered mail addressed to you at your main office within 5 days after demand by you that I make such election, then you may make such election. Judgment upon any award rendered by arbitration may be entered in any court having jurisdiction.

Another similar clause of a different firm is:

This agreement and its enforcement shall be governed by the laws of the State of New York. Any controversy between you and the undersigned arising out of, or relating to this agreement, or the breach thereof, or arising out of transactions with you shall be settled by arbitration, in accordance with the Rules, then obtaining, of either the American Arbitration Association, or the Board of Arbitrators or the Panels of the New York Stock Exchange, as we may elect. If we do not make such election by registered mail addressed to you at your main office within five days after receipt of notification from you requesting such election, then you may make such election. Any arbitration hereunder shall be before at least three arbitrators, and the award of the arbitrators or a majority of them shall be final, and judgment upon the award rendered may be entered in any court having jurisdiction. We agree that notice of, and in, any such arbitration may be sent to us by mail and waive personal service thereof.

The effect of this clause is that the investor agrees that disputes be settled by arbitration rather than by the courts. However, the United States Supreme Court in *Wilko v. Swan* [346 U.S. 427 (1953)] held that a customer of a broker–dealer does not waive the protections of the securities acts by an agreement to arbitrate future controversies. Thus, in spite of having signed the "Customer Agreement," the investors may go directly to court to obtain restitution.

Most securities transactions which do not take place on a stock exchange occur in what is called the over-the-counter market. And most securities brokers who deal with the public in over-the-counter securities such as zero coupon bonds (issued under custodial arrangements) such as TIGRS, CATS, LIONs, etc., are members of the NASD. The NASD, which is based in Washington, D.C., is a self-regulatory organization. The members of its board of governors are from the securities brokerage community and also include some independent persons. The NASD has a

Code of Arbitration Procedure which includes the following provisions:

> The board of governors appoints a director of arbitration (DAC) and a national arbitration committee (NAC). The NAC establishes a pool of arbitrators, composed of persons from within and outside of the securities industry.
>
> The customer–investor must file with the DAC three copies of a submission agreement, three copies of a statement of claim, and, if possible, an indication of the amount claimed and the remedies sought. The DAC then serves the foregoing documents on the broker. The broker has 10 business days to file an answer (containing the broker's defenses and any counterclaim), which DAC then sends to the customer. The customer may then file (within 10 business days) a statement of reply setting forth defenses to the broker's assertions.
>
> The DAC then sets a time and place for an initial hearing. Parties may be represented by counsel, bring witness, documents, and so forth, and have the power of subpoena. Claims involving relatively small sums (less than $2000 at this writing) may be arbitrated solely on the documentary evidence filed by the disputants, unless either of the parties demands a hearing.
>
> All rulings and determinations of the panel are by a majority.
>
> Awards are in writing within 30 days of the close of the hearings and signed by the arbitrators. The arbitrators may assess any costs and fees including but not limited to the expense of the record upon the parties in such manner as they deem to be just and reasonable.

The NASD charges a nominal filing fee to each of the parties to the arbitration.

NASD REGULATIONS TO PROTECT THE PUBLIC

The NASD establishes rules, regulations, and policies to protect the public and regulate the brokerage industry. Some policies of particular potential interest to investors include the following:

> In recommending to a customer the purchase, sale or exchange of any security, the broker shall have reasonable grounds for believing that the recommendation is suitable for such customer upon the basis of the facts, if any, disclosed by such customer as to his other security holdings and as to his financial situation and needs.

(The NASD mentions such violations of NASD rules as: "other fraudulent activities, such as forgery, **non-disclosure or misstatement of material facts,** manipulations, and various deceptions.")

The SEC in the case *Philips & Company and Gerald Bernheimer,* 37 SEC66 (1956) found a broker in violation for, among other activities, making statements that led the customers to believe that their investment was free of risk.

Much of the literature of brokers that I have reviewed concerning zero coupon bonds stresses the safety factor and fails to mention the volatility risk. Persons who have been misled by such propaganda may have a valid claim for recovery of any losses suffered.

> It shall be deemed conduct inconsistent with just and equitable principles of trade for a broker/dealer to enter into any transaction with a customer in any security at any price not reasonably related to the current market price of the security or to charge a commission which is not reasonable.

Probably the most accurate measure of the current market price for a zero coupon bond is the price at which a major dealer like Salomon Brothers was selling comparable bonds on the same day at the same time. Salomon is a strictly institutional firm and does not deal with the public. The price at which it sold CATS to other brokers is a good indication of the market. And the price at which your broker sold to you, as compared to the Salomon price, indicates the amount of the markup or spread. Salomon's pricing may be judged relative to the other institutional sales as well as relative to the theoretical spot rate curve.

The Board of the NASD has stated that it would be impractical and unwise, if not impossible, to define specifically what constitutes a fair spread on each and every transaction because the fairness of a markup can be determined only after considering all of the relevant factors. Under certain conditions a markup in excess of 5 percent may be justified, but, on the other hand, 5 percent or even a lower rate is by no means always justified (e.g., may be too high). The Board of the NASD states that a higher percentage of markup customarily applies to a common stock transaction than to a bond transaction of the same size.

FEDERAL SECURITIES LAWS

Rule 10b-5, issued pursuant to the Exchange Act of 1934, states:

> It shall be unlawful for any person, directly or indirectly, by the use of any means of instrumentality of interstate commerce, or of the mails, or of any facility of any national securities exchange: (1) to employ any device, scheme, or artifice to defraud, (2) **to make any untrue statement of a material fact or to omit to state a material fact necessary in order to make the statements made, in the light of the circumstances under which they were made, not misleading,** or (3) to engage in any act, practice, or course of business which operates or would operate as a fraud or deceit upon any person, in connection with the purchase or sale of any security.

Section 15 of the Exchange Act of 1934 [15(c)(1)] specifically applies wording similar to the foregoing to brokers and dealers.

And Rule 15(c)(1-2) relating to the over-the-counter markets, adds: The term "manipulative, deceptive, or other fraudulent device or contrivance" is hereby defined to include **any untrue statement of a material fact and any omission to state a material fact necessary in order to make the statements made, in the light of the circumstances under which they are made, not misleading,** which statement or omission is made with knowledge or reasonable grounds to believe that it is untrue or misleading.

IF YOU WERE VICTIMIZED

If you feel that you have been victimized, you can take action. First, try to obtain satisfaction by writing to the head office of the brokerage firm that you feel has wronged you. Second, write to the NASD or the stock exchange (where the transaction took place or the broker is a member) and ask them to send you the rules of arbitration and the necessary papers to file a claim. Third, when you have received and reviewed such information, you might want to consult an experienced securities lawyer. Securities law is a highly specialized field, and you would be well advised to seek the services of an attorney who specializes in securities law.

The NASD is located at 1735 K Street, N.W., Washington DC 20006.

The New York Stock Exchange is located at 11 Wall Street, New York, NY 10005.

Appendix C

Bureau of the public debt: The safety of book-entry treasury securities

The following statement has been issued by the Bureau of the Public Debt in response to inquiries received from investors concerning the safety of Treasury securities issued in book-entry form:

First, it is understandable that some investors should feel uneasy about obligations that are not evidenced by certificates. The fact is, however, that this concern is somewhat paradoxical, given the fact that the book-entry system was, in part, developed precisely because it substantially reduces the exposure to loss. Prior to the adoption of the book-entry system, which has been in existence since 1968, there had been widespread losses of definitive, i.e., physical, securities from banks, securities dealers, etc.

Second, the Treasury has not had a single claim of loss of a book-entry security, such as a bond, note or bill. While its experience has been certainly reassuring, this does not mean that the Department is unconcerned about the safety of the system. It cannot but be concerned since a book-entry Treasury security represents a direct obligation of the United States. This means that the payment of principal and interest thereon is guaranteed by the Government.

Third, a book-entry security can be likened to a bailment. Legally, it represents property held in custody for the account of an owner by the book-entry depository, i.e., commercial bank or other institution, but the security is not part of the latter's assets. Therefore, if the bank or other financial institutions should fail, the book-entry securities it holds for customers could not be reached by its creditors. The owners should arrange, in such a case, to have any unmatured accounts transferred to another bank or other depository.

Fourth, since neither the Federal Reserve nor the Treasury maintains ownership records of the book-entry securities held by commercial banks, etc., if a dispute should arise as to the status of a Treasury obligation between a customer and custodian institution, the Treasury would normally expect that the matter will be settled by the parties involved. If the dispute should persist, the Department would be prepared, either directly or through the

Federal Reserve, to have the matter investigated so that the matter can be satisfactorily resolved.

Fifth, where an investor, for whatever reason, prefers to have his/her Treasury bills held by the Department, arrangements can be made to have them maintained by the Bureau of the Public Debt. It should be pointed out that the Treasury's book-entry system is a limited one. For example, the accounts may only be held in the name of individuals in a single name, or jointly with another person. Also, most transactions can only be conducted through the mails, since the records are centrally maintained by the Bureau. Perhaps even more important is the fact that bills held at the Bureau cannot be pledged as collateral. In order to sell or to trade such a bill prior to maturity, it must first be transferred out of the Bureau accounts to a bank or other institution designated by the owner.

Sixth, although the Treasury book-entry system enjoys the participation of some 800,000 investors, by far most Treasury securities are held in book-entry form in the commercial sector. The determination as to which book-entry system should be used in the case of Treasury bills depends on the investor's own needs.

Index